NASH-Shit blaster

P.C. BLACK
FENDER TELE

E 321406

CHAMELEON

ST. BLUE

DEFINITELY

THE OFFICIAL STORY OF

JOE ELLIOTT // PHIL COLLEN // RICK ALLEN // RICK SAVAGE // VIVIAN CAMPBELL

DEFINITELY

THE OFFICIAL STORY OF

JOE ELLIOTT//PHIL COLLEN//RICK ALLEN//RICK SAVAGE//VIVIAN CAMPBELL

GENESIS PUBLICATIONS LIMITED SINCE 1974

ISBN: 978-1-905662-79-1

Genesis Publications Ltd
Genesis House
2 Jenner Road, Guildford
Surrey, England, GU1 3PL

10 9 8 7 6 5 4 3 2 1

This book first appeared as a limited edition of
1,500 numbered copies, signed by Joe Elliott, Phil Collen,
Rick Allen, Rick Savage and Vivian Campbell

www.genesis-publications.com

FOREWORD BY BRIAN MAY

In 1981, Queen were in the studio in Munich recording the *Hot Space* album, and I nipped out to catch a local show. Some friends of mine, Ritchie Blackmore's Rainbow, were playing, and who should be supporting them but a precocious bunch of lads called Def Leppard. I got there late and I missed them. Afterwards I poked my head round their dressing room door and said, 'Hi guys, I just wanted to say hello because I missed you and I'm really sorry. I'm Brian May from Queen.' And they said, 'No shit,' which was nice. We've got on well ever since!

A few months later I was in Los Angeles and noticed that Def Leppard were playing the wonderful LA Forum. I'd just been working with another bunch of young lads whose sole aim was to sound like Def Leppard, so I'd done some research on them and this time I wasn't going to miss the Def Lepp show. After all these years, words still fail me. I'd seen many great acts storm the Forum, and we'd had many a memorable Queen night there too. But I had NEVER seen the whole place on its feet for the whole show the way it happened that night. It was a riot – a triumph of epic proportions! This time, poking my head round their dressing room door was different! I was a bit lost for words, but they just said, 'Why don't you come up and play with us tomorrow?' So I did ... and 'Travelin' Band' has never been the same for me since. I hardly need to mention that if it hadn't been for Joe's timely backwards drag on my collar I would have been fried by their pyro flames at the end of the show. But that was just part of the experience!

I regard these guys as great friends, almost like family. Joe and I in particular have shared many precious and fun moments, snatched among the madness of touring life. We have a strong bond and he's one of my dearest pals. When Steve Clark died, Joe says that the first phone call he got was from me. And when the news came out of Freddie's passing, the first phone call I got was from Joe.

These guys as a band are some of the most charismatic crowd-pleasers ever, but they're much more than that. They also embody great musicianship, a rare instinct for memorable riffs and choruses, and the magic of a raw power that never gets old. They have it all.

The press, particularly in the UK, has not always been kind to Def Leppard. It was as if they were being attacked for making hit records. Their success seemed to make them uncool in some people's eyes. But songs like 'Photograph', 'Pour Some Sugar on Me' and 'Love Bites' – real songs that people can sing and carry in their heads – are the reason that Def Leppard will be remembered in hearts and minds long after all of us have left this Earth.

Def Leppard have a unique spirit. It's not just about survival. They have grown deeper and wiser over the years, and their canon really means something. It makes you cry. It makes you laugh. Makes you rock before you have time to think about it. Def Leppard are original, inimitable and, well, I'm gonna say immortal.

Enjoy journeying with them in this book.

One morning in March 1985, I stood at the bottom of a flight of stairs in an apartment in Holland, struggling to hold up my end of a young British rock band's history to that point: a steamer trunk packed with the archaeology of Def Leppard's first eight years in records, tours and general, jubilant chaos, collected by singer Joe Elliott with a clear eye for destiny and the devotion to historical detail that always marks the true fan. After an overnight flight from New York, I had arrived in Oud-Loosdrecht, a village in the north of the country, to interview the band members for a book published two years later as *Animal Instinct*. The trunk was just in from the band's hometown, Sheffield, where it had been in the care of Elliott's parents. The Leppards had been in Holland for several months, commuting to a studio in nearby Hilversum for what already seemed like the eternal process of making their fourth album, the followup to 1983's platinum-busting *Pyromania*. They would eventually – and rightly – call it *Hysteria*.

Once we got that trunk up the stairs into the lounge of Elliott's rented apartment – Malvin Mortimer, the band's legendary Welsh road manager, was tugging on the other end – the memories and wonder of Def Leppard's growing up and going nuclear came roaring back as the singer dug through the contents and marvelled at what he had saved. There were show flyers, detailed gig diaries and local news stories from the band's hard graft in the pubs and working men's clubs of Sheffield. ('The Young Lions of Rock', boasted one club ad.) Backstage passes, tour itineraries and record-label correspondence charted the Leppards' high-speed rise, at the leading edge of the so-called New Wave of British Heavy Metal and on early life-changing tours of America. And there was an endless parade of press clippings – breathless raves and turning-point features in the UK music papers and the first US rock magazines to get on the train, as well as a few sour notices that Elliott had obviously kept for comic relief.

'It was what we wanted,' he told me later, summing up the long miles in ambition and dedication that had already filled that trunk in 1985 – the years of 'driving through snow to play to 15 people; touring as an opening act. It wasn't overnight success. When it started kicking in, it was just, "Well, this is how it's supposed to be."'

Now you get to feel the way I did that morning: like you're falling into that trunk, except it's a lot deeper and you have the entire band – Elliott, bassist Rick Savage, drummer Rick Allen and guitarists Phil Collen and Vivian Campbell, along with the late, dearly missed guitarist Steve Clark and even the early guitarist Pete Willis – to bring the stories, laughs and confessions. *Definitely* is Def Leppard's first official biography in their own words and images covering the full ride so far, right up to the pop-craft writing, sing-along aura and vintage glam-metal stomp of their 2022 album *Diamond Star Halos* – continuing proof that the Leppards, inducted into the Rock and Roll Hall of Fame in 2019, are still facing forward. Quitting, as you learn at every crossroads in this book, has never been an option. And they've had plenty of chances.

Rock and roll loves a good back story; I can vouch for that. And this band has given me plenty to write about over the years. Here is a saga that, even by the standards of my profession, is extraordinary in its whiplash between massive, diligently won success and cycles of trial and loss that seem like some constant, divine test of will.

It's also striking to discover again, in these pages, how Def Leppard have fought through disaster and sorrow with a defiance grounded in friendship and their faith in the mission. 'The reason everybody joined the band,' Allen once told me, 'was purely to play.' Life, in all of its glory and calamity, happens to everyone. But the music that follows here could not have been made by any other band. And getting it done – more than that, getting it done right whatever the odds – was always the first and most important reward.

I get flashbacks of my own here. The live shots put me back in the house, at my own stops on the trail. I was often on assignment; I always got rocked. The looning on the road reminds me that Def Leppard have never taken their stardom too seriously – but never at cost to the work. And I remember walking up those two flights of stairs in the Portland Works – the so-called 'Spoon Factory' off Bramall Lane in Sheffield – when Andy Smith, the band's first roadie and driver, gave me a guided tour of their home turf. The smell of sour milk that Smith remembered from containers used for tea breaks at rehearsals, then left forgotten behind an amp or a chair, was long gone. Yet it was not hard to imagine the freedom the young Leppards felt in that ruin in 1977 and 1978, to dream big and write their own ticket in riffs, choruses and commitment.

And, yes, that's me on page 101 – my original March 1983 review of *Pyromania* in *Rolling Stone*, just before the whirlwind. I often like to make this distinction about my journalism: I don't write about stars, I write about musicians. Some of them happen to be stars – or become stars along the way. Def Leppard hit that jackpot on a truly historic scale. But they did it – and keep doing it – as musicians: an enduring band of writers, players and brothers.

And that story, as you will see, is definitely not over.

CONTENTS

JOE ELLIOTT: The first gig I ever went to was T. Rex at the Sheffield City Hall on 23 October 1971.

Next I saw the Faces in 1972, but only the first three songs. I was only 12 and I had to leave to meet my parents outside the City Hall at 10.30. Normally that was kicking-out time, but the band didn't come on until 10.20. They said they'd been fogged in at Heathrow, but I think they were fogged in at the Dog and Duck. I didn't see another gig until Hunter Ronson in March 1975.

I had four paper rounds, two in the morning before school and then two after school. I would get 50 pence per round per week. And I'd get 50 pence pocket money off my dad for sweeping the backyard. So that was £2.50 a week, which was enough for an album or a gig ticket.

I was at every concert at the City Hall until 1979. I saw hundreds and hundreds of gigs – everybody, from the cool bands like Hunter Ronson, Sparks, Be-Bop Deluxe, Lynyrd Skynyrd, Thin Lizzy and UFO to Joan Armatrading, Supertramp and Rick Wakeman. I used to go with my schoolmate Andy, who became my lifelong buddy. Then when Def Leppard started in 1977 the whole band would go to gigs en masse.

There was a huge, 400-pound guy called Jan Kaminski who was the in-house photographer for the City Hall and we used to buy photos off him. One day he asked us, 'Do you want to be able to get in for free?' And we said, 'Are you kidding?' He sold us a press pass and all we had to do was flash it at one of the penguins at the door and he would reluctantly let us in.

It wasn't just the City Hall, it was the Top Rank, Sheffield Polytechnic ... I saw the Stiff 'Greatest Stiffs Live' tour with Wreckless Eric, Ian Dury, Nick Lowe, Larry Wallis and Elvis Costello. I saw the Clash one week at the Top Rank and Styx the week after. What a contrast! We really did see everything there, from the Jam to the Scorpions to AC/DC. You name it, I saw it. At the Top Rank gigs, you didn't get a ticket stub, you just paid and walked in. It was like a bingo hall.

There was also a fantastic club on a Sunday night called Improvisions, where you saw bands that were either on the way up, like the Pat Travers Band, Adam and the Ants, and Siouxsie and the Banshees, or that were on the way down or never quite made it, like the Pink Fairies, the Edgar Broughton Band, Boxer, Crawler, Moon and Trapeze.

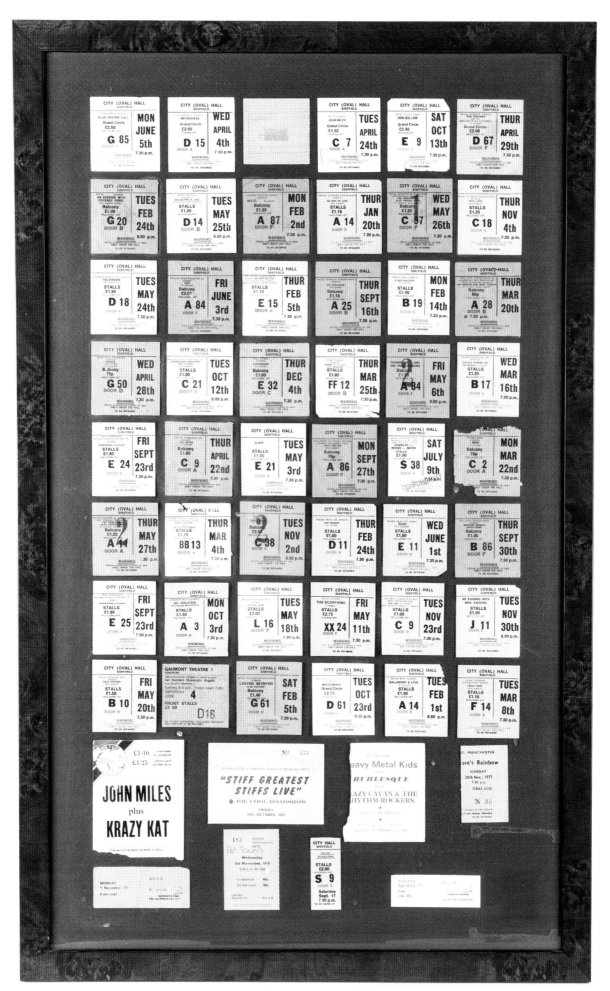

JOE ELLIOTT

NICKNAME	: TOO RUDE TO MENTION!
BIRTHDAY	: 1ST OF AUGUST
STAR SIGN	: LEO
PLACE OF BIRTH	: SHEFFIELD, ENGLAND
EDUCATED AT	: KING EDWARD VII COMPREHENSIVE SCHOOL, SHEFF.
HEIGHT, WEIGHT	: 6'0", ANYTHING BETWEEN 147 AND 154 LBS
COLOUR HAIR	: LIGHT BROWN
COLOUR EYES	: GREEN
MARRIED	: ONLY TO THE BAND
BROTHERS, SISTERS	: NONE
CAREER BEFORE MUSICIAN	: VAN DRIVER
MUSICAL INFLUENCES	: MOTT THE HOOPLE, T REX, BOWIE, ZEP
FIRST GIG	: PLAYING ELVIS IN A SCHOOL PLAY WHEN I WAS 11
FIRST GIG WITH DEF LEPPARD	: WESTFIELD SCHOOL, SHEFFIELD, JULY 1978
FIRST VINYL APPEARANCE WITH DEF LEPPARD	: THE DEF LEPPARD E.P., SEPT. 1978
ANY OTHER VINYL APPEARANCES	: ALL DEF LEPPARD
TYPE OF MICROPHONE USED	: USUALLY A SHURE SM58
INTERESTS	: MUSIC, SOCCER, NIGHTCLUBBING
FAVORITE BAND	: MOTT THE HOOPLE
FAVORITE SINGER	: PAUL RODGERS, ROBERT PLANT, DAVID COVERDALE
FIRST RECORD BOUGHT	: "SUGAR, SUGAR" BY THE ARCHIES! (1968)
FIRST CONCERT SEEN	: T REX, SHEFFIELD CITY HALL - 1971
BEST CONCERT SEEN	: HUNTER/RONSON BAND, SHEFFIELD CITY HALL - 1975
HEROES	: IAN HUNTER, HARRISON FORD, LAUREL AND HARDY, TONY CURRIE
HEROINE	: MARILYN MONROE
FAVORITE FILMS	: ANY CHEECH AND CHONG, CADDYSHACK, RAIDERS OF THE LOST ARK, E.T., PORKY'S
FAVORITE BOOK	: DIARY OF A ROCK'N'ROLL STAR BY IAN HUNTER PRIVATE EYE MAGAZINE
FAVORITE FOOD	: EGGS, BEANS ON TOAST, BARBEQUED RIBS
FAVORITE DRINK	: LAGER, VODKA, PINA COLADA
FAVORITE COLOUR	: RED AND BLACK
FAVORITE CAR	: PORSCHE TURBO
MOST ENJOYABLE PART OF WORK	: ON STAGE
MOST HATED PART OF WORK	: STUDIOS
FUNNIEST EXPERIENCE	: MY OLD HEADMASTER GETTING BOMBED (I'LL TELL YOU ABOUT IT SOMEDAY)
WORST EXPERIENCE	: SEEING MY MASTER TAPES MANGLE UP WHILE MAKING "PYROMANIA"
IDEAL HOME	: SOMEWHERE I CAN PLAY MY STEREO AS LOUD AS I LIKE
IDEAL HOLIDAY	: NO PEOPLE, HOT SUNNY BEACH WITH A CLEAR SEA
DREAMS	: NO TAXMAN, DEF LEPPARD BIGGER THAN THE STONES!
AMBITIONS	: TO MAKE DEF LEPPARD BIGGER THAN THE STONES!

JOE ELLIOTT: At school, I got grilled by my careers officer, 'What do you want to do, boy, when you grow up?'

Well, I wanted to be either a footballer or in a band but, even at the age of 15, I realised that the band was a better option because making it in sport is all about discipline, whereas rock and roll is as much to do with your vibe and attitude as the amount of work you put in. There's inspiration as well as perspiration.

I had an instinctive drive to be involved in music, whereas I would just dabble in sports like football and tennis and golf. I would do anything to get into a gig – climb a drainpipe, squeeze through the toilet window. And I'd also do anything to get my hands on a record, including stealing it if necessary.

I had a £5 Broadway drum kit from a junk shop which I played in the attic, much to our neighbour's annoyance. I could keep a regular beat, but that was about all. I started playing guitar when I was eight. My mother had bought one from a catalogue and she taught herself to play Americana music like Pete Seeger and Joan Baez. I was fascinated watching her fingers move. I told my parents that I wanted a guitar and, quite rightly, they said, 'Well, learn to play first, then we'll think about it.' I had my mum teach me some chords and we played from a tune-a-day book.

I never had the discipline to sit on the edge of my bed and go widdly, widdly for eight hours a day. I didn't care about playing lead guitar. I was only doing it for my own amusement, and as a way to accompany my voice.

I also wrote my first song when I was eight years old. It was called 'Going Forever' and was about a girl leaving me. I was obviously heavily influenced by the Sixties pop-rock bands that were on BBC Radio One at the time, who were all singing about girls leaving them.

'Going Forever' had minor chords for the verse, then it went major on the chorus. Proper songwriters, like Neil Sedaka, will tell you that's the way to go. But I didn't know; it was almost like I was channelling a songwriter from a previous life.

At about the age of 12 I tried to write a rock opera about a girl called Katrina, named after Alice Cooper's snake, which I saw on the back cover of the *Killer* album. I didn't get very far, but I remember one of the songs was called 'Acid Bath'. I was obviously a little bit influenced by horror movies and the Who's song 'The Acid Queen' from *Tommy*.

By this time, I was besotted with T. Rex and David Bowie. I was always intrigued by the way Bowie wrote songs. He'd move up a semitone from an E minor to an F, which was something you might find in European cabaret music like Jacques Brel and Marlene Dietrich, but not so much in rock and roll.

I only knew half a dozen chords. Once you learn to bridge, then you can shift your fingers any way you want. I didn't sit down and play religiously for hours at a time. I would just pick it up, put it down, pick it up, put it down. The next day I'd want to try something different.

Because my dad was a wannabe musician who could play a bit of piano and a bit of guitar, he was very supportive. He wanted me to take my music further than he had. Having said that, I don't think my parents would have been happy if I'd said I was going to join a band when I left school. They might have been OK if I'd said I was going to music college, but I didn't. I went to work in a factory – Osborn-Mushet Tools – because that's what you did if you lived in Sheffield. It was a steel city. If you lived on the outskirts, you'd work in a coal mine; but if you lived in the centre, it was factory life for you.

If you were lucky, you'd get a job in the office so you didn't have to go on the shop floor, which is what I did. I started off in the buying department, and then I ran the basement store. By the age of 17 I was ordering everything that was needed for the factory, from soap and hand towels to the boilers and grinding wheels for the shop floor. I had that job down to a fine art. It was an eight-hour day, but I could do the work in two hours.

JOE ELLIOTT: Def Leppard came from a chance meeting. One evening in August 1977 I missed the bus home after work. Instead of following the bus route, I walked along a quieter street that went the same way. As I was walking up the street, I saw Pete Willis walking down to his house. I knew Pete through my friend Craig – they went to Tapton Comprehensive whereas I went to King Edward's on the other side of the fence, but we'd see each other after school and at weekends.

I knew that Pete played guitar and so when I bumped into him I asked if he wanted to get a band together. He said, 'No, I kind of got one, but we're looking for a singer.' I said, 'I'll do it.'

RICK SAVAGE: When I was 13 or 14 I used to go to the youth club of Tapton School every Tuesday night. Whoever had a guitar or whatever would come in and start playing. It wasn't a band as such, it was just a congregation of people who were learning to play.

From that I got to know Pete Willis. After a year or so we decided to do something more serious. I brought in Tony Kenning, who had been playing drums for a couple of years, and that was the nucleus of our band, Atomic Mass. What we didn't have was a singer. Everybody wanted to play guitar. Fortunately, Pete knew Joe and he was enthusiastic to be a lead singer.

JOE ELLIOTT: Rick ('Sav'), Tony and Pete came to my mum and dad's house, and we went up to my bedroom. They'd brought a few albums and I played some of mine. Sav was massively into Queen and I introduced them to stuff that they'd never heard, like UFO, Montrose, Heavy Metal Kids – they were a massive favourite of mine – and a bit of punk as well. They were very impressed with my record collection and that's pretty much how I got the gig. I didn't sing in front of them; I just talked a good game, liked the right kind of music and I was tall.

By the time they left we were a band. We hadn't played or sung a single note to each other, but they came to that house as three kids and they left as three members of Def Leppard.

When Pete said they were thinking about calling the band Accracy, I just said, 'That's shit.' They were shocked that I was so opinionated. 'You got anything better?' And I said, 'Yeah, what about Deaf Leopard?'

The name was inspired by a collage I'd done at school that had a leopard on it and a cut-out of the word 'deaf'. I just caught sight of it on my bedroom wall when challenged to come up with a band name – those two concepts came beaconing out at me from the paper. I thought Deaf Leopard sounded great phonetically and a few weeks later Tony suggested we spell it phonetically too, which was when we noticed the similarity to Led Zeppelin.

Pete just went, 'Deaf Leopard?' But Sav and Tony thought it was pretty cool. We instantly had three votes to one. So, from the start, the band was a cooperative. It wasn't Pete's band, which he was hoping it would be, it was a four-way thing. Whoever came up with the best idea would, in theory, win the vote.

I had an insane enthusiasm. When you're an only child obsessed with music by the age of three or four, as I was, your imagination runs wild. You make all the decisions by yourself and you don't have to compromise because it's all in your head. So, I'd already formed this whole vision for a band.

But if I had caught the bus that day, it wouldn't have happened. I'd still be in Sheffield with 3.2 kids, a big belly and a bald head!

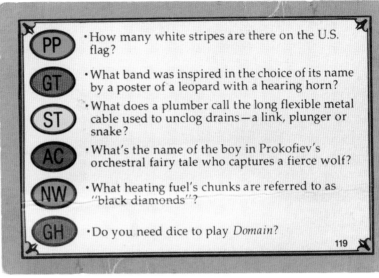

- PP · How many white stripes are there on the U.S. flag?
- GT · What band was inspired in the choice of its name by a poster of a leopard with a hearing horn?
- ST · What does a plumber call the long flexible metal cable used to unclog drains—a link, plunger or snake?
- AC · What's the name of the boy in Prokofiev's orchestral fairy tale who captures a fierce wolf?
- NW · What heating fuel's chunks are referred to as "black diamonds"?
- GH · Do you need dice to play *Domain*?

119

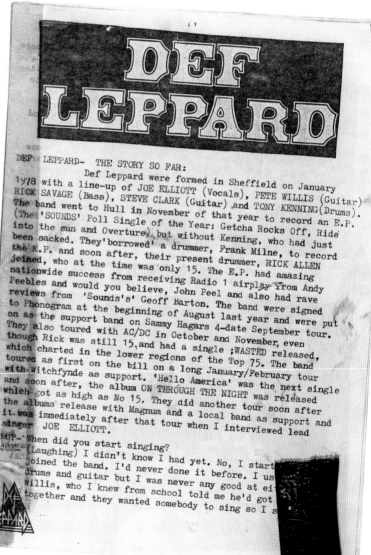

DEF LEPPARD

DEF LEPPARD- THE STORY SO FAR:

Def Leppard were formed in Sheffield on January 1978 with a line-up of JOE ELLIOTT (Vocals), PETE WILLIS (Guitar) RICK SAVAGE (Bass), STEVE CLARK (Guitar) and TONY KENNING (Drums) The band went to Hull in November of that year to record an E.P. (The 'SOUNDS' Poll Single of the Year: Getcha Rocks Off, Ride into the sun and Overture) but without Kenning, who had just been sacked. They 'borrowed' a drummer, Frank Milne, to record the E.P. and soon after, their present drummer, RICK ALLEN joined, who at the time was only 15. The E.P. had amazing nationwide success from receiving Radio 1 airplay from Andy Peebles and would you believe, John Peel and also had rave reviews from 'Sounds's' Geoff Barton. The band were signed to Phonogram at the beginning of August last year and were put on as the support band on Sammy Hagars 4-date September tour. They also toured with AC/DC in October and November, even though Rick was still 15,and had a single ;WASTED released, which charted in the lower regions of the Top 75. The band toured as first on the bill on a long January/February tour with Witchfynde as support. 'Hello America' was the next single and soon after, the album ON THROUGH THE NIGHT was released which got as high as No 15. They did another tour soon after the albums' release with Magnum and a local band as support and it was immediately after that tour when I interviewed lead singer JOE ELLIOTT.

When did you start singing?
(Laughing) I didn't know I had yet. No, I start joined the band. I'd never done it before. I us drums and guitar but I was never any good at ei Willis, who I knew from school told me he'd got together and they wanted somebody to sing so I s

RICK SAVAGE: We were all heavy rock fans before we formed the band. I could listen to punk, and I thought the Pistols were brilliant, but we'd all grown up on heavy rock and we were anxious to keep it going. And if we had played punk we might have disappeared without a trace, because everybody was doing it.

Looking back, I think coming in during the punk era actually helped us because there were only a couple of bands that were playing our type of music – us and Iron Maiden. People probably took a little bit more notice of us because we stood out.

Scrapbook created from a wallpaper sample book by Joe Elliott's mother, Cindy, containing photographs and clippings that document the early days of Def Leppard

RICK SAVAGE

NICKNAME	: SAV
BIRTHDAY	: 2ND OF DECEMBER
STAR SIGN	: SAGITTARIUS
PLACE OF BIRTH	: SHEFFIELD
EDUCATED AT	: TAPTON COM., SHEFFIELD
HEIGHT, WEIGHT	: 5' 11", 10 STONE 10 LB (150 LBS)
COLOUR HAIR	: ANYTHING FROM DARK BROWN TO RED TO PURPLE
COLOUR EYES	: BLUE
MARRIED	: NO!
BROTHERS, SISTERS	: 2 BROTHERS, NO SISTERS
CAREER BEFORE MUSICIAN	: TECHNICIAN WITH BRITISH RAIL
MUSICAL INFLUENCES	: BRIAN MAY, LED ZEPPELIN
FIRST GIG	: AT SCHOOL WHEN I WAS 14 PLAYING LEAD GUITAR
FIRST GIG WITH DEF LEPPARD	: SOME SCHOOL DANCE
FIRST VINYL APPEARANCE WITH DEF LEPPARD	: THE DEF LEPPARD E.P.
ANY OTHER VINYL APPEARANCES	: NONE
TYPE OF BASS GUITAR	: FENDER PRECISIONS, HAMER STANDARD & CRUISE BASS
INTERESTS	: ALL SPORTS ESPECIALLY SOCCER; THE UNKNOWN
FAVORITE BAND	: TOO MANY TO MENTION; EARLY QUEEN IN PARTICULAR
FIRST RECORD BOUGHT	: "PROPOGANDA" BY SPARKS
FIRST CONCERT SEEN	: URIAH HEEP – 1974
BEST CONCERT SEEN	: LED ZEPPELIN – 1974
HERO	: NOBODY IN PARTICULAR
HEROINE	: NOBODY IN PARTICULAR
FAVORITE FILMS	: BOGART, EASTWOOD, BRONSON FILMS
FAVORITE BOOK	: ANYTHING ON THE UNKNOWN
FAVORITE FOOD	: STEAK, BEANS
FAVORITE DRINK	: FREE!
FAVORITE COLOUR	: BLUE, BLACK
FAVORITE CAR	: PORSCHE
MOST ENJOUABLE PART OF WORK	: DOING GOOD SHOWS
MOST HATED PART OF WORK	: TRAVELLING EARLY IN MORNING OR RIGHT AFTER SHOWS
FUNNIEST EXPERIENCE	: CARRYING PETE WILLIS AND HIS ENTIRE BEDROOM SUITE OUTSIDE WITH THE SCORPIONS; PETE DID NOT EVEN NOTICE!
WORST EXPERIENCE	: PLAYING READING FESTIVAL AND WAITING FOR PYROMANIA TO BE RELEASED
DREAMS	: YES, THANKS
AMBITIONS	: TO BE HAPPY, EVERYTHING ELSE IS SECONDARY

Richard Savage scores the first goal for Sheffield Boys against Manchester in the English Schools' F.A. Trophy Quarter-Final Replay at Bramall Lane on 8th March.

(Photo by courtesy of Sheffield Newspapers)

LYDGATE CITY FINALISTS 1971-1972

HANDBOOK
Season 1976-77

RICK SAVAGE: I've always loved music, right from watching *Top of the Pops* as a kid. My interest in playing guitar came from my elder brothers. I'm the youngest of three sons, seven years adrift of the next youngest, so my brothers were a big influence on me. My father was a semi-professional pianist who would play in clubs and bars on the weekends. By the time I was ten, I had learned to play 'Maggie May' by Rod Stewart on the acoustic guitar – I picked it up really quickly. From then on, I just wanted to keep playing and keep improving.

While I was learning my guitar, I was also playing football to a pretty high level. I was signed to Sheffield United and played for their youth team, despite being a Sheffield Wednesday fan. (To my mind, the only two teams in Sheffield worth mentioning are Sheffield Wednesday and Sheffield Wednesday Reserves.) But then there was a sliding doors moment when it became obvious which direction I was going to choose.

Sheffield United told me they didn't think I was going to be quite good enough to become a professional. And very soon after that, I met Joe for the first time. So, almost overnight, I went from budding footballer to budding rock god. It saved my life, because I don't know what else I would have done. I was working for British Rail at the time, but I didn't see much future in that.

I was the original guitar player and Pete Willis was the other, but we couldn't find a bass player to save our lives. Pete was a better guitar player than I was, so I volunteered to play bass just until we found someone. And I guess we never did, so I kept the gig!

There's still absolutely no chance of me getting anywhere near six strings within the current line-up because Phil Collen and Vivian Campbell are two of the best rock guitar players in the world.

JOE ELLIOTT: Tony found us a rehearsal room in a place called Portland Works, which was originally a bunch of miniature factories, each consisting of one man making his own cutlery or whatever. By the mid-Seventies, the steel industry was imploding. You could now buy 100 knives and forks from China for the price of one made in Sheffield, so the steel workers were retiring and all the factories were falling to bits.

Portland Works became a hive of art, and Sheffield in the late Seventies became like Liverpool in the early Sixties. Straight Eight rehearsed across the room from us. I wouldn't be surprised if some of the guys from ABC were down there at some stage in other crappy little bands. The Thompson Twins were from nearby Chesterfield, and then, of course, there was the Human League. I used to see Phil Oakey a lot in Record Collector in Broomhill. We would be flicking through stacks of vinyl and pulling out the same Mick Ronson albums. (Here's a pub quiz question for you: what three things do the Human League and Def Leppard have in common? The answer is: both bands are from Sheffield; they've both released an album called *Hysteria*; and they've both covered the Mick Ronson song 'Only After Dark'.)

The rehearsal room in Portland Works was probably 30 feet by 15 feet, and the rent was £1 each a week. We could well afford that because we all had day jobs, pulling in around £15 each. Knock off a fiver for board and our mums washing our clothes and that left £10 to spend.

Most bands had rehearsal spaces where they could play for two hours and then they had to strip out their gear and take it home. We wanted to be able to leave everything there – not least because the room was on the top floor. It was bad enough having to lug our gear up and down two flights of stairs every time we had a gig.

We went to town decorating the place and getting it just the way we wanted it. We had posters of Peter Gabriel and Bowie and *Sounds* articles taped to the wall. We set up a little table in the corner with a kettle and a record player so we could listen to stuff as well as play.

Portland Works
Sheffield

JOE ELLIOTT: We would rehearse after work, starting at about seven and going on until eleven. Then we'd run along to a pub called the Sheldon and buy one pint with four straws. We'd discuss what we'd been doing that evening and how we were going to conquer the world, with all the exuberance you have when you're 18 years old.

Often, I didn't get home until one in the morning and then I had to get up for work at seven. I would keep going until about ten and then pass out for a bit on sacks of dirty overalls in the back of the stores. They made a great mattress. The guys I worked with let me get away with it because they thought I was funny, the wannabe kid rock star, the only guy on the factory floor with long hair.

The first song we learned to play together was 'Suffragette City'. This was a song I'd been listening to since I was 12. I didn't even need a lyric sheet, I could just blare it out. Then we branched out into Thin Lizzy songs like 'Jailbreak' and 'Rosalie'. We used to do 'Only You Can Rock Me' by UFO. I think we had a go at 'Hot Blooded' by Foreigner. We did a couple of Pat Travers tunes, like 'Rock 'n' Roll Susie'. We even did 'Pretty Vacant' by the Pistols. Although it was obvious we were never going to be a punk band ourselves, we did take a lot of the ethos along with us – we went for short guitar solos rather than massively long ones, for example.

We also started writing pretty much straightaway. I wrote lyrics and melodies; the other guys wrote the music (with an occasional contribution from me). I think the first song we ever wrote was 'Ride into the Sun', which became the first track on *The Def Leppard EP*. Sav and I were alone together at Portland Works. It wasn't supposed to be a rehearsal day, but we'd gone down there anyway just to hang. He wrote the riff, and I started singing melodies and writing words down. We had the song written that night in one long stream of consciousness. Then we played it to the guys the next day and there it was, our first song.

Pete had the riff for 'Getcha Rocks Off', so we played around with that next. I started making noises until words came out. Then we had another song. It was always music first, melody and lyrics second. I was never walking in with a load of poetry, saying, 'Put some music to this, boys.'

We were a four-piece band all the way up to Christmas 1977 when we did our first gig at the rehearsal room in front of a select bunch of mates. We played the six or seven songs that we had, and tried to make a show of it by wrapping crepe paper over the light bulbs and wearing stage clothes while the 'audience' just sat cross-legged on the floor a foot and a half in front of us. Hilarious, but they were really impressed. It was reassuring to know that all the work we'd been doing was leading somewhere.

But the most important thing was that we were impressing ourselves. We were writing our own tunes. Tony was a decent drummer. Sav had become a really good bass player. Pete was a fantastic guitar player. I was still a pretty average singer, but I was getting better.

JOE ELLIOTT: It was thanks to Pete that Steve Clark joined Def Leppard. On top of work and the band, Pete was also doing an educational course at college. One lunchtime in January 1978, he was in the college common room. Just as he reached for a copy of *Guitar Monthly* off the coffee table, this skinny blond lad came into the room. They looked at each other, 'You play?' 'Yeah, I play.' They got talking and Pete invited him to come down to the rehearsal room.

I arranged to meet Steve outside Virgin Records. It was fucking freezing, and I was wearing an army surplus trench coat and a flat cap. I looked like a classic Yorkshireman. Around the corner, about five minutes late – and that would be his thing, forever – came this vision. He weighed about 120 pounds. He had the tightest blue jeans you've ever seen, white clogs like the ones his hero Brian Robertson of Thin Lizzy used to wear, white socks, a little white T-shirt that was about four inches short of his jeans so his navel was on display, and a dirty jacket that was about six inches from meeting in the middle. He had long, blond, curly hair and he was carrying a guitar case.

He was 17, and he already looked like a total rock star.

We shook hands, and then we talked as we walked the ten minutes to the rehearsal room. He met everyone else, sat on this crappy couch that we'd found on the street and watched us play the few songs that we did. He couldn't stop himself smiling. I remember him saying it was the first time he'd ever met like-minded people. He loved the fact that we had a proper set up – we'd even got the drums on a riser.

After a while we took a break and Steve started jamming on some Zeppelin on his own (Jimmy Page was his guitar hero, along with Zal Cleminson from the Sensational Alex Harvey Band and Alex Lifeson from Rush). Somebody then suggested that we play 'Free Bird' by Lynyrd Skynyrd because we all knew it. We'd never played it, but we all knew it.

In 'Free Bird' you have three different guitarists soloing individually. Well, Steve played all three parts on his own right to the end of the song. Our jaws were on the ground. I just blurted out, 'Well, he's in then.' Pete said, 'Don't you think we should talk about it first?' I stared at him and said, 'Are you kidding?' It was like finding a diamond and saying, 'Well, I'm not sure about this.' Steve was perfect for us.

Instantly, a crack opened up in my relationship with Pete; he didn't like me being so forthright, and I didn't like him being so conservative. My view was, we were a rock band, not a government. We were supposed to take risks.

Luckily, Tony and Sav thought the same way, so now we had two guitarists, like Thin Lizzy. We split the solos between Pete and Steve, began to incorporate guitar harmonies, and before long we started writing songs with Steve.

One day, Steve was running late for rehearsal as usual. We could hear the click, click, click of him galloping up the steel-tipped stairs, then he burst through the door. Shushing us with a finger to his lips, he went straight over to his stack, plugged his Gibson copy in and stood with it slung low and his legs three feet apart like an upside-down Y. Then he belted out this incredible riff, which he'd had singing around in his head and was desperate not to forget.

We worked out an arrangement together and I started on the lyrics. Pete didn't like one of my verses so I rewrote it. And that was 'Wasted', Steve Clark's first Def Leppard song.

STEVE CLARK: I wrote 'Wasted' on the way to a rehearsal. I'd been with the group about two weeks and I was just sat on the bus without my guitar when I came up with this riff. I belted into the rehearsal room, told everyone to shut up and then I worked it out. It was done in five minutes.

Steve Clark Joe Elliott
DEF LEPPARD

A	DATE · · N.R [ ] YES [ ] NO	B	DATE · · N.R [ ] YES [ ] NO

A side:
- Train Kept A Rollin
- Nobodys Fault But Mine
- Black Dog
- In The Evening
- The Rain Song
- Hot Dog
- All My Love

B side:
- Trampled Underfoot
- Since I've Been Loving You
- Achilles Last Stand
- White Summer
- Kashmir

LED ZEP MANNHEIM 7-2-80 2/2 / VARIOUS

Cassette tapes featuring Led Zeppelin, from Steve Clark's personal collection

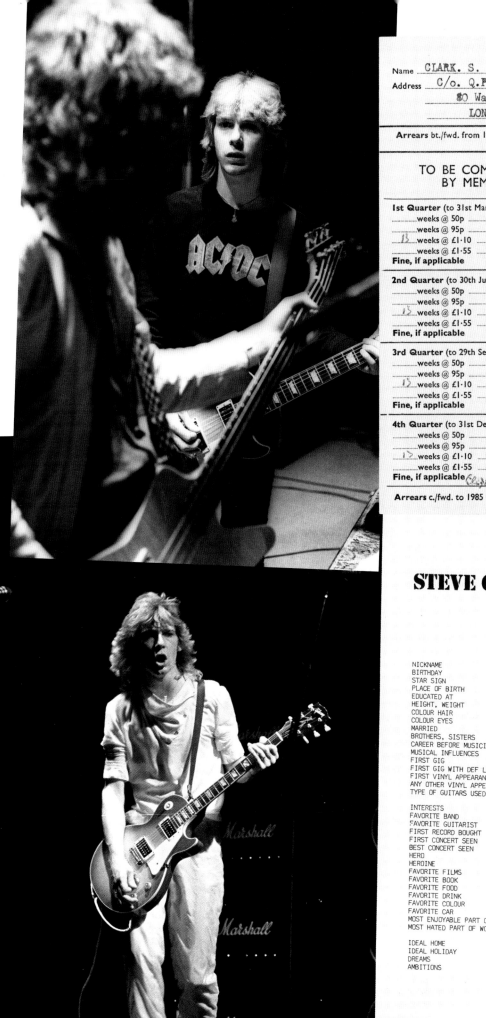

STEVE CLARK

NICKNAME	: Steamin'
BIRTHDAY	: 23rd of April
STAR SIGN	: Taurus
PLACE OF BIRTH	: Sheffield
EDUCATED AT	: Wisewood School
HEIGHT, WEIGHT	: 5'10", 9 stone 2 lbs (128 lbs)
COLOUR HAIR	: Blond
COLOUR EYES	: Blue
MARRIED	: No
BROTHERS, SISTERS	: 2 brothers, no sisters
CAREER BEFORE MUSICIAN	: Lathe operator
MUSICAL INFLUENCES	: Led Zep, Beatles, Classical
FIRST GIG	: Old folks home (Sheffield)
FIRST GIG WITH DEF LEPPARD	: School dance
FIRST VINYL APPEARANCE WITH DEF LEPPARD	: Rocks Off E.P.
ANY OTHER VINYL APPEARANCES	: None
TYPE OF GUITARS USED	: 3 Gibson Les Pauls, Hamer Double Neck, Hamer Junior, (Strat and Tele in studio)
INTERESTS	: Art, Archeology
FAVORITE BAND	: Led Zeppelin
FAVORITE GUITARIST	: Jimmy Page, Zal Cleminson
FIRST RECORD BOUGHT	: Shadows E.P.
FIRST CONCERT SEEN	: The Sensational Alex Harvey Band
BEST CONCERT SEEN	: Led Zeppelin
HERO	: Not really got any
HEROINE	: Not really got any
FAVORITE FILMS	: Depends on mood
FAVORITE BOOK	: Depends on mood
FAVORITE FOOD	: Bacon and eggs
FAVORITE DRINK	: Vodka, Lucozade
FAVORITE COLOUR	: Blue
FAVORITE CAR	: Morgan, 'E' type Jaguar
MOST ENJOYABLE PART OF WORK	: Playing live gigs
MOST HATED PART OF WORK	: Long stretches doing the same thing (becomes too routine)
IDEAL HOME	: Victorian house with studio
IDEAL HOLIDAY	: Cruise down the Nile
DREAMS	: To be rich and happy
AMBITIONS	: Improve as a musician, have more success

STEVE CLARK: The good thing about Def Leppard when I joined is I'd been trying to find other musicians with the same enthusiasm as myself and they were very determined from day one. They didn't want to go to the pub and then just rehearse for 30 minutes. They made it quite clear that every night we'd rehearse for three hours, then we'd have a drink after. And they were really keen to write their own songs. They never just wanted to be a club band covering Thin Lizzy songs or top 20 hits to make a little bit of money on the side of their day job. Their aim was always much higher than that.

JOE ELLIOTT: In the summer of 1978, the whole band went on holiday to the Norfolk Broads. You could rent a boat for £120. We took along our friend Nick Cartwright, who became our sound engineer. While we were there, we found out that UFO were playing the Gaumont Theatre in Ipswich, which was only 20 miles down the river from where we were. We moored as close as we could, took a taxi in, and got tickets right at the back of the hall.

It was a fantastic gig. Other than the fact that they had a keyboard player, UFO were exactly the kind of band we wanted to be.

We came out of there, got back to the boat and Steve, hammered, uttered the immortal words, 'That's it, if we don't do a gig within the next couple of weeks, I'm leaving.' He'd seen Pete Way, Phil Mogg and the insane vision that was Michael Schenker posing in his boots with his Flying V, and that was it.

The first thing I did when we got back to Sheffield was visit our mate Bill Coupland, who was kind of our first unofficial manager. In full panic mode, I said, 'We've got to do a gig, we've got to do a gig *now*.'

STEVE CLARK: I was desperate to play live, but the rest of the guys in the group just wanted to keep on rehearsing and polishing and polishing. In ten years' time I didn't want to still be rehearsing in that bloody spoon factory.

I'd probably had one light ale too many and I threatened to leave if we didn't do a gig soon. Joe was very good about it. He said, 'All right, I guess that's it. Let's do our first show.'

JOE ELLIOTT: That first gig was on 18 July 1978 at Westfield School in Mosborough, at their end-of-term party. We couldn't believe we were actually going to be playing in front of a proper audience. Andy and my other good schoolmate, Ian, borrowed their dads' cars, and we loaded all the gear in the back. We were so nervous we smuggled in some beer for Dutch courage.

It was a gymnasium, half seven at night in July so it was broad daylight. The kids were sitting on chairs all the way round the outside of the hall. There was nobody down the front, and they looked at us like we were aliens – probably because they all loved the Bee Gees or Donna Summer. We opened with one of our own songs, 'World Beyond the Sky', which we later abandoned, never to be heard again. Steve came out, struck the pose, did a Pete Townshend windmill and ...

... nothing.

He'd forgotten to turn on his standby. So he went, 'Oops', flicked the switch and started again. Of course, everybody laughed at us but we got through the song and then the other 45 minutes of material, which is pretty much all we had, and then we went back behind the stage into a big classroom which was our dressing room.

The teacher came in, said, 'Thanks, lads,' and gave us five quid out of his pocket. Then we started hearing chants of 'More! More!' coming through from the gym, so the teacher said, 'I think you need to go out there and do another one.' All we had left was 'Jailbreak'. Luckily it had been in the charts, so we came out and played it and all these kids rushed down to the front and started headbanging. That told us what kind of songs we needed to play.

JOE ELLIOTT: We kept on gigging with the material we had, while writing more songs all the time. Sav and I would write the commercial stuff, Pete the more bluesy, heavy stuff, and Steve came out with the very angular, weird stuff, like the music for 'When the Walls Came Tumbling Down', the lyric for which was based on a brilliant poem about the end of the world by my mate Andy.

By November 1978, we'd probably done about seven or eight gigs. We played working men's clubs where they expected us to do covers. We never did that, we just played our own! But those venues used to pay proper money – £350 for a gig – whereas at a rock bar we'd get £20. Playing the working men's clubs subsidised our playing where we needed to play to get noticed.

RIDE INTO THE SUN (Savage/Elliott)

I'm revvin' up my engine, doin' hundred and four
I've got the throttle open, she won't take no more
'cause I'm ridin', I'm ridin' into the sun

We're shootin' down the highway, got my baby behind
She holds onto my hips, and drives me out of my mind
'Cause I'm ridin', I'm ridin' into the sun

Chorus: We've gotta make it, make it by midnight
           and if we take it, you know that it's alright
           but if we break it, no need to get uptight,
           Just ride, just ride into the sun

We're cruisin' and we're boozin', we're havin' some fun
We're chasin' through the country, got the blues on the run
'Cause we're ridin', we're ridin' into the sun

It's such an easy feelin' with the wind in my hair
I'm burning up the rubber, and I don't really care
'Cause I'm ridin', I'm ridin' into the sun

Chorus:

Chorus:

GETCHA ROCKS OFF   (Savage/Elliott/Clark/Willis)

Well, we were gettin' ready just the other night
when a knock on the dressin' room door
gave way to a leather jacket little girl
who we'd never ever seen before.
In her red satin' dress and her high heeled shoes
well, she took us all by surprise
and when she asked us what we wanted to do
well, she said it with her eyes

JUST GETCHA ROCKS OFF !

Well when we finally took the stage, there she was
but she wasn't on her own
because she'd brought some friends, maybe five or six
yeah, she must have been on the 'phone
and when they started dancin' and jumpin' around
well we could'nt believe our eyes
because they'd got the whole damned audience rockin'
and they'd got us paralysed

JUST GETCHA ROCKS OFF !

The Overture (Savage/Elliott/Clark/Willis)

And with this message, that I bring to you
A beacon of light, to see you through
For time is on our side.

And a holy man, does say to me
To always be blind, and never to see
Its not the way he planned it, oh no.

The time has come to gather up your thoughts
For you have said your peace
The Lords of light will change this place
From famine into feast
The buildings that once stood so tall have crumbled to the ground
The silver warriors who came in force are nowhere to be found.

Time is the essence the priests do say
To restore your faith in man
For the job you do and the roll you play
Will help rebuild this land
Through empty streets and dusty fields, we'll fight for what we need
Protected by our swords and shields, we can replant the seed

The roads ahead are long and winding
In which the bandits thrive
But we have the power of finding
Illusion to keep us alive
So through the valleys and over the hills
We'll march and sing in rhyme
We'll fight until we lose our will
For essence is our time.

The man the moon, the darkened sky
The morning dew reflecting in my eye
The rising mist the tempered earth
They're just reminders of what life's worth.

And with this message, that I bring to you
A beacon of light, to see you through
For time is on our side.

Special thanks to our Mixer Man
Mr. Nick Cartwright whose name
was thoughtfully left off the
E.P. cover !

Joe"Zeff"Elliott   Steve Clark   Pete Willis

Rick Savage

Frank Noon

Side One

RIDE INTO THE SUN
                    Savage/Elliott

GETCHA ROCKS OFF
                    Savage/Elliott
                    Clark/Willis

Side Two

THE OVERTURE
                    Savage/Elliott
                    Clark/Willis

Recorded at Fairview Studios
              Hull   Nov. 1978

Pete Willis – guitar (lead ●)
Steve Clark – guitar (lead ●)
Joe Elliott – lead vocals
Rick Savage – bass guitar & vocals
Frank Noon – drums

Engineered by Roy Neave
              & Keith Herd
Produced by Def Leppard
Art work by Dave Jeffery
Photography by John Wood

33⅓ rpm

Thanks to
Tony Kenning
Paul Ainsbury
Kevin Clark
Ian Flint
Russ Major
Craig Robertshaw
Andy Smith
Keith Strong
Pete Titterton
Dave Walker
Gary Ward
Rent-a-Crowd

Frank Noon – courtesy of
" The Next Band "

The Def Leppard EP
Recorded: November 1978
Released: January 1979

THE DEF LEPPARD EP

JOE ELLIOTT: *I know that certain members of this band have said that they spent forever gluing together the 1,000 picture sleeves for our debut EP. Bullshit! They may have done 100, but my mum and I did the other 900. Each sleeve came as a single sheet, which you had to fold in half and then you had to cut a quarter-inch piece off the back so you could fold the front flat and glue it with Pritt. The first 100 copies had a lyric sheet, which I ran off on the photocopier at work – I nearly got fired when they found out.*

BLUDGEON RIFFOLA RECORDS

DEF LEPPARD

33 ⅓ RPM

SRTS/78/CUS 232-A
STEREO

1. RIDE INTO THE SUN
(Savage/Elliott)
2. GETCHA ROCKS OFF
(Savage/Elliott/Clark/Willis)

(Copyright Control)

BLUDGEON RIFFOLA RECORDS

DEF LEPPARD

33 ⅓ RPM

SRTS/78/CUS 232 B
STEREO

THE OVERTURE
(Savage/Elliott/Clark/Willis)

(Copyright Control)

JOE ELLIOTT: One of the other local bands around at the time was a three-piece called the Next Band. One time we saw them play and they were selling an EP of four of their songs. I was friendly with Frank Noon, the drummer, who told me they'd recorded the songs in Hull at a place called Fairview Studios, sent them off to be pressed up in Cambridge, then had some sleeves made and sold them for a pound.

I presented all the information to the rest of the guys and begged my dad to lend us the £150 we'd need for the session. Bless him, he emptied his bank account.

Just before we were due to record the EP, we had to fire Tony because he'd stopped turning up to rehearsals. He wanted to go to the movies with his girlfriend instead. We told him it was her or us and, sadly for him, he picked her. With so little time to find a new drummer, I asked Frank if we could borrow him. He had barely a week to learn three songs from scratch.

We were booked in the studio over a weekend, so we drove to Hull on the Friday and got bollocksed drunk but not so drunk that we couldn't play the next day.

We set up in the morning and ran through the songs while the knob-twiddlers were getting the sound balances right. By the end of Saturday, we had all the backing tracks and guitar solos recorded. I started singing Saturday night and got two of the songs done, and then on Sunday I had to go back in early to finish the third one. We'd picked three songs that would show different sides of the band. 'Ride into the Sun' was a pop-rock song; 'Getcha Rocks Off' was very hard, not out-and-out heavy metal but leaning that way; and 'The Overture' was epic – it had all sorts of stuff in it: acoustic bits, fast bits, quiet bits, dual guitar harmonies, a bit of Rush, a bit of Bowie. It was eight minutes long and all over the shop.

I probably finished singing by noon on Sunday, and then we had four hours for mixing before we ran out of money. But we got it done.

We ran off two cassettes and took the master tapes with us, and paid the studio bill: £148.50. It was getting dark by the time we left to go back to Sheffield, three band members in one car and two in the other, our mates driving, and one of the cassettes in each car. Using what was left of my dad's money, we stopped off and got £1.50's worth of fish and chips to share between the lot of us, and we drove home listening to the cassette over and over again on the car stereo, going, 'We've done it, we've made a record.'

JOE ELLIOTT: When we got back we made copies so everybody could play it to their mums and dads and friends, and then we had to go through the process of pressing it onto vinyl. If you sent a cassette to an A&R man it would be one of the 300 he was going to receive that week. They just became paperweights and door stops. So we figured, naively, that if we sent a seven-inch vinyl single with a picture sleeve to a record company, they'd at least take the time to listen to it.

I was still working at Osborns then, sharing an office with a lady called Jenny Taylor. We got on quite well, so I told her I needed £450 to get 1,000 records pressed. She offered to lend us the money but she wanted £600 back. I had no other options, so I accepted. Our plan was to send copies off to all the music papers and rock radio stations, and then sell the rest so I could pay back Jenny Taylor's £600 and my dad's £150. At a pound a copy, we'd need to sell 750 just to break even.

Keith Strong was a reporter at the *Sheffield Star* who did a Thursday night pop page. We managed to use him quite brilliantly over the years to include Def Leppard announcements in his news articles. When we sent him a copy of the EP, he wrote about it and even included the phone number to ring if you wanted to buy one. Virgin Records wanted 25 pence for every copy they sold, so I went to Revolution Records, which was run by a guy called Pete Martin, who I'd been buying records off for years. He just sold them and gave us a straight pound, so we loved him.

THE DEF LEPPARD EP

JOE ELLIOTT: The Monday after recording our EP, we woke up to being a four-piece band without a drummer. We offered Frank the job, but he stayed loyal to the Next Band.

I always felt a little insecure as a singer, so to justify my existence I felt I had to do a bit more than everybody else. I was the guy who organised everything and, even back then, I was good at it. I realised that we couldn't afford to take out an advert for a new drummer in the *Sheffield Star*'s entertainment page so I rang Keith Strong and asked him if he would put it in his column. So, there was this little article, 'Leppard Loses Skins'. It said, 'Def Leppard have parted company with Tony Kenning, so if there are any drummers out there interested in joining …' and it had my mum and dad's phone number at the bottom. We literally had one phone call and it was from Rick Allen.

We invited him to come and audition at the rehearsal room. The weird thing was that on the night he came to audition, Tony turned up and said he'd changed his mind and wanted his job back. But once we heard Rick play, we were blown away. It was a no brainer. Even Tony realised.

Rick had only just turned 15. I was 19, and the rest of the guys were 17 and 18. Three or four years is a big age gap when you're a teenager. When you're 18, you can drink. When you're 15, you're still at school. It was something we were aware of, but his ability to play overrode any concerns we had. We offered him the job on the spot. He came as a package with his brother Robert, who took over as sound engineer from our friend Nick Cartwright, because he was more qualified to do it, in fairness. Robert eventually became our road manager for three years, up until the end of the Pyromania tour.

Rick had to finish his education, otherwise his parents would have been prosecuted, but there was a loophole that if he went to school in Scotland he technically only needed to attend for one day a week. So, once a week, he would catch a train to Scotland, do nothing and come back. He was supposed to do this until he was 16, but he stopped bothering when we signed our first record deal, on 5 August 1979, long before his 16th birthday.

Rick's parents were happy to go along with all this. Their attitude was, let him be a musician and if he falls flat on his face he can catch up with his education later. All our parents were very supportive, but the rest of us had day jobs until we signed our record deal. Although we were only working for about three years, that was long enough to make us realise that work is hard and hard work is even harder.

RICK SAVAGE: There were so many things that could go right or wrong but as long as the band had total belief in itself and we were willing to spend enough hours playing guitar or whatever it is that we each did, then if we didn't make it at least we could say we'd given it 100 percent. And that's what we've always done.

JOE ELLIOTT: I got fired from Osborns. The final straw was being caught playing cricket in the basement stores with a Bakelite knob and a piece of wood from a skip. After that I got a job for six months driving for an ironmongery firm. I was delivering things like door handles, letterboxes and hinges to building sites. They gave me a little Ford Escort van, which they let me take home at the end of the day.

After three months they put me on the Leeds/Bradford run and gave me a bigger van. Not massive, but big enough to get all the gear in for gigs. Things went really well until I turned up at work one day and my manager said, 'What was your van doing in Mansfield last night?' And I said, 'I don't know.' He said, 'Well, maybe it had something to do with the gig you were playing in the pub next door to the boss's house.' What are the chances?

RICK ALLEN

NICKNAME	: NONE
BIRTHDAY	: 1ST OF NOVEMBER
STAR SIGN	: SCORPIO
PLACE OF BIRTH	: DRONFIELD, ENGLAND
EDUCATED AT	: HENRY FANSHAW SCHOOL, DRONFIELD
HEIGHT, WEIGHT	: 5' 9", 145 LBS
COLOUR HAIR	: AUBURN
COLOUR EYES	: GREEN
MARRIED	: SINGLE
BROTHERS, SISTERS	: ONE OLDER, ROBERT - COVERS BOTH!
CAREER BEFORE MUSICIAN	: MUSICIAN
MUSICAL INFLUENCES	: JOHN BONHAM, BILLY COBHAM, ETC.
FIRST GIG	: FRONT ROOM AT HOME WITH MY FIRST BAND
FIRST GIG WITH DEF LEPPARD	: CLIFTON HALL, ROTHERHAM, DECEMBER 1978
FIRST VINYL APPEARANCE WITH DEF LEPPARD	: "WASTED/HELLO AMERICA" SINGLE-1979
ANY OTHER VINYL APPEARANCES	: JOHNNY KALENDER E.P. - 1978
TYPE OF DRUMS USED	: LUDWIG
INTERESTS	: MOTORCYCLES, CARS, DRIVING AND DRUMS!
FAVORITE BAND	: DEF LEPPARD
FAVORITE DRUMMER	: TOMMY ALDRIDGE
FIRST RECORD BOUGHT	: "SPIRIT IN THE SKY" - NORMAN GREENBAUM
FIRST CONCERT SEEN	: SLADE
BEST CONCERT SEEN	: SLADE
HERO	: SUPERMAN
HEROINE	: STEPHANIE POWERS
FAVORITE FILMS	: E.T., AN OFFICER AND A GENTLEMAN
FAVORITE BOOK	: HITCHHIKER'S GUIDE TO THE GALAXY
FAVORITE FOOD	: MY MUM'S
FAVORITE DRINK	: PINT OF BITTER
FAVORITE COLOUR	: RED
FAVORITE CAR	: LAMBORGHINI
MOST ENJOYABLE PART OF WORK	: PLAYING LIVE
MOST HATED PART OF WORK	: TRAVELLING
WORST EXPERIENCE	: BADLY CUT HAND
IDEAL HOME	: FARM OR RANCH IN THE COUNTRY
IDEAL HOLIDAY	: TRIP TO THE MOON ON SKYLAB
DREAMS	: WET ONES!
AMBITIONS	: TO BE SUCCESSFUL AND BE RESPECTED AS A MUSICIAN

Name _ALLEN.R.J.C._   Branch Mem. No. _3491_

Address _C/o. Q.Prime Inc.,_   R.O. No. _264140_

30 Warwick Gardens,   Date of Admission _21/10/79_

LONDON. W14 8PR.

Arrears bt./fwd. from 1983 £ _____   Credit bt./fwd. from 1983 £ _Clear_

TO BE COMPLETED BY MEMBER		£	p	THESE COLUMNS ARE TO BE ENTERED ONLY BY BRANCH OFFICIAL		
				Amount Paid for each Qtr.	Date Paid	Branch Stamp
1st Quarter (to 31st March)						
____weeks @ 50p						
____weeks @ 95p						MUSICIANS' UNION SHEFFIELD BRANCH
13 weeks @ £1·10		12	50			
____weeks @ £1·55						
Fine, if applicable						
2nd Quarter (to 30th June)						
____weeks @ 50p						
____weeks @ 95p				£100·00	3 MAR 1984	MUSICIANS' UNION SHEFFIELD BRANCH
13 weeks @ £1·10		12	50			
____weeks @ £1·55						
Fine, if applicable						
3rd Quarter (to 29th September)						
____weeks @ 50p						
____weeks @ 95p						MUSICIANS' UNION SHEFFIELD BRANCH
13 weeks @ £1·10		12	50			
____weeks @ £1·55						
Fine, if applicable						
4th Quarter (to 31st December)						
____weeks @ 50p						
____weeks @ 95p						MUSICIANS' UNION SHEFFIELD BRANCH
13 weeks @ £1·10		12	50			
____weeks @ £1·55						
Fine, if applicable	Paid to 1985	50	00			

Arrears c./fwd. to 1985   £ _—_ p   Credit c./fwd. to 1985   £ _50:00_ P

RICK ALLEN: My father was a fan of big band music, so I grew up listening to a lot of Glenn Miller and people like that. Then I started getting into more contemporary stuff: Carole King, Elton John, Willie Nelson, all different types. That set me up really well. I wasn't necessarily looking to get into a rock band – I saw myself as more of a jazz drummer to begin with. I was influenced by Billy Cobham and the really technical way he played. I saw him at the Roundhouse in London very early on, before I even joined Def Leppard.

I went for lessons with this guy called Kenny Slade, a local Sheffield drummer who had spent quite a bit of time around Joe Cocker. He was key to setting me on the right track. Kenny fancied himself as a jazz drummer and he played like that, so I followed suit.

My brother came home from school one day with a copy of Deep Purple's *Made in Japan* that he had borrowed from one of his friends, and that got me into Ian Paice. Ian brought a technical aspect to rock drumming that was pretty unusual. I'd air drum along to the record, but I kept the traditional grip that Kenny Slade had taught me. That combination of jazz and rock influences left me with a unique style, which suited those early Def Leppard songs pretty well.

I stuck with traditional grip all the way through until I lost my arm. I could never get into matched grip for some reason. It just didn't feel right, and I could play all those really cool little press rolls and drags with my left hand that I could never have achieved with matched grip.

JOE ELLIOTT: John Peel came to Sheffield University to do a DJ set, and I jumped up on stage and he nearly shat himself – I think he thought I was going to kill him. I handed him a copy of the EP and said, 'Play this,' and he said, 'Well, I don't know what it is, but write your phone number on it and I'll take it back home and give it a listen.'

The following Monday at about ten past five, my mum answered the phone.

She said, 'Joe, there's a John Peel on the phone for you.' He said, 'I played your record and I really like it. I'm going to play a song at ten past seven tonight.' So, of course, I had to spend the next two hours telling the band and everybody else I knew. He ended up playing a song a night for five nights.

Things were starting to pick up pace. I went to see Pete Martin at Revolution Records to find out how many copies of the EP he'd shifted. He'd only sold three, but he'd played it to a friend, Frank Stuart-Brown, who worked for a record company, really liked it and thought he could get some money for us to do some more demos. Pete and Frank also wanted to manage us.

Frank wasn't an A&R man, he was the guy that drove round with a boot full of records delivering to the record stores, but he was obviously a music fan. The two of them were very enthusiastic, and more than a little naive, but what else did we have going for us at the time? We needed somebody to help us get to the next stage; I couldn't do it all on my own.

'Basically it's just down to the fact that we're all posers. We all want to go onstage, wear dinky white boots, tight trousers and have all the girls looking That's us, that's it. We're arrogant

THE NEW WAVE OF BRITISH HEAVY METAL — PART TWO

BY DEAF BARTON

PIX BY ROSS HALFIN

FIRST became aware of the existence of Def Leppard back in November of last year when Joe Elliott, knowing of my slight bias towards music of the heavy metal genre, sent me a cassette of three numbers the band had just laid down in Hull's Fairview studios. 'We've recorded these songs for an EP which will be ready about Christmas,' ran the accompanying note on 'Def Leppard' headed note paper. 'Hope you enjoy it, glad to hear your comments. Sorry about the awful writing.'

Intrigued by the hype-less, friendly letter, I played the tape and was astounded by its excellence. From the bouncy, infectious 'Ride Into The Sun' through the raw rock excitement of 'Getcha Rocks Off' up to the Rush-style epic 'Overture', the package livewire crackled with youthful energy and enthusiasm. Irrefutable evidence that HM is not an old man's game. I was very impressed by the trio of tunes and made a promise to myself to go up and see Def Leppard play live at the earliest opportunity.

Unfortunately, time sped by and it's somehow taken six months for this 'earliest opportunity' to arrive. Still, while I'd been dithering around in London subbing Dave Angry copy for half a year, matters proceeded apace for the Def Ones in Sheffield. Having consolidated their line up as Joe Elliott (vocals), Pete Willis (guitar), Steve Clark (guitar), Rick Savage (bass) and Rick Allen (drums — a mere 15 years old and the newest recruit) the band watched with pride as their EP, aided by notices in Sounds and radio play by Andy Peebles and (grudgingly) John Peel, sold out and became a much sought after item.

A highpoint was reached a couple of months back when the band headlined at Sheffield Polytechnic, drew a 500 strong crowd and enjoyed a rapturous reaction. Prior to that gig, they'd only ever really been part of a headbanging, adulatory crowd ... it gave them the greatest kick to be on the receiving end for the first time in their lives.

But sadly this night at the Workingmen's Club the punters are a little thin on the ground, most of the Sheffield fans having taken their imaginary guitars with them down to the City Hall to see Status Quo.

The club initially reminds me of my old school dining room; uninviting, high ceilinged, lots of light-coloured wooden tables and chairs, little cliques of people huddled haphazardly around. But then again you could never buy a scotch and coke for 30p there (let alone a double for 54p) and so it is that the scholastic comparisons fade rapidly and the atmosphere becomes warm, comfortable ... and more than a little hazy.

DEF LEPPARD burst onstage at about 10 p.m. and your immediate impression is how good they look: from left to right guitarist Pete Willis, diminutive but cool in white shirt and grey satin strides; tall, lanky Joe Elliott, garbed in a full silk shirt and the aforementioned narrow, figure-hugging 'leather' pants; drummer Rick Allen, barechested and already slick with sweat atop his riser; and bass player Rick Savage and guitarist Steve Clark, resplendent in leather/leopard skin combination outfits, both possessors of fine heads of tightly curled blond hair. Eminently presentable; not a single pair of time warp Angel Witch style loon pants in evidence, thank God.

And the music? High powered heavy rock played to a degree of tightness usually only achieved after a half-dozen gruelling American tours. Neat duelling guitars and a titanic rhythm section, the skinsman putting weaklings like Les Binks to shame with his mallet to the skull drumwork. I must admit to being surprised again: the EP, good as it is, doesn't even hint at Def Leppard's live dynamism.

Kicking off with the punchy 'Glad I'm Alive' the band cavort around the stage with wild abandon, belying their tender years by exuding confidence and professionalism. 'Rosalie' follows, making the Thin Lizzy version sound like something off a 99p Woolworths album, and before you have time to catch your breath 'Ride Into The Sun' erupts from the PA, the hoary old 'driving at high speed' lyrical chestnut sounding fresh and alive once more: 'It's such an easy feelin' with the wind in my hair/I'm burnin' up the rubber and I don't really care/'Cos I'm ridin, I'm riding into the sun'.

Joe Elliott hasn't got a great voice but he has got presence and, really, that's half the battle. 'This next song is about destruction, like all heavy metal songs,' he says, announcing the masterful 'The Day The Walls Came Tumbling Down', musically fast and ambitious with words that somehow bring to mind Sabbath's 'Into The Void'. Synth rumbles (meant to indicate the collapse of the walls') lead us into 'Answer To The Master' which in turn acts as a scene-setter for the evening's highlight, 'Overture'. So much stronger than the EP version, tonight 'Overture' is given the magnum opus treatment, its words — 'The sun, the moon, the darkened sky/The morning dew reflecting in my eye/The rising mist, the dampened earth/They're just reminders of what life's worth' — recalling the bleak optimism of Rush's classic '2112'.

The rest of the set passes by in a flash; 'Beyond The Temple', 'Sorrow Is A Woman', 'Emerald' (out-Lizzying the original once again), 'Heat Street' ('I'll anybody's ever walked down a street at night and been really scared 'cos you

CONTINUES NEXT PAGE

JOE ELLIOTT is aged 19. He's singer in a young heavy rock band called Def Leppard. He holds down a day job driving a van and delivering odd bits of machinery. After work he spends his time with the group.

They've been practising five evenings a week for the past 18 months or so. Recently they've stepped up their schedule and now rehearse for four hours a night, five nights a week and on Saturday and Sunday afternoons. Joe Elliott lives with his parents in Sheffield. His dad works fixing radios and cassette players into cars and is easy going, seems quite content to allow his son to do as he pleases. His mum, however ... well, the first impression you get is that she doesn't approve of his activities.

"People keep phoning up about this bloody record," says Joe Elliott's mum, referring to a self-financed and distributed three track Def Leppard EP. "Where's St Albans? Miles away!" I thought it was. Someone called up from there today and asked about the record. I had to tell him that I didn't know anything about it."

One of the songs on the EP, the basic, bruising 'Getcha Rocks Off', is figuring strongly in HM charts throughout the land. Joe Elliott's mum doesn't rate it.

"I can't understand why people like that 'Getcha Rocks Off'," she complains. "I think it's horrible. What does it mean, anyway?"

Onstage, Joe Elliott enjoys strutting about in tight leather trousers. Well, not leather exactly. They cost him £15 and are plastic, in fact. They're a bit more shiny than the genuine article, but not so much as you'd really notice.

Joe Elliott's mum doesn't reckon much to her son's macho posing. "I think he sticks his bum out too much," she remarks.

But after a while you get the feeling that all these displays of displeasure are something of a front, that she is really proud of her son, although for her own reasons she does her best not to show it. For tonight Joe Elliott's parents have trooped up to the Crookes Workingmen's Club to see Def Leppard perform. And if his mother really does disapprove, why is she biting her lip and looking tense? Why is she nervously fidgetting in her seat instead of sitting still and scowling?

JOE ELLIOTT: Once the EP came out and John Peel played it, people who had previously ignored us started to take notice.

I'd written to Geoff Barton at *Sounds* magazine a couple of times, but couldn't persuade him to make the trip up the M1 – until he heard the EP, and then he was all over us. He and the photographer Ross Halfin came up in June 1979 to do a feature when we played the Crookes Working Men's Club.

Crookes Working Men's Club
Sheffield, 5 June 1979

Geoff Barton's Sounds *review*

THE DEF LEPPARD EP

RICK SAVAGE: This was actually quite a big gig for us because Joe and I literally lived a stone's throw away. So that in itself created its own little pressures. You're playing in your own community, wondering how the gig's going to go down. Your parents are going be there and their friends and our friends. It was one of the stepping stones for us to get to the next level.

JOE ELLIOTT: Ross and Geoff got hammered on cheap beer and whisky, so they were down the front headbanging while everybody else in the audience was sat there wondering what the hell was going on. Then they came backstage to our dressing room and Ross pissed in the sink.

Geoff got us a brilliant middle-page spread and then all the record companies came sniffing.

RICK ALLEN: We were certain that if we could get the backing we could be quite successful.

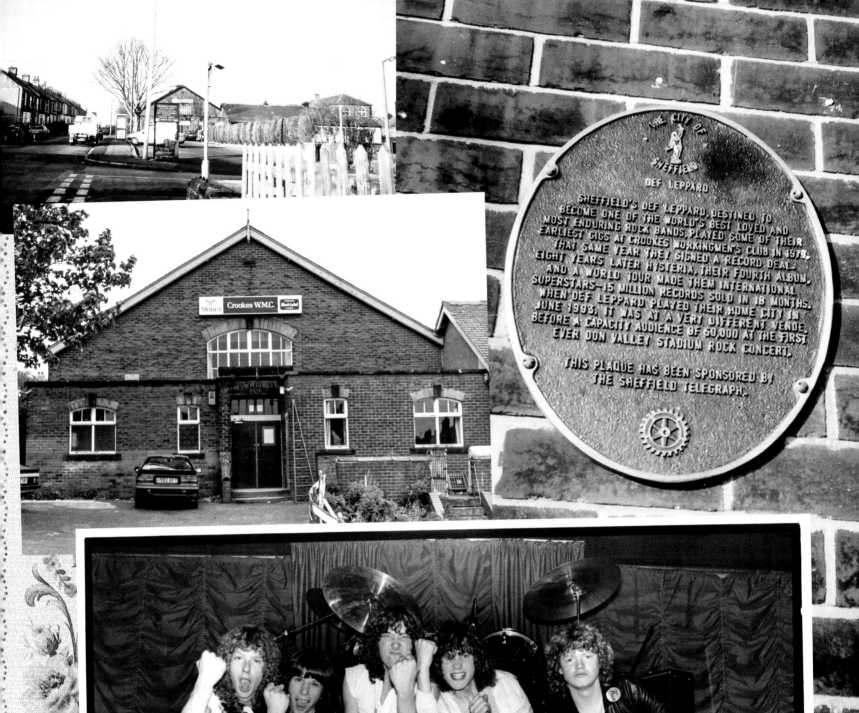

THE CITY OF
SHEFFIELD

DEF LEPPARD

SHEFFIELD'S DEF LEPPARD, DESTINED TO
BECOME ONE OF THE WORLD'S BEST LOVED AND
MOST ENDURING ROCK BANDS, PLAYED SOME OF THEIR
EARLIEST GIGS AT CROOKES WORKINGMEN'S CLUB IN 1979.
THAT SAME YEAR THEY SIGNED A RECORD DEAL.
EIGHT YEARS LATER HYSTERIA, THEIR FOURTH ALBUM,
AND A WORLD TOUR MADE THEM INTERNATIONAL
SUPERSTARS—15 MILLION RECORDS SOLD IN 18 MONTHS.
WHEN DEF LEPPARD PLAYED THEIR HOME CITY IN
JUNE 1993, IT WAS AT A VERY DIFFERENT VENUE,
BEFORE A CAPACITY AUDIENCE OF 60,000 AT THE FIRST
EVER DON VALLEY STADIUM ROCK CONCERT.

THIS PLAQUE HAS BEEN SPONSORED BY
THE SHEFFIELD TELEGRAPH.

DEF LEPPARD

STEVE CLARK: Basically, we were all fucking posers. We all wanted to go out on stage, pose in our dinky white boots and tight trousers and have all the girls looking at our bollocks. That was us. We liked showing off.

RICK ALLEN: We were trying to do something different. In every picture in the papers of a punk or New Wave band, all the members would be snarling, trying to look as horrible as possible. We weren't like that. We tried to look good, have style.

We were just exploring what made us feel good. I think Pete Willis was partly responsible for those really unusual early riffs. I just followed suit. I wanted to explore all the stuff that I'd learned in drum lessons.

JOE ELLIOTT: Pete and Frank were doing their best. They got us a gig at the Retford Porterhouse, where 11 A&R men came to see us, including Dave Dee from EMI and Dave Bates from Polygram. Soon there was a bidding war between six or seven labels.

EMI wasn't one of them, which I think was my fault. I was having a drink after the gig when this big guy sitting down the bar said to me, 'You don't move much for a singer, do you?' I replied, 'Fuck off, you fat ****.' Turned out that was Dave Dee.

DAVE BATES: The band came on and my jaw hit the floor. I'd heard they were young, but crikey, they were just school kids! Then when they opened up, the second shock hit me: wow, they sure could play. After the show a few of the other labels went backstage to schmooze. I made a brief introduction and left. The plan was to spend more time with them when none of the other labels were around. When they played in Middlesbrough the next night, I think I was the only record company person there and so after the show I got them all to myself. Turns out these young lads were also massive music fans, so we discussed our favourite bands, albums, singles and live shows. Only two weeks later I went to the young drummer's parents' house to sign the band. As Rick was only 15, his dad, Geoff, had to sign on his behalf.

JOE ELLIOTT: Years later, we found out that a copy of the EP had somehow ended up on the desk of Cliff Burnstein, the head of A&R at Mercury Records in Chicago. Mercury and Polygram were sister labels. When Cliff heard our EP, he'd called his Polygram counterpart, Dave Bates, and said, 'Under no circumstances let this band sign to another label.' So we'd already got the Americans in our back pocket, but we had no idea.

We were given a £100,000 advance, and when that leaked into the press things started to go a bit shit-shaped for us. Everybody thought that we were lording it in limos, but they didn't realise what we had to use that money for. It was a loan to record our first album, do a photo shoot, buy some stage clothes and maybe get some real Gibson guitars. We couldn't just buy a house with it.

I remember queueing with Steve outside the Wapentek club where we used to drink every week. We were standing there and these kids started gobbing on us, and saying, 'You fucking don't deserve that record deal.' That's when Steve and I realised that we'd outgrown Sheffield.

BLUDGEON RIFFOLA RECORDS

DEF LEPPARD

33⅓ RPM
A

MSB 001
STEREO
MSB 001 A

1. RIDE INTO THE SUN
(Savage/Elliott)
2. GETCHA ROCKS OFF
(Savage/Elliott/Clark/Willis)

(Copyright Control)

BLUDGEON RIFFOLA RECORDS

DEF LEPPARD

33⅓ RPM

MSB 001
STEREO
MSB 001 B

THE OVERTURE
(Savage/Elliott/Clark/Willis)

(Copyright Control)

Def Leppard give up day jobs shock

DEF LEPPARD, a young Sheffield heavy metal band and *Sounds* discoveries, have signed with Phonogram in a five figure deal.

The band's first tour duties as Phonogram artists will be as support to ex-Montrose man Sammy Hagar on his upcoming British gigs, dates for which were announced last week. Also in the pipeline is a Radio One 'In Concert' show and a one-off appearance at Newcastle Mayfair on August 10.

Their upcoming release is likely to be a single, the A-side to be either stage favourite 'Wasted' or a new number called 'Rock Brigade'.

Commenting on the signing, Def Leppard's lead singer Joe

DEF LEPPARD's Joe Elliott

Elliott said: "All the band got very drunk when we heard. We're all very pleased. This is it, full-time work from now on. No more day jobs for us."

LEPPARD WON'T CHANGE THEIR SPOTS: Metal merchants **Def Leppard**, recently signed to Phonogram, could well have become labelmates with such wondrous acts as **XTC, Kevin Coyne** and **Supercharge** instead. In other words, they could well have found themselves on Virgin, of all companies.

In the early days when they were still negotiating a deal, Virgin supremo **Richard Branson** called Leppard manager **Frank Stewart-Brown** and asked snootily: "Why haven't you phoned us?" Stewart-Brown replied: "Why haven't *you* phoned *us*?" Branson suddenly had very little to say . . .

Radio Hallam present several of their usual programmes live on Friday but on Saturday among the attractions are leading local rock band Def Leppard in concert, and top pop group The Dooleys, who top the Hallamland spectacular bill.

HEAVY METAL

1 SPACE STATION NO 5, Montrose, from 'Montrose', WEA
2 STARGAZER, Rainbow, from 'Rainbow Rising', Polydor
3 WHOLE LOTTA ROSIE, AC/DC, from 'If You Want Blood', WEA
4 LOVE TO LOVE, UFO, from 'Lights Out', Chrysalis
5 WHOLE LOTTA LOVE, Led Zeppelin, from 'Zeppelin II', WEA
6 CHILDREN OF THE GRAVE, Black Sabbath, from 'Masters of Reality', Vertigo
7 DOWN DOWN, Status Quo, from 'On the Level', Vertigo
8 BASTILLE DAY, Rush, from 'Archives', Mercury
9 HIGHWAY STAR, Deep Purple, from 'Made In Japan', Purple
10 GETCHA ROCKS OFF, Def Leppard, Bludgeon Riffola EP
11 JUST THE TWO OF US, Thin Lizzy, Vertigo 45 B-Side
12 YOURS IS NO DISGRACE, Yes, from 'Yessongs', Atlantic
13 VICTIM OF CHANGES, Judas Priest, from 'Sad Wings of Destiny', Gull
14 LIGHTS OUT, UFO, from 'Lights Out', Chrysalis
15 EASY LIVIN', Uriah Heep, from 'Demons and Wizards', Bronze
16 A MAN I'LL NEVER BE, Boston, from 'Don't Look Back', Epic
17 CAN'T GET ENOUGH, Bad Company, from 'Bad Company', Island
18 ROCK THE NATION, Montrose, from 'Montrose', WEA
19 LOGICAL SONG, Supertramp, from 'Breakfast In America', A&M
20 BLOWING FREE, Wishbone Ash, from 'Argus', MCA

Compiled by the Penthouse HM Disco, Dixon Lane, Sheffield 1.

Def Leppard are getting to the stage where they'll soon be able to command an audience of AC/DC size themselves. They're getting out of the kindergarten school of heavy metal and knocking off the rough edges. Joe Elliot's fast emerging as Sheffield's answer to Robert Plant and the rest of the band aren't short on positive theatrics. Tonight Hammersmith Odeon, next year the world.   ROBIN SMITH

Pic. by G. Leighton

JOE ELLIOTT: Now that we were signed to Polygram, we started playing bigger venues all over the country. We did our first London show in mid-September, opening for Sammy Hagar at the Hammersmith Odeon. Geoff Barton gave us a stonking review in *Sounds*: 'Watch them go, watch them rise, catch them wherever you can. Keep your cool, you Leppards, you will become the success story of the decade.'

Just before that, we played Club Lafayette in Wolverhampton. Cliff Burnstein had come over from America to see us, so it was unfortunate that my trousers split. I had to do the entire gig with my legs crushed together. I certainly didn't move around much that night! It didn't seem to put Cliff off. He saw us as a rough diamond to be polished.

NEW Wave of British HM hits the ... nes this week with Def Leppard (above) ... rting US rocker Sammy Hagar at ...

PHONOGRAM LIMITED · LONDON

phonogram

129 Park Street
London W1Y 3FA
Telephone: 01-491 4600
Telex: Phongm 261 583
Registered in England
Company No. 586873
Registered office address
Abacus House Gutter Lane
London EC2V 8AH

21st September 1979.

Dear Dan

DEF LEPPARD

Enclosed is a cassette of 7 demo recordings by this new five year signing. The band spent last week in Olympic Studios, London, recording their next single "Wasted" which also appears among the demo titles.

Needless to say we in London are very excited about Def Leppard. Their first release, originally on the band's own Bludgeon Riffola label sold over 20,000 and was re-issued on Vertigo reaching No.84 in the UK charts. For a first single, not a bad achievement. These sales were reflected in the strong support the band received when they supported Sammy Hagar at the Hammersmith Odeon last Sunday - they went down a storm.

Now comes news that they will support AC/DC in October and November on another UK tour. With four nights (1st to 4th November) at the Odeon again, there is room for you to choose a date on which to check them out. By that time <u>Wasted</u> will have been released (October 19th) and will herald the first LP which is set for February 29th.

Definately a strong band : technically, musically and visually - something the Japanese have already come to appreciate. Don't be the last to know.... I'll see you there!

Best regards,

Marek

PS. Bob Sherwood has the tape

S. L. G. Gottlieb, Chairman · K. N. Maliphant, Managing · D. M. Baker · P. A. Bond · P. R. Schellevis · W. G. Williams

*Opening for Sammy Hagar
Hammersmith Odeon, London
16 September 1979*

JOE ELLIOTT: When we got the support slot on AC/DC's Highway to Hell tour the following month Pete Martin and Frank Stuart-Brown thought it was down to them, but we actually had Cliff to thank (not that we knew it at the time). Cliff had big plans for us but he needed to make sure that we were as good as our EP, so he recommended us to his friend Peter Mensch, who was AC/DC's manager at the talent agency Leber-Krebs. If we were opening for AC/DC, Peter could watch us like a hawk every night and report back to Cliff.

AC/DC wanted Maggie Bell as their support act, so Mensch had to persuade them to take us instead. Once they came round to the idea, they were fine with us. They weren't very social, apart from Bon Scott, who lent us money and bought us drinks. He was the only one we saw much. Angus Young came into our dressing room, played Steve and Pete's guitars for about ten minutes, wished us good luck, then left.

STEVE CLARK: We supported AC/DC, playing to about 10,000 seats, before we even had a record out, so we've been used to learning as we go.

JOE ELLIOTT: On that tour it started to become really obvious that Pete and Frank were way out of their depth. When Frank suggested that we needed a gimmick, Pete Willis sarcastically said, 'Maybe we could stop the set, bring out a table and do some card tricks?' And he said, 'Yes! Something like that.' So that's when we asked Peter Mensch to manage us. He agreed, but pointed out that it was going to cost us a lot of money to buy ourselves out of our contract with Pete and Frank.

We thought it was worth it. Steve was reluctant in the beginning because Pete Martin was his drinking buddy, but he eventually came round to the idea. At Leber-Krebs, we were part of the same roster not only as AC/DC but also Ted Nugent, Aerosmith, the Scorpions and the New York Dolls. To be a British band with American management weight behind us felt amazing.

Another big advantage of being managed by Peter Mensch was that he was able to introduce us to Mutt Lange, who had produced the *Highway to Hell* album for AC/DC. Peter asked Mutt to come and see this opening act he'd just signed. Standing by the mixing desk at Bingley Hall in Stafford, Mutt could see our potential although he felt we still needed a lot of polish. I'd been a huge Mutt Lange fan long before AC/DC. Down in the rehearsal room, we were playing records he'd done with bands like the Boomtown Rats, Supercharge and the Motors. I would've loved Mutt to have produced our first record. But he was happy to do the second album once he'd heard the first one and seen us live a few more times.

RICK SAVAGE: I think Mutt was attracted by the challenge of working with an unproven group like us.

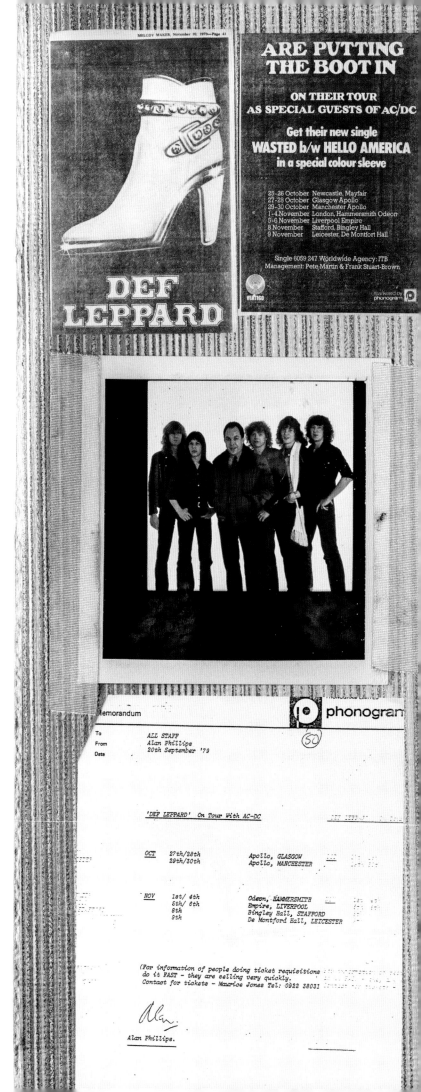

DEF LEPPARD

AMERICAN TALENT INTERNATIONAL LTD
888 SEVENTH AVENUE   (212) 977-2300
NEW YORK, N.Y. 10019

Recording Exclusively For

mercury

A product of Phonogram, Inc.

On Through the Night
Recorded: December 1979
Released: 14 March 1980

ON THROUGH THE NIGHT

JOE ELLIOTT: *I'm sure we're not the only band that has had the indignity of just being told what our debut album cover was going to be. It never occurs to you as kids to worry about the album design. The record company told us they'd take care of it, and that's exactly what they did.*

There was no discussion. It was just, 'Here's your album cover.' A truck carrying a giant guitar travelling around the moon. Not exactly what we had in mind, but we had bigger fish to fry at the time.

To me, band names and album covers are a bit like horse names in horse racing. If you ever actually stopped and thought about them, you'd realise how stupid they were. But at the end of the day, it doesn't matter. It's just something that the commentator can scream out down the final furlong. So, covers aren't really that important, but they are important enough for us to say that it was never going to happen again.

JOE ELLIOTT: *On Through the Night* was produced by Tom Allom, who was great. His brief from the label was to just capture our energy. We'd been playing some of those songs for 18 months and we weren't in any mood to change anything. That first album was like a diary of who we were and what we'd done up to that point.

We were buzzed at the choice of studio. Startling Studios was in Ringo Starr's house near Ascot. It had been owned by John Lennon back in the *Imagine* days and he had built the studio there before selling the place to Ringo when he went to live in New York. I drew the long straw and had John's bedroom, which was amazing.

We were in there for about three weeks in December 1979. We moved in just as Dr. Hook were moving out. There was a two-hour crossover period during which we played pool with those guys and smoked hash for the first time.

One problem was that we didn't have enough music. When we went in the studio we were two songs short. We were already re-recording 'Overture', which was on the EP, and we were doing a faked live version of 'Rocks Off' where we just stole some crowd audio from somewhere. So, we came up with 'It Don't Matter' and 'It Could Be You' while we were there.

We spent too much time on the guitar overdubs, and as a result the album ended up a bit too smooth. It also left me with way too little time for the vocals. I had to blast through the whole record in four days, three songs a day. For an unschooled but very enthusiastic singer, it was hard. I couldn't take a day off. If my voice went crap, I had to just sing crap.

RICK SAVAGE: We had very little idea of how the vocal would fit. We just compiled a collection of interesting guitar riffs and then told Joe to sing over them. After that we all became a little more conscious of what Joe had to do.

Because we'd been playing all but two of the songs live for a year or so, the songs as they stood were all they needed to be. Rick and I recorded all the bass and drums in a day. Then we just needed to do some guitar overdubs and the lead vocals, but we ended up spending the next three weeks putting more and more stuff on the backing track that really shouldn't have been there. It was naivety on our part, but I also don't think that we were very well directed by our producer.

STEVE CLARK: It was like painting a picture without knowing when to stop.

RICK SAVAGE: We used to get drunk every night and still try to record. We were kids playing at being musicians and you can hear that on the album. I will always defend *On Through the Night* to a certain extent because it's who we were at the time. The songs are great but I wish that we'd recorded them differently.

HEAVY METAL

1	6	**GREEN GRASS HIGH TIDES**, The Outlaws, from 'The Outlaws', Arista
2	7	**THE BOUNTY HUNTER**, Molly Hatchet, from 'Molly Hatchet', Epic
3	2	**WARRIOR**, Riot, from 'Rock City', Ariola
4	3	**THE GREEN MANALISHI (WITH THE 2-PRONGED CROWN)**, Judas Priest, CBS 12" Limited Edition 45
5	8	**STALLIONS OF THE HIGHWAY**, Saxon, from 'Saxon', Carrere
6	13	**STARGAZER**, Rainbow, from 'Rainbow Rising', Polydor
7	5	**ROCK BABY**, Moxey, from 'Ridin' High', Warner Bros
8	16	**LIGHTS OUT**, UFO, from 'Strangers In The Night', Chrysalis
9	18	**GETCHA ROCKS OFF**, Def Leppard, Maxi-Single, Bludgeon Riffola
10	14	**ANTHEM**, Rush, from 'Archives', Mercury
11	15	**THE CLOCK STRIKES TEN**, Cheap Trick, from 'Cheap Trick In Color', Epic
12	9	**ANOTHER PIECE OF MEAT**, Scorpions, from 'Lovedrive', Harvest
13	10	**PARALYSED**, Ted Nugent, from 'State of Shock', Epic
14	11	**SPACE STATION NO 5**, Montrose, from 'Montrose', WEA
15	1	**WANG DANG SWEET POONTANG**, Ted Nugent, from 'Double Live Gonzo', Epic
16	—	**MEGLOMANIA**, Black Sabbath, from 'Sabotage', Phonogram
17	4	**WAR PIGS**, Black Sabbath, from 'Paranoid', Phonogram
18	19	**RED**, Sammy Hagar, from 'All Night Long', Capitol
19	12	**PROWLER**, Iron Maiden, Demo Tape
20 =	—	**BIG TEASER**, Saxon, from 'Saxon', Carrere
20 =	—	**ERUPTION**, Van Halen, from 'Van Halen', WEA

Compiled from record requests at the Bandwagon Heavy Metal Soundhouse, Kingsbury Circle, London NW9.

HEAVY METAL

1 **WHOLE LOTTA ROSIE**, AC/DC, from 'If You Want Blood', Atlantic
2 **STARGAZER**, Rainbow, from 'Rainbow Rising', Polydor
3 **SPACE STATION NO. 5**, Montrose, from 'Montrose', Warner Bros
4 **BAT OUT OF HELL**, Meat Loaf, from 'Bat Out Of Hell', Epic
5 **JUST THE TWO OF US**, Thin Lizzy, from 'Previously Unreleased', Vertigo
6 **ROCK BOTTOM**, UFO, from 'Phenomenon', Chrysalis
7 **THE LOGICAL SONG**, Supertramp, from 'Breakfast In America', A&M
8 **OVERKILL**, Motorhead, from 'Overkill', Bronze
9 **WHOLE LOTTA LOVE**, Led Zeppelin, from 'Zeppelin II', Atlantic
10 **CHILDREN OF THE GRAVE**, Black Sabbath, from 'Masters Of Reality', Vertigo
11 **ANOTHER PIECE OF MEAT**, Scorpions, from 'Lovedrive', Harvest
12 **MYSTERY SONG**, Status Quo, from 'Blue For You', Vertigo
13 **BASTILLE DAY**, Rush, from 'Archives', Mercury
14 **VICTIM OF CHANGES**, Judas Priest, from 'Sad Wings Of Destiny', Gull
15 **DON'T LOOK BACK**, Boston, from 'Don't Look Back', Epic
16 **GYPSY**, Uriah Heep, from 'Best Of Uriah Heep', Bronze
17 **GETCHA ROCKS OFF**, Def Leppard, Bludgeon Riffola EP
18 **CAN'T GET ENOUGH**, Bad Company, from 'Straightshooter', Island
19 **SPEED KING**, Deep Purple, from 'In Rock', Harvest
CAT SCRATCH FEVER, Ted Nugent, from 'Cat Scratch Fever', Epic

Compiled by Penthouse HM Disco, Dixon Lane, Sheffield 1.

CRACKER OF the week. Def Leppard, the fantastic up and coming rock band certainly sound as good as they look! Please print a picture of any one of them as my pictures are getting faded with so much handling! Do you think the lead singer ever takes off the clingy leather jeans he wears? If he has any trouble in removing them to go to bed at night, he knows who to contact! Def Leppard's no. 1 fan — **Christine Fletcher, Lochgilphead, Argyllshire.**

DEF LEPPARD: 'Wasted' (Vertigo). Def Leppard are, apparently, "out of their brain and going insane" and even "wasting their time and doing a line". They're also, apparently, about 15 years old. I find this remarkable. Like the sons of the aristocracy—H M clones Def Leppard are able to adopt the attitudes of their elderly peers even before their adolescence is over — in fact adopting a Black Sabbath attitude before fully realising the benefits that such posturing could lead to. They'll have a breakdown when they find out. Otherwise it's brilliant heavy metal by numbers by young talented musicians — just what we all need a dose of from time to time. Def Leppard will get their dose when they're older.

ANTHEM, Rush, from 'Archives', Mercury
GREEN GRASS AND HIGH TIDES, The Outlaws,
rom 'Outlaws', Arista
GETCHA ROCKS OFF, Def Leppard, Bludgeon
Riffola maxi-single
LIGHTS OUT, UFO, from 'Strangers In The Night',
Chrysalis
STALLIONS OF THE HIGHWAY, Saxon, from
rom 'Saxon', Carrere
STARGAZER, Rainbow, from 'Rainbow Rising',
Polydor
MEGALOMANIA, Black Sabbath, from 'Sabotage',
Vertigo
BIG TEASER, Saxon, from 'Saxon', Carrere
WARRIOR, Riot, from 'Rock City', Ariola
THE GREAT WHITE BUFFALO, Ted Nugent, from
Double Live Gonzo', Epic
RED, Sammy Hagar, from 'All Night Long', Capitol
THE BOUNTY HUNTER, Molly Hatchet, From 'Molly
Hatchet', Epic
YOU REALLY GOT ME, Van Halen, from 'Van Halen',
Warner Bros
ROCK BABY, Moxy, from 'Ridin' High', Warner Bros
ANOTHER PIECE OF MEAT, Scorpions, from
Lovedrive', Harvest
ROCK CITY, Riot, from 'Rock City', Ariola
CAPTURED CITY, Praying Mantis, demo tape
HOME SWEET HOME ALABAMA, Lynyrd Skynyrd,
from 'First . . . and Last', MCA
PROWLER, Iron Maiden, demo tape
LOST IN HOLLYWOOD, Rainbow, from 'Down To
Earth', Polydor

*Compiled from record requests at the
Heavy Metal Soundhouse, Kingsbury Circle, London NW9*

BACKS TO THE WALL, Saxon, from 'Saxon',
Carrere
ROCK YOU TONIGHT, Marseille, from 'Marseille',
Mountain
SECRET OF THE DANCE, Gillan, from 'Mr
Universe', Acrobat

5- 1. 80

WASTED, Def Leppard, from '45 A-Side', Vertigo
LADIES MAN, April Wine, from 'Harder . . .
Faster', Capitol
BOMBER, Motorhead, from 'Bomber', Bronze
SPACE STATION NO 5, Sammy Hagar, from '45
A-Side', Capitol
OVER THE TOP, Motorhead, from 'Bomber 45 B-
Side', Bronze
BIG BROTHER, Samson, from 'Survivors', Laser
VICTIM OF CHANGES, Judas Priest, from
Unleashed In The East', CBS
CAPTURED CITY, Praying Mantis, from 'demo
tape'
EL CID, Cozy Powell, from 'Over The Top', Ariola
THIS PLANET'S ON FIRE, Sammy Hagar, from
Street Machine', Capitol
GENOCIDE, Judas Priest, from 'Unleashed In the
East', CBS
PARADISE, McKitty, from 'demo tape'

JOE ELLIOTT: We hated being pigeonholed as part of the New Wave of British Heavy Metal (NWOBHM). Iron Maiden and Judas Priest were great bands, but they were metal and we weren't. My go-to phrase was, 'In Liverpool there was the Mersey Sound, then there was the Beatles.' We were drums, bass, two guitars and vocals, so on that basis you could say that we were the same as the Rolling Stones. But that would be as ridiculous as saying that we were heavy metal.

The same thing happened a few years later when we got lumped in with hair metal in America. We couldn't believe it. In 1987 you had Bon Jovi, Poison, Mötley Crüe, Warrant and a bunch of other bands all over MTV. We'd spent the previous two and a half years in Holland living next door to a windmill. It wasn't exactly the Sunset Strip. I didn't get it then, and I still don't get it. I'm not knocking those other bands. They're great at what they do. I just don't think we sound like them. We use acoustic guitars and pianos and orchestras. We have harmonies. If anything, we're a baby Queen, with the power of *Back in Black* when we do 'Rocks Off'. That was always our blueprint: Queen meets AC/DC.

Melody Maker

February 2, 1980   20p weekly   USA $1.25

↑ DEF LEPPARD: HEAVY METAL'S NEW WAVE?
by ALLAN JONES (p. 28–30)

U.K. TOUR '1980'

56   **ON THROUGH THE NIGHT**

Drowning in the deep end

Martha *and the* Muffins · Cherie Currie

Sounds

HAS THE LEPPARD CHANGED ITS SPOTS?
The Def boys scoop our Poll. But Mr. Barton is worried.... See pages 16—20

JOE ELLIOTT: We spent the first four months of 1980 touring the UK, from Aberdeen at the top down to St Austell at the bottom and calling at all points in between. We sold out the university and club circuit in January and February, then did really well in the theatres in March and April. *On Through the Night* went into the UK top 20. And after all that, we got accused of selling out to the Americans.

The rot started to set in as early as March, when Geoff Barton did a follow-up article in *Sounds* – 'Has the Leppard changed its spots?' I think he was upset because I didn't pick him up at the train station like I had when he came to see us play the working men's club the previous summer. We had people to help with things like that, because by then I had other things to do. He wouldn't have got picked up at the station by Phil Mogg if he was coming to see UFO.

In fairness to Geoff, he's publicly apologised numerous times for that piece and it didn't do us any lasting harm. In fact, it was probably character-building.

Colonel Tom and the lame Leppard

Leppard falling on Def ears

JOE ELLIOTT: Touring America was amazing, although edged with a bit of sadness because of the negative attitude towards us back home at the time.

It was the first time I'd left the country – I didn't even have a passport until then. The furthest I'd ever been was London.

When we landed in Los Angeles on 18 May we had to carry Pete Willis off the plane because he was so drunk. Sadly, that kind of behaviour on tour would lead to his departure from the band a couple of years later.

First stop was Sunset Boulevard. The record company decided to give us the five-star treatment, so they put us up in the Chateau Marmont. As we were checking into the hotel, right behind the reception desk there was a photograph of Led Zeppelin sitting on the steps that we'd just walked up. We had to pinch ourselves.

After a quick shower Steve and I went straight to the Rainbow. We didn't even have jet lag – we were young and full of beans. I wanted to go upstairs to see the private room where the original Hollywood Vampires hung out – Alice Cooper, Keith Moon, Harry Nilsson and the rest.

The guy behind the bar said, 'Can I help you, boys?' We said, 'Yeah, two vodka and oranges, please, mate.' And he said, 'Y'all mean a screwdriver?' As full-on Yorkshiremen, we replied, 'No, if we wanted a screwdriver we'd go to a fucking hardware store. We want two vodka and oranges.'

As we carried on with this light-hearted kerfuffle, the sound of our accents attracted the attention of four girls sitting in the far corner of the bar. They came over and said, 'Y'all English?' Nice, because the accent put everybody off outside of Sheffield.

'Yes, we're from Sheffield.'

'Are you in a band?'

'Yes, we're in Def Leppard.'

'We're coming to see you tomorrow night.'

And I got laid that night. Without even trying. Couldn't get a look in with an English girl. I thought to myself, 'I like this place.'

JOE ELLIOTT: For the first two weeks of the tour, we were supporting Pat Travers. The first gig was at Santa Monica Civic. What I remember most is being very nervous because it was our first ever gig in America and we didn't want to mess up. It didn't help that we hadn't been able to do a soundcheck or line check. But as we walked out on the stage and the house lights went down, there was a cheer. Now, there's always a cheer when the lights go down, even if it's just an announcer coming out, so we knew that the cheer wasn't for us, but we also heard people shouting out some of our song titles. It was encouraging to realise that there were people in the crowd who knew who we were.

RICK ALLEN: Everybody was singing the words to our songs. We were like, 'What's going on here?'

JOE ELLIOTT: Most of the shows we did with Pat were in 2,000- or 3,000-seater theatres, but when we got to Portland, Oregon we were in an 11,000-seater arena. It was mind-blowing.

When we went on stage, the whole place flickered with cigarette lighters. Cliff Burnstein was friends with a Portland DJ called Gloria Johnson and he'd given her an exclusive – she was the first US DJ to ever play Def Leppard. After that, she fell in love with the band and played us to death on her show. So there must have been a lot of people in the crowd who had heard some of our songs and maybe even bought the album.

We went down an absolute storm that night and we realised for the first time what the potential was for the band. If the rest of the country picked up Def Leppard the way that Portland had, we could become the next British band to break America – following on from amazing artists like the Beatles, the Stones, the Who, the Kinks, Led Zeppelin, Black Sabbath and David Bowie. We were almost bigger than T. Rex had ever been in America and we had barely started.

DEF LEPPARD - U.S. TOUR 1980

MAY	20	SANTA MONICA, CALIFORNIA	CIVIC CENTER	(with PAT TRAVERS
	21	FRESNO, CALIFORNIA	WARNERS THEATRE	" BAND)
	23	RENO, NEVADA	CENTENNIAL COLISEUM	"
	24	OAKLAND, CALIFORNIA	OAKLAND AUDITORIUM	"
	25	SAN FRANCISCO, CALIFORNIA	WARFIELD FOX THEATRE	"
	26	SACRAMENTO, CALIFORNIA	MUNICIPAL AUDITORIUM	"
	27	DAY OFF		
	28	EUGENE, OREGON	COLISEUM	"
	29	PORTLAND, OREGON	COLISEUM	"
MAY	31	HOUSTON, TEXAS	COLISEUM	(with JUDAS PRIEST)
JUNE	1	SAN ANTONIO, TEXAS	COLISEUM	"
	2	CORPUS CHRISTI, TEXAS	COLISEUM	"
	3	DAY OFF		
	4	AMARILLO, TEXAS	CIVIC CENTER	"
	5	DAY OFF		
	6	MIDLAND, TEXAS	CHAPARAL CENTER	"
	7	EL PASO, TEXAS	COLISEUM	"
	8	DAY OFF		
	9	TUSCON, ARIZONA	COMMUNITY CENTER	"
	10	ALBUQUERQUE, NEW MEXICO	CIVIC CENTER	"
	11	DAY OFF		
JUNE	12	DES MOINES, IOWA	MEMORIAL AUDITORIUM	(with TED NUGENT
	13	MADISON, WISCONSIN	DANE CIVIC CENTER	and SCORPIONS)
	14	MILWAUKEE, WISCONSIN	ARENA	
	15	CHICAGO, ILLINOIS	ROSEMONT HORIZON	"
	16	DAY OFF		
	17	ST. LOUIS, MISSOURI	CHECKERDOME	"
	18	KANSAS CITY, MISSOURI	KEMPERER ARENA	"
	19	DENVER, COLORADO	McNICHOLS ARENA	"

CONTEMPORARY COMMUNICATIONS CORPORATION

0019

65 WEST 55TH STREET
NEW YORK, NEW YORK 10019
(212) 765-2600

)019

as of 6/6/80

TED NUGENT/SCORPIONS/DEF LEPPARD

JUNE 20 - 21	(TED NUGENT/OFF ROAD RACE - LOS ANGELES)			
	22	PHOENIX, AZ	COMPTON TERRACE	DON FOX
	23	off		
	24	MIDLAND, TX	CHAPPARAL	MIKE CLARK
	25	SAN ANTONIO, TX	HEMISFAIR ARENA	JACK ORBIN
	26	DALLAS, TX	REUNION ARENA	LOU MESSINA
	27	HOUSTON, TX	SUMMIT	LOU MESSINA
	28	BATON ROUGE, LA	CENTROPLEX	DON FOX
	29	SHREVEPORT, LA	HIRSCH COLISEUM	DON FOX
JULY	1	MEMPHIS, TN	MID-SOUTH COLISEUM	BOB KELLY
	2	NASHVILLE, TN	CIVIC AUDITORIUM	ROBERT STEWART
(tentative)	3	COLUMBIA, SC	CAROLINA COLISEUM	CECIL CORBETT
	4	LAKELAND, FL	CIVIC CENTER	JACK BOYLE
	5	JACKSONVILLE, FL	VETERANS COLISEUM	SIDNEY DRASHIN
	6	HOLLYWOOD, FL	SPORTATORIUM	JACK BOYLE
	7	off		
	8	CHARLOTTE, NC	COLISEUM	CECIL CORBETT
	9	GREENSBORO, NC	COLISEUM	PHIL LASHINSKY
	10	NORFOLK, VA	SCOPE PLAZA	PHIL LASHINSKY
	11	off		
	12	NORFOLK, OH	LEGEND VALLEY (outdoors)	BELKIN
	13	LARGO, MD WASHINGTON CAPITOL CENTER		DAVE WILLIAMS, Cellar Door
	14	PHILADELPHIA, PA	SPECTRUM	LARRY MAGID
	15	NEW HAVEN, CT	COLISEUM	CROSS COUNTRY
	16	BUFFALO, NY	MEMORIAL AUDITORIUM	LARRY NATHAN

CONTEMPORARY COMMUNICATIONS CORPORATION

65 WEST 55TH STREET
NEW YORK, NEW YORK 10019
(212) 765-2600

DEF LEPPARD ITINERARY

JULY 15-17	NEW YORK CITY	HOWARD JOHNSON 851 EIGHTH AVE. NEW YORK, NY	#212-581-4100
17-19	ROCHESTER, NY	HOLIDAY INN DOWNTOWN 120 MAIN STREET E. ROCHESTER, NY	#716-546-6400
19-20	CLEVELAND, OH	HOLIDAY INN LAKESIDE 111 LAKESIDE AVE. CLEVELAND, OHIO	#216-241-5100
20-21	DAYTON, OH	SHERATON DOWNTOWN 21 SOUTH JEFFERSON DAYTON, OH	#513-223-2100
21-22	WHEELING, W. VA	HOLIDAY INN ROUTE 4 ST. CLAIRSVILLE, OH	#614-695-0100
22-23	TOLEDO, OH	HOLIDAY INN RIVERVIEW SUMMITT & JEFFERSON TOLEDO, OH	#419-243-8860
23-24	KALAMAZOO, MI	SHERATON INN 3600 CORK STREET KALAMAZOO, MI	#616-385-3922
25-27	CHICAGO, IL	HOLIDAY INN CITY CTR. 300 EAST OHIO STREET CHICAGO, IL	#312-787-6100
27-29	DUBUQUE, IA	HOLIDAY INN 1111 DODGE STREET DUBUQUE, IA	#319-556-3340
29-31	CLEVELAND, OHIO	HOLIDAY INN 2160 EUCLID AVE. CLEVELAND, OH	#216-696-5175
July 31-AUG 1	PITTSBURGH, PA	CROSSGATES INN FORBES AVE & McKEE PL OAKLAND, PA	#412-683-6000
1-2	NEW YORK CITY	GRAMERCY PARK HOTEL 2 LEXINGTON AVE NEW YORK CITY	#212-475-4320

DEF LEPPARD ITINERARY CONTINUED...

| AUGUST 2-3 | BOSTON, MA | HOWARD JOHNSON
777 MEMORIAL DRIVE
CAMBRIDGE, MA | #617-492-7777 |
| 3-4 | SYRACUSE, NY | HOLIDAY INN
701 EAST GENESEE ST.
SYRACUSE, NY | #315-474-7251 |

JOE ELLIOTT: As well as giving us a huge shot of confidence, our experience in Portland showed us how important radio was.

We did promotion – tons of it – until it got to the point where it was affecting us on stage. They'd send me to a studio an hour and a half away and then I'd have to drive back to the venue in roasting heat with the air conditioning on, so by the time I got out of the car I had no voice left for singing. By the time *Pyromania* came out, we were getting choosy. We'd do MTV, we'd do *Rolling Stone*, but we weren't going to do the *Arkansas Dogwalkers Weekly*.

ENGLAND'S HEAVY METAL EXPLOSION

WELCOME
ASSEMBLIE
OF DOGS

HELLO AMERICA

Holiday Inn Lakeside
CITY CENTER

Cleveland, Ohio

1111 Lakeside Avenue
Downtown Cleveland, Ohio 44114

Leppard spotted in USA . . .

SUMMER ROCK 1980

JOE ELLIOTT: Chateau Marmont had been to show us what LA was all about. They say drug dealers give people their first six weeks of supply free to get them hooked, and then they start charging. It was like that. For us it was all shared rooms in Holiday Inns after that, but we hardly noticed. That didn't change until 1983, when we started headlining. Even when we started the Pyromania tour and Phil Collen had joined the band, he was sharing with Steve and I was sharing with Sav.

After we finished with Pat Travers, we did two weeks with Judas Priest and then six weeks with Ted Nugent and the Scorpions, who were both also managed by Leber-Krebs. By now Cliff had left Mercury to join Peter Mensch at the agency. Sometimes the bands we were playing with were staying in the same hotels as us. I remember one time on that tour we had a day off in a Holiday Inn somewhere in the Midwest. When we went down to the pool Ted Nugent was in there already, and he was the headline act.

THE READING REPORT

Reading's metal mayhem

HEAVY METAL, new wave and old, dominates this year's Reading Festival, which is being staged from August 22-24.

UFO and Whitesnake will headline two of the three nights (though which has still to be decided) and the special guests will include Wishbone Ash, Gillan, Ozzy Osborne's new band and Iron Maiden.

Backing them up with a kerranggg will be Def Leppard, Magnum, Angel City from Australia, Girl, Sledgehammer and Tygers Of Pang Tang.

Def Leppard have as many lights as UFO. Leppard have just completed a successful American tour. They have a No 50 album in America. But Def Leppard didn't win the crowd. Sid Headbanger thinks that they've had too much too soon and they've been whisked away by a slick American Godfather. There's a great feeling of resentment against the Leps and they were greeted by beer cans and derision.

But it was a set that proved they're not pubescents any more as they thundered through 'Rock Brigade' with poses a go go and 'Me And My Wine'. — Elliott on Robbie Plant impersonations. He tried to be mates with the crowd but it didn't work and an encore was not wanted. 24 Aug, 1980

READING became the 1980 Can Festival when several warm-up bands and the audience itself faced a dense and dangerous barrage of jagged-edged cans and other missiles.

Experienced Reading watchers were surprised at the extent and ferocity of the bored fans' assault as can battles built up from one side of the audience to another, injuring people in the middle ground as well as some of those in the target area.

24.8.80

Page 6 — New Musical Express 26th July, 1980

20th NATIONAL ROCK FESTIVAL

READING ROCK '80

FRIDAY 22 AUGUST
RORY GALLAGHER AND HIS BAND
from Switzerland KROKUS
9 BELOW ZERO
FISCHER-Z
PRAYING MANTIS
HELLIONS
01-BAND
RED ALERT
SPECIAL GUESTS GILLAN

SATURDAY 23 AUGUST
UFO
IRON MAIDEN
FROM AUSTRALIA ANGEL CITY
'Q'TIPS · SAMSON
BROKEN HOME
WRITZ · HEADBOYS
TRIMMER & JENKINS
SPECIAL GUESTS
PAT TRAVERS BAND

SUNDAY 24 AUGUST
Whitesnake
DEF LEPPARD
GARY MOORE'S G-FORCE
MAGNUM
BUDGIE
GIRL · TYGERS OF PANTANG
SLEDGEHAMMER
PENCILS
SPECIAL GUESTS OZZIE OSBOURNE'S BLIZZARD OF OZ

£12.50

★ SPECIAL WEEKEND TICKETS ★
including VAT. Camping and car parking at no extra charge.
★ IN ADVANCE ONLY ★

RICK SAVAGE: People believe what they read. That's why we got the cans at Reading.

Whitesnake, Def Leppard & Slade bang heads at the British Woodstock of heavy metal

Leppards back on the prowl

JOE ELLIOTT: It's gone down in legend that when we came back home to play the Reading Festival, we got booed off. That's bullshit. You've only got to listen to the BBC radio broadcast of our set to realise that. The BBC don't fake audience sounds. It's true that some people threw stuff at us – cabbages, bottles of piss – but every single band on the bill, including the headliners, got the same. It was a badge of honour. Among those 30,000 kids, there were probably pockets of people telling us to fuck off. But the majority liked our set and were there for us.

There had been one or two naysayers in the press, including Geoff Barton of course. Then a few readers started writing letters to the editor saying Def Leppard had sold out. So there was some animosity towards us, but it didn't show itself at Reading.

While Reading wasn't the unmitigated disaster that it's been built up as over the last 40 years, it's fair to say that our popularity in the UK flattened off at a point when we were expecting it to continue growing.

The other thing about Reading was that we were supposed to follow Ozzy Osbourne, but he pulled out and was replaced by Slade. They were on for 45 minutes, and every song in their set was a number one – including 'Merry Xmas Everybody', which they played in August. It was their day. We did OK, but we were a bit of an anti-climax after that. It would be a bit like Supertramp following the Sex Pistols.

But we had balls – and we were naïve, in a good way. We went out there, full throttle, and pretended that we were the only band playing that day. You just have to bluff your way through those situations.

Reading Festival
24 August 1980

JOE ELLIOTT: After Reading we went to Europe for three weeks in September/October with the Scorpions. We were due to start *High 'n' Dry* with Mutt Lange after that, but he was delayed doing *Foreigner 4*.

So, we had this hole where we were supposed to be working on the new record. We did get together to write some songs and come up with new riffs and bits and pieces, but the start date kept getting shifted on a month and then another month.

To relieve the boredom, I decided we should do some gigs, which was the most stupid idea I've ever had for the band because nobody else was really interested. We put some shows on in December at little clubs. Whereas we'd sold out the Nottingham Boat Club in January and there were 700 people queuing round the block to get in, 11 months later 87 people turned up. It was the same in Chesterfield at the Aquarius, and everywhere else – just handfuls of people.

During that period, we went back to square one – penniless and living with mum and dad. We didn't even have the rehearsal room at Portland Works anymore. I spent a lot of the winter working on a muddy building site with my girlfriend's father just to earn enough money to be able to give my mum some board and buy a pint now and again. We'd had a UK top 20 album, almost a top 50 album in America, we'd sold out Sheffield City Hall as headliners, and now six months later I was carrying bricks up a ladder.

I felt bloody miserable. We still had the prospect of Mutt Lange doing our next record to look forward to, but meanwhile we were freezing our balls off rehearsing in a paper mill in Dronfield that was owned by Rick's mum's boss. We had space heaters, but, even with fingerless gloves, the guys were struggling to play the guitar.

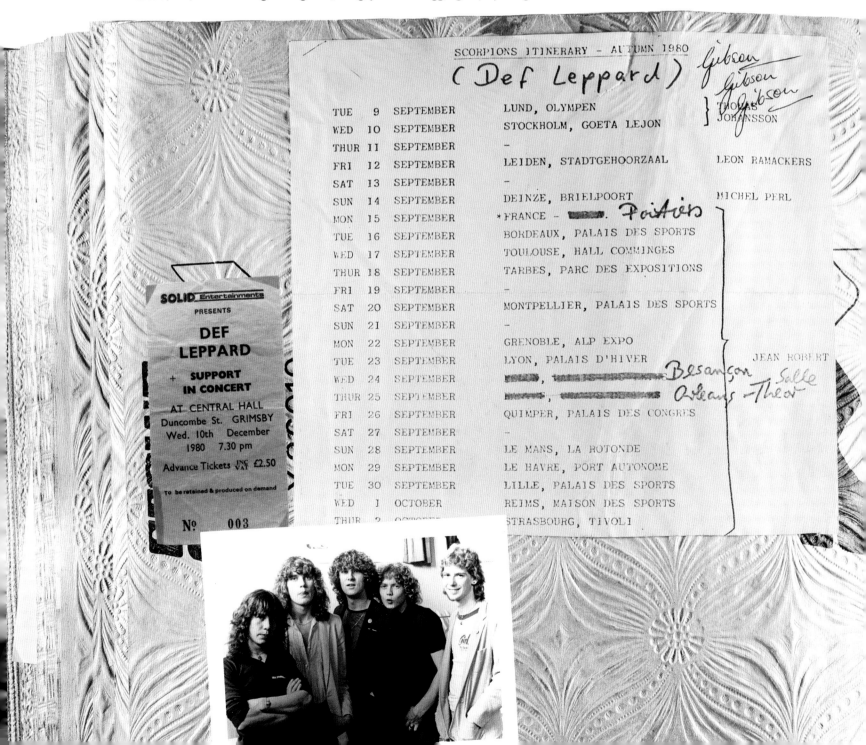

1. LET IT GO
2. ANOTHER HIT AND RUN
3. HIGH 'N' DRY (SATURDAY NIGHT)
4. BRINGIN' ON THE HEARTBREAK
5. SWITCH 625
6. YOU GOT ME RUNNIN'
7. LADY STRANGE
8. ON THROUGH THE NIGHT
9. MIRROR, MIRROR (LOOK INTO MY EYES)
10. NO NO NO

PRODUCED AND MIXED BY ROBERT JOHN "MUTT" LANGE

ORIGINAL COVER BY HIPGNOSIS

PolyGram

POLYGRAM RECORD OPERATIONS

FROM: Jerry Jaffe
TO: All Local & Regional Promotion Mgrs.
DATE: July 6, 1981
SUBJECT: DEF LEPPARD

Here is the much anticipated test pressing of Def Leppard's second album High & Dry.

What a magnificent piece of hard rock craftsmanship harnessed by the redoubtable Mutt Lange whose only two other production credits this year are Foreigner and AC/DC.

The Rock Department recommends the following tracks for immediate ear-catching:

"Let It Go"
"High & Dry"
"Bringing On The Heartbreak"
"Lady Strange"

I am sure the quality of this record will impel both you and radio to discover even more great music but this will do for starters. The first Def Leppard album sold over 200,000 units, which is quite an accomplishment in the age of economic depression and meager record sales. This one should break them to superstars.

Enclosed for your edification are the tracking sheets from last May during the height of Def Leppard's airplay run. Note where the act was an airplay success and where work needs to be done.

To help spread the word and to substantiate our commitment, we have ordered 300 Def Leppard tour jackets (in assorted sizes, Don Masters). Each of you will receive one and you shall have an ample supply to grease all your influential AOR programmers.

Final promotional points:

a) postcard announcing the imminent release of the Leppards has just gone out to radio.

b) Cliff Burnstein of Leber-Krebs Management, and a PolyGram alumnus, shall help coordinate the promotional effort and we all welcome Cliff's assistance and good fellowship.

PolyGram Record Operations, A Division of PolyGram Corporation • 810 Seventh Avenue • New York, N.Y. 10019 • (212) 399-7100
Casablanca Records, Inc. • PhonoGram Inc. • Polydor Incorporated • PolyGram Classics Inc. • PolyGram Distribution, Inc.

Above left: The band are presented with gold RIAA awards for High 'n' Dry, December 1982. Manager Peter Mensch is kneeling to Phil Collen's right.

POLYDOR INCORPORATED CASS.
ALBUM LABEL COPY AND MASTERING INSTRUCTIONS

A POLYGRAM COMPANY

LABEL	MERCURY	ARTIST	DEF LEPPARD	ALBUM NO. MCR-4-1-4021
TITLE	HIGH 'N' DRY		INTL # 7150 045	

— TO APPEAR ON LABEL — TITLES, CREDITS, PERFORMANCE RIGHTS & TIME		— NOT ON LABEL — PUBLISHER & MASTER NO.
SIDE NO.	MGS NO.	

SIDE ONE

LET IT GO
ANOTHER HIT AND RUN
HIGH 'N' DRY (SATURDAY NIGHT)
BRINGIN' ON THE HEARTBREAK
SWITCH 625

TOTAL TIME: 20:42

SIDE NO.	MGS NO.	

SIDE TWO

YOU GOT ME RUNNIN'
LADY STRANGE
ON THROUGH THE NIGHT
MIRROR, MIRROR (LOOK INTO MY EYES)
NO NO NO

TOTAL TIME: 21:48

Produced by Robert John "Mutt" Lange

℗ 1981 Phonogram Ltd.

NOTES:

REC. IN UK   MUSIC: POP   PRICE: 8.98
TERRITORY: USA   NOTE: NON-DOLBY!!
7/9/81 jy

HIGH 'N' DRY

JOE ELLIOTT: *We chased down Hipgnosis to do the cover for High 'n' Dry. Storm Thorgerson and his partner at Hipgnosis had done all of UFO's sleeves. We were also aware of the fact that they'd done Zeppelin's Presence album and, of course, they were known for their Pink Floyd covers. We wanted to jump on the coattails of the big boys, thinking that it might help us become a big boy too.*

Storm offered us seven or eight different ideas based around the title High 'n' Dry, including the one that we ended up using – of a diver suspended high in the air above an empty (i.e. dry) pool.

We found out later that the High 'n' Dry cover concept had been rejected for Ummagumma by Pink Floyd in 1969. Something similar happened when we did the album cover for Retro Active with Hugh Syme, although this time we were the ones doing the rejecting. One of the ideas Hugh showed us was of an old lady hanging babies up to dry on her washing line. We all said, 'My God, that's hideous.' Then, lo and behold, it appeared on a Megadeth cover a year later.

High 'n' Dry was the first of a run of covers through to Adrenalize that have an obvious common thread in terms of colours and graphic style. It's all part of the big picture, like what KISS, Thin Lizzy and Yes did with their logos.

High 'n' Dry
Recorded: February–June 1981
Released: 6 July 1981

JOE ELLIOTT: In February 1981, we finally got the call to go down to London to start work on the new album, and that's when the record company started kicking money back into the band. Luckily, Battery Studios in Willesden had live-in quarters, two terrace houses glued to the side of the studio, so the band had somewhere to stay. We were at John Henry's rehearsal studios for a month, and then we recorded for three months with Mutt in Battery Studios. So, we were down in London from February to June 1981.

With the greatest respect to Tom Allom, who was a brilliant producer, Mutt Lange is in an orbit of his own. Tom just allowed us to be who we were. We recorded the songs as we'd been playing them live, wrote two new ones, and that was *On Through the Night*.

Mutt was much more willing to intervene. He would literally say, 'Stop right there. OK, that section, just take it out. It's not up to scratch.' We'd never had anybody say that to us before. When we were writing stuff, if someone felt like a section wasn't working it would take a week for us all to agree. But Mutt would say it right there and then.

So, for example, we had three new songs which we had played at Reading: 'When the Rain Falls', 'Lady Strange' and 'Medicine Man'. 'When the Rain Falls' got rewritten as 'Let It Go', because Mutt said it was too fast, the lyrics sucked and we needed to turn it into an anthem like 'Highway to Hell'. He liked 'Lady Strange', but we still had to edit one section out and put a new section in. 'Medicine Man' ended up on *Pyromania*, rewritten as 'Rock! Rock! (Till You Drop)'. It was the same kind of thing with 'Bringin' On the Heartbreak': musically it stayed pretty similar to the original and the melody survived, but he put a chorus in it and told us to improve the lyrics.

Mutt was a great judge in that respect, but it took us a long time to get used to somebody tearing our art to pieces. We were naive, and we didn't realise that that's how it is when you're working with a top-class producer.

When we heard the finished album, we were absolutely blown away. The parallels with *Highway to Hell* were obvious: the two albums were recorded, 18 months apart, in the same room with the same producer and the same engineer. We loved the fact that our record sounded a bit like AC/DC, but we also loved the fact that we had sections in our songs – massive harmonies and jangle guitars – that they wouldn't go anywhere near.

RICK ALLEN: It was the first time we all experienced really, really hard work. When a band comes out with their first record, those songs have already been worked and reworked and polished in front of audiences. But by the time they do their second album, a lot of the songs are being created in the studio. We brought all our ideas to the table. Mutt really helped us shape the songs on that record and develop our own sound. It was a better version of ourselves. I thought it sounded way better than the first record. Mutt showed us the fantastic direction we could go in.

RICK SAVAGE: On the first album, Tom Allom let us put all our own ideas forward, so there wasn't much discipline but it was good fun. The second and third albums with Mutt were a lot harder work and less fun, but the result was better.

JOE ELLIOTT: Even though it didn't sell as well as *On Through the Night* in the UK, *High 'n' Dry* got fantastic reviews. It only reached 26 in the album charts, and during the UK leg of the tour we were playing to half-empty theatres. Things went quiet for us at home until 1986. Even *Pyromania*, which sold 6 million copies in America, didn't chart in the UK when it was first released.

Looking back now, I actually don't like my vocals on *High 'n' Dry* too much. They're fine on songs like 'Let It Go', 'Bringin' On the Heartbreak' and 'You Got Me Runnin''. But I find them a bit grating on 'No No No' and 'High 'n' Dry'. It sounds like I was trying too hard – but in 1981 screamy, shouty lead vocalists were the in thing, so I wasn't the only one.

By the time we got to *Pyromania*, I realised that I was actually a pop singer not a rock singer. When we did our covers album *Yeah!* more than 20 years later, I was singing songs by Blondie, ELO and Roxy Music, not Led Zeppelin or Black Sabbath.

I wasn't Robert Plant or Ozzy Osbourne or Paul Rodgers. Eventually, I became Joe Elliott, but on *High 'n' Dry* I was still trying to discover my real voice.

JOE ELLIOTT: Our first gig on the High 'n' Dry tour, opening for Ritchie Blackmore's Rainbow in Gothenburg, was an absolute disaster. Because the album had taken longer than expected to record, we hadn't had a chance to rehearse properly. I didn't even turn up at the venue until about three hours before the gig, because I was in the studio with Mutt finishing off the vocal for 'Me and My Wine', the B side of 'Bringin' On the Heartbreak'. That song is a real throat-ripper, so I was in no condition to sing by the time I got on stage.

I was so shit-scared, I begged them to open with the instrumental 'Switch 625' just to ease myself in. We were playing on muscle memory, and we must have been awful. Apparently, the reviews were atrocious – and rightly so.

Apart from Gothenburg, my strongest memory of that European tour is playing the bullring in Barcelona in early July. Rainbow were headlining again and UFO were also on the bill. Phil Mogg got into a full-on fist fight in the dressing room area, which was a big tent with screens to separate the individual dressing rooms. The fight started at one end and then the screens all fell down like dominoes. Everyone grabbed their guitars to stop them getting trashed and ran out into the open.

The headliners were supposed to go on at midnight, but Blackmore didn't want to play that late so he made us go on after him. Once Rainbow had played their last note, everybody turned round and started to leave. Our lighting engineer blasted out a white strobe over the audience, which made everybody stop and come back, and the roadies got our gear on stage in a matter of minutes. Weirdly, we ended up headlining that show and most people stayed.

Def Leppard prowls again

DEF LEPPARD (above) undertake their first British tour for over a year next month to coincide with the release of their second album, 'High 'N' Dry', which is released by Vertigo on July 6.

The band have just completed work on the album with producer Mutt Lange who has also been working with AC/DC and Foreigner which is why Def Leppard's recording has got behind schedule.

The tour opens at Bristol Colston Hall on July 13 and continues at Birmingham Odeon 14, Derby Assembly Rooms 16, Bradford St Georges Hall 17, Newcastle City Hall 18, Edinburgh Odeon 19, Sheffield City Hall 20, Liverpool Royal Court 22, Manchester Apollo 23, Wolverhampton Civic Hall 24, London Hammersmith Odeon 25.

Tickets for all gigs are £3.25, £3.00 and £2.75 except Derby and Wolverhampton which are £3.25.

HIGH 'N' DRY
New album
Produced by MUTT LANGE

DEF LEPPARD

SPECIAL OFFER*

If you present your ticket stub from any of the eleven tour dates at any HMV store you will receive an extra 50p reduction on the album which will really leave you High 'n' Dry.

TOUR DATES

13 JULY BRISTOL *Colston Hall*	20 JULY SHEFFIELD *City Hall*
14 JULY BIRMINGHAM *Odeon*	22 JULY LIVERPOOL *Royal Court*
16 JULY DERBY *Assembly Hall*	23 JULY MANCHESTER *Apollo*
17 JULY BRADFORD *St. George's*	24 JULY WOLVERHAMPTON *Civic Hall*
18 JULY NEWCASTLE *City Hall*	25 JULY HAMMERSMITH *Odeon*
19 JULY EDINBURGH *Odeon*	Concerts promoted by M.C.P.

*Offer closes August 31st.

JOE ELLIOTT: From August to November 1981 we were in America, first supporting Ozzy Osbourne and then, from mid-September, a Southern rock band called Blackfoot.

Touring with Ozzy was brilliant. Being able to watch Randy Rhoads every night was a privilege. And Ozzy and Sharon were big supporters of ours, so they really looked after us. We got soundchecks, we got the lights. In fairness, we were always treated well by the bands we opened for.

STEVE CLARK: Ozzy was well established and his fans had grown up with him. The kids in the audience could relate to us because we were around the same age as them, but the older people found it harder to look at a young band like us and respect us.

JOE ELLIOTT: My best memory is the last night when we were in Daytona Beach, Florida. We drove the bus onto the beach and it got stuck and had to be towed off (eating heavily into our tour profit, no doubt). There was an end-of-tour party in Tommy Aldridge's room, who was Ozzy's drummer at the time. Someone from Ozzy's camp was setting fireworks off on the balcony, aiming them down at the pool where there were still people sitting around having drinks. The cops came and tried to round up everyone who was in Tommy's room, but Tommy was having none of it. It began to dawn on us that we could get into deep shit, so we snuck off like naughty schoolboys through the adjoining door into the next room.

JOE ELLIOTT: Two days after finishing the Ozzy tour, we were in Georgia opening for Blackfoot. There's no way on earth that anybody would have put us on that tour unless it was literally the only option available. It was like when Jimi Hendrix opened for the Monkees. They were great guys, don't get me wrong, but their audience didn't look like they would take to us. They were Southern boogie boys – cowboy hats, cowboy boots, flared trousers, the whole bit – whereas we looked like T. Rex. It was a little weird, but we actually went down OK.

In fact, at one particular gig in Denver, Colorado, Blackfoot refused to go on after us because the crowd was full of Def Leppard fans. There were two shows that night. For the first show, we opened as normal; but for the second show, they wanted us to close things out. That was fine by us as long as we got paid the headline fee, but their management wasn't having it. At first, we refused to go on. But we soon realised that it wouldn't do us any good to disappoint the 1,500 kids out there who had come to see us. So, we sucked it up and performed. I was so fired up after everything that had gone on beforehand that I jumped off the stage during the instrumental section of 'Getcha Rocks Off', ran through the crowd to the mixing desk and pulled Robert Allen's trousers down. I don't know what I was thinking; it was just something I did because I could.

JOE ELLIOTT: Pete Willis and Steve Clark were very different guitarists. Pete was a technician, whereas Steve was more of a slop-meister, and I mean that in the best possible way. Steve was more interested in what he was writing than how he played it. And that's how it always should be.

The contrast between Pete and Steve worked fine on the first album. Because we were all so excited to be in a band, there wasn't really any arguing about the direction a particular song was taking. If one of us didn't like, say, 'Answer to the Master', we just sucked it up because everybody else seemed to like it.

Things were still OK on *High 'n' Dry*, because both guitarists were taking direction from Mutt rather than throwing their own weight around. Mutt figured them out pretty quickly. He'd say, 'OK, Pete, this is your part. Steve, what have you got that you can do here?' Steve wouldn't necessarily offer anything up to begin with, but Mutt would always know how to coax something good out of him.

By the time we got to *Pyromania*, Pete was really struggling with all the cutting-edge Eighties technology that Mutt wanted us to use. Sav and I were totally in favour of this new direction; Steve and Rick a little less so, but they were still on board; but Pete didn't like it at all. He was much more of a traditionalist. He kept his mouth shut, but his frustration showed itself in other ways.

Although they roomed together on tour, Pete and Steve didn't get on particularly well. They didn't dislike each other, but they were definitely bandmates rather than mates. One time, Steve marched through the adjoining door into the room I was sharing with Sav. He said, 'I can't room with that bastard anymore. He's had a shower and he's used all the towels. He stood on one, he's got one wrapped round his waist, one on his head as a turban, and one over his shoulders. What am I supposed to fucking do?'

The big problem with both Pete and Steve was that they liked to drink too much. Sadly, for Steve it turned out really bad. At that time, though, Pete's drinking was more of an issue than Steve's. It had got to the point where he was going on stage drunk to overcome his stage fright. But then he was too drunk to play, and that caused so many fights – particularly on those long tours of America.

We were all guilty of drinking, but the rest of us never went on stage drunk. After a particularly traumatic show in 1980 where Pete was so hammered that his fingers were falling off the strings, I came running and screaming back into the dressing room and threw a bottle into the shower, smashing it everywhere. I went absolutely apeshit at him. Pete would apologise, he'd be all right for a week, and then he would start to slip again. This just went on and on and on.

JOE ELLIOTT: One night during our tour of Europe in 1981, Pete had gone to bed bollocksed while the rest of us stayed down in the bar. When we went to go up to our rooms, the carpet of the elevator was covered in white powder with these tiny footprints in them. Little high heel size seven boots. We looked at each other and went, 'That's Pete.' We got up to our floor and followed a trail of white powder to Pete's room. He'd set a fire extinguisher off, on his own. When Keith Moon or Keith Richards set a fire extinguisher off they did it for a laugh with a bunch of mates watching. You don't do it on your own. Pete ended up paying for the fire extinguisher to be refilled and to clean up the mess. He's the only guy I've ever known who actually lost money by touring, because whatever money he earned went to replace things that he'd destroyed.

c   - 3 -

11.) BAND FOOD

Food for ten (10) people to be available 1½ hours before Def Leppard
show-time, to consist of light foods i.e.: fruit, cheeses, canapes or
hot and cold hors d'oeuvres, sandwiches, appetizers, salads, deli-trays
and the following beverages:
36 cans of lager
24 cans of Pepsi (no diet beverages)
12 bottles of Perrier water (or similar)
2 litres of Apple Juice
2 litres of fresh Orange Juice
2 litres of Milk (pasteurised)
2 bottles of Piesporter (or similar medium-sweet German white wine)

(all the above to be served in ice buckets)

1 bottle of Vodka

Coffee and Tea-making facilities available in dressing rooms

1 carton of cigarettes (200) i.e. Marlboro, Rothmans, St. Moritz etc.

2 boxes of Smarties

ACCEPTED AND AGREED TO:

PURCHASER: DEF LEPPARD:

BY:.......................   BY:.................................

JOE ELLIOTT: Things had got so bad that I was already thinking about possible replacements. I rang Phil Collen from America to sound him out. I'd met Phil in Sheffield the year before when his band, Girl, opened for UFO at the City Hall. I'd gone backstage and we got on really well. Steve and I went on with him and Phil Lewis, Girl's lead singer, to the Genevieve nightclub where a band called Sledgehammer was playing. After they finished their set, we drunkenly asked if we could use their gear. We got up and played two songs: 'You Really Got Me' by the Kinks and 'Do You Love Me?' by KISS. I was on drums, Steve played bass, Phil C. played guitar and Phil L. sang. Steve fell asleep on the drum riser.

PHIL COLLEN: Joe phoned me up and asked me whether I could learn 16 songs in two days. 'Yeah, of course,' I lied. Then nothing happened. He didn't phone back until a few days later, and said, 'We smoothed it out. But thanks anyway.'

JOE ELLIOTT: Having slept on it, I rang Phil back and said, 'Look, it's not going to happen right now, but we want you in at some stage.'

When we got back from the 1981 tour, we had a band meeting where we told Pete he'd have to go if his behaviour continued. We always forgave him on the road because being on the road is weird. People get up to shenanigans – groupies, drinking, drugs, throwing TVs out of the window. All the cliches.

It was when Pete started messing up during the *Pyromania* sessions that we realised this couldn't go on. I remember getting to the studio one morning, and Mutt was coming out of the control room laughing. He wasn't even angry. Pete had got through two bottles of brandy the day before and was still drunk. He was wearing his guitar back to front and trying to strum the back of it. Then Mutt did start getting angry because Pete was trying to justify himself. I was worried that Mutt might walk, and I couldn't let that happen.

Mutt sent Pete back to Sheffield and told him to sort himself out. But we'd already made the decision that he wasn't coming back.

Peter Mensch insisted that we fire Pete to his face. So poor Russ Major, our drum tech, had to drive him all the way down from Sheffield to a big house in Kensington on the day of the 1982 World Cup final. Pete knew damn well what was going on. We sat him down and said, 'Listen, mate, we're sorry, but we're going to have to fire you.' He offered to go to rehab, but we just said, 'Sorry, Pete. It's too late. You're gone.'

Once he realised we weren't going to back down, he said, 'You know what, it's actually a relief because I'm not really enjoying it anyway.' I think the pressure of working with Mutt on *Pyromania* had got to him.

RICK SAVAGE: I very rarely remember Steve going out to perform the worse for drink. Steve drank after the show, but he never let his drinking compromise what he had to do on stage. As much as I liked Pete when he was sober, I can't say the same for him. It's a question of respect to yourself, to your band members and, most importantly, to your paying public. Pete was given a lot of chances, he really was, but he was starting to become detrimental to the band as a whole.

PETE WILLIS: Things were going too fast for me. I was still enjoying it, but I had started to use drink as a crutch. It wasn't nice to leave the band like that, but if I'd stayed there was a good chance I'd have gone the same way as Steve.

Steve was probably drinking as much as, if not more than, I was, but he was a different type of guy. He wouldn't say boo to a ghost, whereas I gave Mutt a mouthful back when he exploded at me and things went downhill from there.

Once something's been decided like that between a group of friends it can never be the same again. But for my health and maybe my sanity, leaving was the best thing that could have happened to me. Which is a hard thing to say.

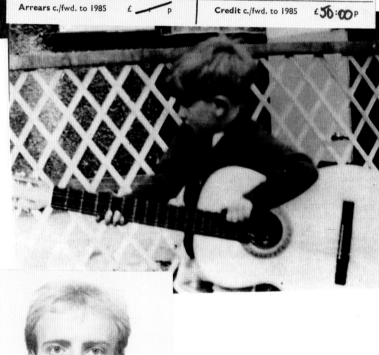

Name	COLLEN P.K.		Branch Mem. No.	45521
Address			R.O. No.	381580
			Date of Admission	15·10·79

Arrears bt./fwd. from 1983 £ _____   Credit bt./fwd. from 1983 £ _____

TO BE COMPLETED BY MEMBER			THESE COLUMNS ARE TO BE ENTERED *ONLY* BY BRANCH OFFICIAL		
	£	P	Amount Paid for each Qtr.	Date Paid	Branch Stamp
1st Quarter (to 31st March)					MUSICIANS UNION LONDON BRANCH
_____ weeks @ 50p					
52 weeks @ 95p	50	00	£100·00	5/3/84	
_____ weeks @ £1·10					
_____ weeks @ £1·55			CLEAR		
Fine, if applicable					
2nd Quarter (to 30th June)					MUSICIANS UNION LONDON BRANCH
_____ weeks @ 50p					
✓ weeks @ 95p			✓	CLEAR	
_____ weeks @ £1·10					
_____ weeks @ £1·55					
Fine, if applicable					
3rd Quarter (to 29th September)					MUSICIANS UNION LONDON BRANCH
_____ weeks @ 50p					
✓ weeks @ 95p			✓	CLEAR	
_____ weeks @ £1·10					
_____ weeks @ £1·55					
Fine, if applicable					
4th Quarter (to 31st December)					MUSICIANS UNION LONDON BRANCH
_____ weeks @ 50p					
✓ weeks @ 95p			✓	CLEAR	
_____ weeks @ £1·10					
_____ weeks @ £1·55					
Fine, if applicable					

Arrears c./fwd. to 1985 £ _____ p   Credit c./fwd. to 1985 £ 50·00 p

PHIL COLLEN

NICKNAME	: NOT TELLING
BIRTHDAY	: 8TH OF DECEMBER
STAR SIGN	: SAGITTARIUS
PLACE OF BIRTH	: LONDON
EDUCATED AT	: SIR GEORGE MONEUX SCHOOL, LONDON
HEIGHT, WEIGHT	: 5'8", 9½ STONE (133 LBS)
COLOUR HAIR	: BLOND
COLOUR EYES	: GREEN (SOMETIMES!)
MARRIED	: NO
BROTHERS, SISTERS	: NONE
CAREER BEFORE MUSICIAN	: DESPATCH RIDER
MUSICAL INFLUENCES	: QUEEN, AEROSMITH, BOWIE, ZEPPELIN, ETC.
FIRST GIG	: PUB IN LONDON
FIRST GIG WITH DEF LEPPARD	: MARQUEE CLUB, LONDON - FEBRUARY, 1983
FIRST VINYL APPEARANCE WITH DEF LEPPARD	: "PYROMANIA"
OTHER VINYL APPEARANCES	: "SHEER GREED" AND "WASTED YOUTH" WITH GIRL
TYPE OF GUITARS USED	: IBANEZ, GIBSON LES PAUL, FENDER STRATS
INTERESTS	: GUITARS
FAVORITE BAND	: AC/DC
FAVORITE GUITARIST	: GARY MOORE
FIRST RECORD BOUGHT	: "MOTT" BY MOTT THE HOOPLE
FIRST CONCERT SEEN	: DEEP PURPLE AT THE RAINBOW THEATRE, LONDON
BEST CONCERT SEEN	: BOWIE, LONDON '73; MOTT/QUEEN LONDON '74
HERO	: JIMI HENDRIX
HEROINE	: NO ONE AS YET
FAVORITE FILMS	: A CLOCKWORK ORANGE; RAIDERS OF THE LOST ARK
FAVORITE BOOK	: EARTHLY POWERS BY ANTHONY BURGESS
FAVORITE FOOD	: SPICY
FAVORITE DRINK	: BANANA MILKSHAKE
FAVORITE COLOUR	: BLACK
FAVORITE CAR	: 'E' TYPE JAGUAR
MOST ENJOYABLE PART OF WORK	: PLAYING LIVE
MOST HATED PART OF WORK	: WAITING AT AIRPORTS
FUNNIEST EXPERIENCE	: MEETING JOE ELLIOTT!
WORST EXPERIENCE	: BIKE ACCIDENT AT 16
IDEAL HOME	: WORLD CRUISER
IDEAL HOLIDAY	: INDIA, EGYPT OR ANYWHERE HOT
DREAMS	: FREQUENTLY WET!
AMBITIONS	: THE OBVIOUS

PHIL COLLEN: I was born in 1957 in London, which was such a fertile ground for music. You'd have access to the pirate radio stations like Radio Caroline and Radio Luxembourg and they would play such cool stuff.

I used to pretend to be Paul McCartney in our back shed with the kid next door (he was John Lennon). We had plastic Beatles wigs and tennis rackets. My cousin left a guitar in the house, but I never really played it. There's a picture of a four-year-old me picking it up, left-handedly, funnily enough, even though I'm right-handed.

Growing up, I got into everything, from the stuff on the radio like the Monkees and the Beatles to more progressive music like Pink Floyd, Deep Purple and Zeppelin. That was a whole other dimension. I loved all kinds of American music – Motown, Aretha Franklin, Jimi Hendrix. And, because there was a huge West Indian community in London, especially in east London where I lived, I got into reggae too.

I went to my first concert when I was 14: Deep Purple at the Rainbow. It changed my life. I was in the front row and I touched Ritchie Blackmore's hand. His guitar playing was out of this world, and it still is. From that point on, all I wanted to do was play guitar. Then I saw David Bowie on *Top of the Pops* and that changed everything again, because all of a sudden I had a feeling that this artist was writing songs for me. I understood what he was getting at. And then it was T. Rex and the Faces and Roxy Music. I delved into loads of other stuff, like jazz guitar playing – I remember going to Ronnie Scott's when I was a kid.

So, all these different inspirations – soul, reggae, prog rock, glam rock, jazz – were being thrown into the pot. It was funny, because when I met Joe years later we had very similar record collections.

I got my first guitar for my 16th birthday. I pestered my mum and dad, and they borrowed money to buy their little only child a Gibson SG. I've still got it. I used to play it all the time – never put it down – and I slept with it next to my bed.

I taught myself how to play. Within my ever-growing record collection, I had the best teachers in the world: Jimi Hendrix, Jimmy Page, Jeff Beck, Ritchie Blackmore. I would put those records on and listen, take the needle off and learn the bits I liked. I wouldn't learn the whole song, I just made a collage of bits and pieces until I could actually play and write songs of my own.

You often hear people talking about how they used to hate their parents when they were teenagers, but I always loved mine. They were great. My dad was my roadie. When we started doing gigs, we'd be playing places like the Ruskin Arms in East Ham and my dad would load up all our shit into his van. My mum was really supportive too. When we went to a careers interview at school and I announced that I wanted to be a guitar player, the careers officer said, 'Well, you can't really be that. You could work in a music shop or a music factory or something.' Afterwards, my mum, who never used to swear, said, 'Fuck them. You do what you want.'

FRONT IMAGES
HAVE TO BE
TAKEN FROM
EXISTING
FILM AS EXPLAINED

Pyromania
Recorded: January–
November 1982
Released: 20 January 1983

PYROMANIA

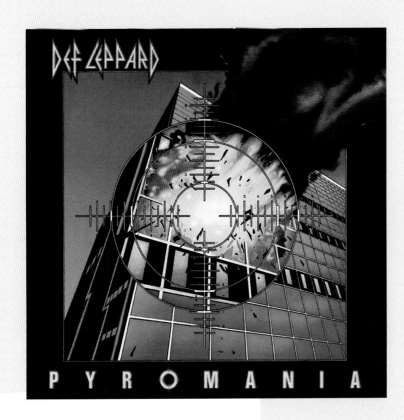

JOE ELLIOTT: *Having scratched our Hipgnosis itch, we decided to try something else for Pyromania. We hooked up with Andie Airfix after Peter Mensch saw his cover for the Thompson Twins'* Here's to Future Days. *We went on to use him for Hysteria and Adrenalize as well. Graphic artists have their own style. Roger Dean did designs for Yes where you couldn't see the name of the band on the album cover in the shop. There would be chopped-off bits of planet that looked like broccoli coming through the sky. But you'd know it was Roger Dean and therefore you'd know it was Yes.*

With his distinctive comic book style, Andie had a similar kind of aura in the Eighties. The Pyromania cover literally looked like it had been lifted out of a graphic novel. It was a very striking image, but it came back to haunt us after 9/11 to a point where I remember thinking we should get the label to make a statement saying that any represses of the album would have a different cover. It was frighteningly similar, but time passed. We were advised that it wasn't necessary to change the image because, historically, it was nothing to do with 9/11. It's not like we were visionaries who had seen this coming. So, we left it alone.

DEF LEPPARD

"PYROMANIA"

Side 1
Rock Rock (Till you Drop) - Clark/Savage/Lange/Elliott
Photograph - Clark/Willis/Savage/Elliott/Lange
Stagefright - Savage/Elliott/Lange
Too Late for Love - Clark/Lange/Willis/Savage/Elliott
Die Hard the Hunter - Lange/Clark/Savage/Elliott

Side 2
Foolin - Clark/Lange/Elliott
Rock of Ages - Clark/Lange/Elliott
Action! Not Words - Lange/Clark/Elliott
Comin' Under Fire - Lange/Clark/Willis/Elliott
Billy's Got a Gun - Clark/Savage/Willis/Elliott/Lange

All songs Def- Lepp Music/Zomba Music Publishers Ltd.

Lyrics as follows.

PHIL COLLEN: About a year after Joe's first phone call, he called me again and asked if I wanted to come down and play some solos on their album. He told me that Pete's drinking had reared its head again and they'd asked him to go home. I thought he was still in the band because he'd played on some of the tracks. So, when I went down initially I thought I was just helping my friends out. I didn't realise it was an audition, so I didn't feel any pressure. Then, the next day I went in and played a solo on 'Stagefright' and the first take ended up on the record.

JOE ELLIOTT: When Phil came in to play on 'Stagefright', we didn't hover in the control room looking through the glass. No one needs that kind of pressure. We took ourselves off to the kitchen area and drank tea. After about 15 minutes, Mutt came rushing out and said, 'You gotta come and hear this,' and he played us Phil's solo. We felt like we'd found our Eddie Van Halen.

Phil was also a fantastic singer. Listen to him singing 'Stay with Me' on the *Yeah!* album and he sounds exactly like Rod Stewart. With Phil on board, we could do all the vocal harmonies live that had been a struggle for Sav, Steve and me. A good example is 'Bringin' On the Heartbreak', which we hadn't been able to play during the High 'n' Dry tour for that reason. We played 'Heartbreak' live for the first time in 1983 and we've been playing it ever since.

PHIL COLLEN: I only ever wanted to be a guitar player when I was a kid but I would also sing along to my favourite bits of songs while I was teaching myself guitar. It could be Stevie Wonder or Sly and the Family Stone or whatever. So, later on, when I was asked to sing, I had the confidence to do it straight away. A lot of people don't sing because they feel embarrassed, but I'd already crossed that bridge without even realising it.

When Mutt found out I could sing, he had me on all the backing vocals. There's this little two-part harmony feature that Joe and I do all the time. We do it pre-chorus on 'Animal', 'Foolin'', 'Too Late for Love'. We introduced that in those first sessions. And then Mutt got me playing on all the other tracks, beefing things up with my style of guitar.

It was so much fun working with them and with Mutt. It was totally inspiring, and the record sounded amazing. Before I knew it, I was on tour with them. It all went so quickly. But I don't think Joe officially asked me to join the band until 2000.

JOE ELLIOTT: So, Mutt gave the thumbs up and Phil was in the band. On *Pyromania*, Pete played all the rhythm guitars, with embellishments from Phil, and Steve and Phil shared the solos.

Steve and Phil became the inseparable 'Terror Twins'. I was almost jealous because Phil was my mate and now he was running off with Steve. There was a moment where Steve became really intimidated by Phil's technical ability and didn't think he could live up to it, but it was Phil himself who was able to talk him down off the ledge. He said, 'Steve, we complement each other perfectly. Your off-the-wall guitar playing is what makes this band work.' The pair would also show what a great writing team they were on *Hysteria*. Steve and Phil was something else.

RICK SAVAGE: Phil is more jazz/rock-oriented than Pete ever was. He's what we call a speed freak; occasionally he tries to see how many notes he can put in a five-second solo. And with him being more jazz/rock-oriented he does have a stronger background of chords and what have you. He and Steve complemented each other really well because they had contrasting styles.

DEF LEPPARD'S UNMATCHED TWIN LEADS

A New Lineup And A New Album Propel Metal Mavens To The Top.

PHIL COLLEN: Steve and I never actually talked about our different guitar roles, but he had clear ideas on the subject. He would say, 'In an orchestra the violin plays one part and the cello plays another part, but most two-guitar bands are really boring because they play the same thing.' Mutt felt the same way. He would talk about having counter melodies, where one rhythm does one thing and the other is counter to that. But it was important not to do it gratuitously – it still had to make sense, it still had to be integral.

Keith Richards talks about 'weaving sonic tapestries' with Ronnie Wood. I totally get what he's saying because that's what Steve and I used to do. One of us would play a lead line; the other would play a melodic counter rhythm or canon to it. We would make a guitar orchestration, building up layer upon layer of guitar parts, a bit like Brian May did with Queen.

What made it work so well was that we always knew which role suited each of us better. Steve's playing is so different from anyone I've ever met before. It reminds me of Jimmy Page. It comes in from a different angle, so it was really obvious who was going to do what on any given song. We didn't even need to think about it.

STEVE CLARK: Phil and I know what each other's thinking. We've got such different styles of playing – Phil plays by ear, and I was taught classically – but the two of us blend together really well. You can always tell on record who's playing what.

On *Pyromania* we wanted to get the right guitar sound for every song so we had to do a lot of overdubbing, which is something I hadn't done too much of in the past. On some of the songs we laid down two tracks of Les Paul for the low end, two tracks of SGs for the mid-range and then two tracks of Telecasters for the highs. By mixing them all together we got a full spectrum of guitar sound.

"We wanted to get the right guitar sound for every song," Clark continues, "so we had to do a lot of overdubbing on *Pyromania*, which is something we haven't done too much of in the past. On some of the songs we laid down two tracks of Les Paul for the low end, two tracks of SG's for the mid-range and then two tracks of Telecasters for the highs. By mixing them all together we got a full spectrum of guitar sound."

Clark attributes the quality of Def Leppard's studio sound to producer Robert John "Mutt" Lange (also of AC/DC's *Back in Black* and Foreigner 4, both multi-platinum sellers). "'Mutt' is one of the best producers in rock," the guitarist beams. "Most producers can't explain something from a musician's point of view. 'Mutt' is a trained musician himself and he will change an arrangement around if it's not right. He is able to put himself into a record buyer's position. Besides, when you're working with 'Mutt' you come out of the studio a better musician. This helps when you're playing a concert because you now know the songs inside out and as a result it makes your guitar playing a lot better."

Clark has three guitars with him on the *Pyromania* tour: a '66 Gibson Les Paul Cherry Sunburst Deluxe, a '75 Gibson Les Paul Standard and a brand-new Gibson Les Paul XR-1. Collen, on the other hand, uses a black '81 Ibanez Customized Destroyer with three humbuckers and a precision-made Dave Story Tremolo. "Ibanez built the guitar for me in Japan when I was in Girl," Collen reflects. "I really like the tremolo because once it's clamped you can still fine tune it."

As for special effects, Collen doesn't use any. Clark, though, uses a Boss chorus, a Boss delay and a Morley volume booster. "The effects I use are so slight most people don't realize I have them on," Clark notes. "I don't like real gimmicky effects that totally alter what I'm playing, just subtle ones that enhance my sound."

In the near future Def Leppard will be seeking to enhance its double-ax attack even more. "On our fourth album we will be playing more songs where each guitar will be playing different parts," Clark predicts. "And maybe we'll add a keyboard player for our next tour. But no matter what happens, we're not going to let the success of *Pyromania* get to our heads—no way. We are going to work so hard on our next release that it will be better than anything we've ever done."

—Joe Lalaina

Steve Clark and Phil Collen, 1983 (opposite) and during the Hysteria tour, 1987/88 (above) Right: Steve's guitars, New York City, c. 1988

LABEL __ MERCURY_____	ARTIST DEF LEPPARD	ALBUM NO._____
TITLE __ PYROMANIA		422-810 308-1 M-1

— TO APPEAR ON LABEL — TITLES, CREDITS, PERFORMANCE RIGHTS & TIME	MGS NO.	— NOT ON LABEL — PUBLISHER & MASTER NO.
SIDE NO. 1		
1) ROCK! ROCK! (TILL YOU DROP) (Clark/Savage/Lange/Elliott)	3:53	2-57090
2) PHOTOGRAPH (Clark/Willis/Savage/Elliott/Lange)	4:12	2-57091
3) STAGEFRIGHT (Savage/Elliott/Lange)	3:46	2-57092
4) TOO LATE FOR LOVE (Clark/Lange/Willis/Savage/Elliott)	4:30	2-57093
5) DIE HARD THE HUNTER (Lange/Clark/Savage/Elliott)	6:17	2-57094
Produced by Robert John "Mutt" Lange Engineered by Mike Shipley All songs published by Zomba Enterprises Inc. (BMI) (P) 1983 Phonogram Ltd. (London)		
SIDE NO. 2	MGS NO.	
1) FOOLIN' (Clark/Lange/Elliott)	4:32	2-57095
2) ROCK OF AGES (Clark/Lange/Elliott)	4:09	2-57096
3) COMIN' UNDER FIRE (Lange/Clark/Willis/Elliott)	4:20	2-57098
4) ACTION! NOT WORDS (Lange/Clark/Elliott)	3:52	2-57097
5) BILLY'S GOT A GUN (Clark/Savage/Willis/Elliott/Lange)	5:27	2-57099
Produced by Robert John "Mutt" Lange Engineered by Mike Shipley All songs published by Zomba Enterprises Inc. (BMI) (P)1983 Phonogram Ltd. (London)		

NOTES:			
TERRITORY: USA PRICES:$8.98	REC. IN ENGLAND	1/5/83 EI	
PLANTS: HRM,PRC-R,PRC-C (DJ) MUSIC: POP			

PHIL COLLEN: Working with Mutt is like going into a class where someone's letting you in on all these amazing secrets. He's the most intelligent person I've ever met in my life. You wouldn't know it immediately. It's like peeling an onion. He'll start talking quite normally and then he'll go deeper and deeper until you start thinking, 'Shit! This is above my pay grade.' He's a huge fan of all kinds of music. He grew up in South Africa and he made pop music there. He'd done AC/DC albums and he's always loved country music, so he would combine all these different styles.

Mutt taught us to hear the thread connecting top 40 songs of different eras. I still do it now – picking out the themes that link the Jonas Brothers, Ariana Grande, Drake or whatever to the hits I used to love in 1973. It's knowing how to listen without prejudice.

RICK SAVAGE: What made Def Leppard special was our ability to come up with songs and arrangements that transcended the rock attitude without straying from the rock format. We got into a mind space of not writing verses that went straight to the chorus, which bands still do today. I'd say we almost pioneered the idea of tricking people into thinking they were hearing a chorus before it actually came. We'd have a bucketful of great eight-bar ideas and someone like Mutt, who could see the bigger picture, would know which of them to glue together – sometimes creating progressions or key changes you never would have naturally written. These different ideas on offer created something above the norm. Quite often it would sound bloody stupid ... but when it worked, it was unbelievable!

STEVE CLARK: Mutt is one of the best producers in rock. Most producers can't explain something from a musician's point of view. Mutt is a trained musician himself and he will change an arrangement around himself if it's not right. At the same time, he is able to put himself into a record buyer's position. When you're working with Mutt you come out of the studio a better musician. This helps when you're playing a concert because now you know the songs inside out and as a result it makes your guitar playing much better.

JOE ELLIOTT: Mutt had us building songs from the ground upwards, like architecture. It was following the method of electronic groups like the Human League, or even Bowie when he was working with Brian Eno.

Traditionally, when a rock band creates a song the musicians write the music and record a backing track, then the singer goes into a corner and comes up with some lyrics. But the problem with that is the drummer will start filling all the gaps on the backing track where the singing should be. Then the singer finds that when he comes to sing his next line, which might be really important from an emotional point of view, there's this mad drum fill getting in the way.

So, when we were writing the songs for *Pyromania* we used a drum machine to play a basic track to begin with, then Rick dropped in his drum dynamics at the end once we knew where they should go. People would say, 'You can't do that.' We'd say, 'Just watch us.'

JOE ELLIOTT: It would have been dead easy to come up with another *High 'n' Dry*, but we accepted Mutt's challenge to make a completely new kind of album. In fairness, we'd always been prepared to experiment. We never let a decision about how we were going to do a song live interfere with the creative process in the studio. If Queen had worried about how they were going to play 'Bohemian Rhapsody' live, they would never have written it.

Even Mutt didn't always know what he was doing. We had no idea that the time codes would go out of sync. There were so many panic moments with tapes wearing thin through overuse or crinkling up in the machines. We would lose things that we'd spent days working on. It was a learning curve, but it was worth it.

It took us nine months to record *Pyromania*. At a certain point, we came to the conclusion – or it was probably thrust upon us by management – that we couldn't afford to keep going at Battery Studios. So, we relocated to Battle, just outside Brighton, to a live-in studio that Paul McCartney and Wings used to work in. It was a quarter of the price of Battery Studios.

Even with that saving, by the time we delivered *Pyromania* we owed the record company something like £700,000. Ever since we'd signed the deal in 1979 we'd done everything on credit, and we hadn't sold enough records to clear the debt.

PHIL COLLEN: Mutt's whole thing with Def Leppard was he wanted to make rock for the masses. Hard rock bands turn a lot of people off. Having melodic structure done with integrity as a rock band is really hard. A lot of bands just have harmonies but without the rock intensity to go with it so it sounds lame. He was able to put all that together. And Mutt wasn't just a great producer. He was always the best singer in the room. He sang backing vocals on all of our stuff and he could play any instrument. You'd ask him to play something really hard on the guitar and he would just do it. Music flowed out of him.

JOE ELLIOTT: Mutt was like the sixth member of the band.

Foolin'
Clark/Lange/Elliott

Lady luck never smiles
So lend your love to me, awhile
Do with me what you will
Break the spell take your fill

On and on we rode the storm
The flame has died, the fire has gone
Oh, this empty bed is anight alone
I realised that long ago

Is any body out there? Anybody there?
Does anybody wonder? Anybody care?

Oh, I just gotta know
if you're really there and you really care
'Cause baby I'm not...

F-F-F-Foolin', Ah F-F-Foolin'
Not F-F-F-Foolin', Ah F-F-Foolin'

Won't you stay with me awhile

Close your eyes, don't run and hide
Easy love's no easy ride
Just wakin' up to what we had
Could stop good love from goin' bad

Stagefright
Savage/Elliott/Lange

I said Welcome to my show!
It's just you and me babe,
We got the whole damn night to go

You're holding out on me, while I'm on fire .
If you can't stand the heat, then you should try
Victim of my vices, you know you are
You skate on ice to paradise, stairway to the stars

Stagefright All night, Won't you let go
All night Stagefright, On with the show

You come on like a lady, dressed to kill
Never thought you could be caught, but you will
A little understanding, a little love
A headline act around the back, is what I'm thinkin' of

Stagefright All night, Won't you let go
All night Stagefright, On with the show
Stagefright All night, You're dream starts today
All night Stagefright, Is only a heartbeat away

You're going for my head, you're going down
Gettin' good at being bad, you're hangin' 'round
A fun inspired asylum, toys for the boys
Love on the rocks, forget-me-nots, you got no choice

Action! Not Words
Lange/Clark/Elliott

I'm sick and tired of the damn T.V.
I'm gonna make my own movie
I wanna star in a late night show
And all I need is my video

Shock me! Make it electric!
Shock me! Make it last

Curtain up let the camera roll
It's Automatic it's in control
Got no script baby, ain't no lines
Just me and you and a real good time

Shock me! Make it Electric
Shock me! Make it last
Shock me! Gimme thunder 'n' lightening
Shock me! Oh babe I need it fast

Cause All I want is some...
Action, Action, Action, Not Words
Gimme Action, Action, Action Not Words

C'mon and shock me, let the cmaera roll!

I'll be the hero, you be the star
With your wine and your caviar
No Audition, a starring roll
I'll be your Bogart 'n' You be Monroe yeah

Shock me! Make it Electric
Shock me! Oh Bump and grind
Shock me! Make a night to remember
Shock ｜ ｜ Do it one more time

So cut me in on the Action

Lights, camera, sound, I need Action

Repeat chorus

Too Late
Clark/Lange/Willis/Savage/Elliott

Somewhere in the distance I hear the bells ring
Darkness settles on the town The children start to sing
The lady 'cross the street she shuts out the night
There's a cast of thousands waiting as she turns out the light

But it's too late, too late, too late
Too late for love
Yes it's too late, too late, too late
Too late for love

London boys are staring as the girls go hand in hand
With a pocket full of innocence, their entrance is grand
And the Queen of the dream stands before them all
She stretches out her hand as the curtain starts to fall

Standing by the trap door aware of me and you
Are the actor and the clown just waiting for their cue
And there's a lady over there she's acting pretty cool
But when it comes to playing at life she's always playin' the fool.

Die Hard the Hunter
Lange/Clark/Savage/Elliott

Let's welcome home the soldier boy from (far away, far away)
No angel of mercy just a need to destroy (fire away, fire away)
Let's toast the hero with blood in his eyes .
The scars on his mind took so many lives
Die Hard the Hunter

Welcome home soldier boy
Put down your pistol, yeah, put down your toy
They can take your gun away from you
But never take away your attitude
They can't do that, no, they can't do that

You got no enemy, no front line
The only battles in the back of your mind
You don't know how to change from bad to good
You brought the war to your neighborhood
You can't do that, no, you can't do that

Back in the city, he's a man on the loose
He is the shadow that's following you
He takes no prisoners when he's hunting for game
He's got a bullet and it carries your name

(Die Hard) Caught in a trap
(Hunter)   There's no lookin' back
(Die Hard) He hides in the crowd
(Hunter) Die Hard and Proud

Photograph
Clark/Willis/Savage/Elliott/Lange

I'm outa luck, outa love
Gotta photograph, picture of
Passion killer, you're too much
You're the only one I wanna touch
I see your face everytime I dream
On every page, every magazine
So wild so free so far from me
You're all I want, my fantasy

Oh, look what you done to this rock 'n' roll clown
Oh Oh, look what you've done

Photograph - I don't wan't your...
Photograph - I don't need your...
Photograph - All I've got is a photograph
But it's not enough

I'd be your lover, if you were there
Put your hurt on me, if you dare
Such a woman, you got style
You make everyman feel like a child
You got some kinda hold on me
You're all wrapped up in mystery
So wild so free so far from me
You're all I want, my fantasy

Oh, look what you've done to this rock 'n' roll clown
Oh, Oh, look what you've done

Repeat chorus

You've gone straight to my head.

Clark/Savage/Lange/Elliott

Rock of Ages
Clark/Lange/Elliott

...e up! Gather round
...k this place to the ground
...n it up let's go for broke
...ch the night go up in smoke

...ck on! Rock on!

...ive me crazier, No serenade
...fire Brigade, just Pyromania

...at do you want? What do you want?
...want rock 'n' roll, yes I do
...ng live rock 'n' roll

...t's go, let's strike a light
...'re gonna blow like dynamite
...don't care if it takes all night
...nna set this town alight

...at do you want? What do you want?
...want rock 'n' roll, Alright!
...ng live rock 'n' roll.

...ock of Ages Rock of Ages
...till Rollin', keep Rollin'
...ock of Ages Rock of Ages
...till Rollin', Rock 'n' Rollin
...e got the power, got the glory
...ust say you need it, and if you need it
...ay Yeah!

...'m Burnin', Burnin', I got the fever
...know for sure, there ain't no cure
...o feel it, don't fight it, go with the flow
...imme, gimme, gimme, gimme one more for the road

...hat do you want? What do you want?
...want Rock 'n'Roll, You betcha
...ong live rock 'n' roll

...repeat chorus

...e're gonna burn this damn place down
...own to the ground

Hold onto your hat, hold onto your heart
Ready, get set to tear this place apart
Don't need a ticket, only place in town
That can take you up to heaven and never bring you down
Anything goes! Anything goes!

Women to the left, Women to the right·
There to entertain and take you thru' the night
So grab a little heat and come along with me
'Cause your mama don't mind what your mama don't see
Anything goes! Anything goes!

Rock! Rock! Till you drop
Rock! Rock! never stop
Rock! Rock! Till you drop
Rock! Rock! to the top

Riding into danger, laughing all the way
Fast, free and easy, livin' for today
Gotta lip service, get it while you can
Hot, sweat 'n' nervous love on demand
Anything goes! Anything goes!

Rock! Rock! Give it to me
It's what I got goin' thru' me
Don't ever stop do it to me
Yeah, Rock! Rock! You really move me

Comin' Under Fire
Lange/Clark/Willis/Elliott

Your kind of woman gotta heart of stone
But watch it break when I get you alone
Take a chance, come lay down with me
Oh, I wanna make it

Slow and steady never lost the race
Don't stop runnin', I'm a fool for the chase
Play the game, surrender to me
Baby, I don't wanna fake it

Is it any wonder, you got me comin' under fire?
Comin' like thunder, you know you make me walk the wire

It's so easy to put on a show
Your body says yes but you won't let it go
But my passion it won't slip away
Oh, am I going crazy?

You got me, I'm cornered, my back to the wall
No bed of roses, ain't no bed at all
I'm walkin' the wire, I stumble and fall
I got the message but I ain't gonna crawl

Billy's Got a Gun
Clark/Savage/Willis/Elliott/Lange

Billy's got a gun, he's on the run
Confusion in his mind, the blind leads the blind
Oh, Billy's got a gun, he's gonna shoot you down
He's got evil in his eyes, gotta reason to despise
There's danger in the air

Can you feel it in the air?
Danger (such a strange emotion)
Can you feel it in the air?

Oh, he was locked inside a room, without a door
His innocence, he suffered for
In a world of black and white, they were wrong and he was right
Just looking for a clue, it's a nightmare come true
Searching underground, to track that danger down
Oh, Billy, why you got that gun?

Never give him an even break
Gettin' caught is the chance you take
It could be your last mistake
(You could be so helpless)
As a bird with a broken wing
Like a sheep in a lion's den
Gonna fall but you won't know when

You hear the footsteps in the night, see shadows on the wall
And the ghostly sound of silence, as the mist begins to fall
Then a scream rang out like thunder, but the lightening was too late

As the rain came down on the crimson ground
It was the hidden hand of fate
And a crowd of people gathered round, but Billy couldn't wait

GUNTER GLIEBEN GLAUSEN GLOBEN

RICK ALLEN: Mutt was getting so tired of saying '1,2,3,4' whenever we counted in at the beginning of 'Rock of Ages'. He wanted to inject a bit of humour in there. I guess 'Gunter glieben glausen globen' is some Germanic-sounding language. I wouldn't put it past Mutt because he actually speaks Dutch.

When it came to mixing the song, we all decided to keep the count on there.

Every time we play 'Rock of Ages' live, Joe gives me the job of saying, 'Gunter glieben glausen globen'.

99

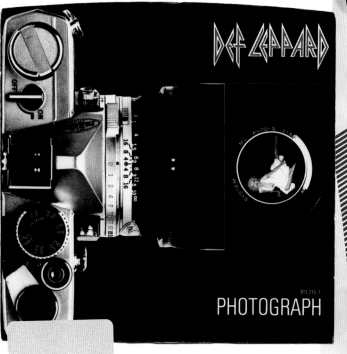

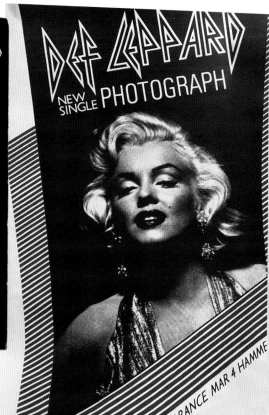

PHOTOGRAPH

DEF LEPPARD

NEW SINGLE PHOTOGRAPH

JOE ELLIOTT: 'Photograph' ate up more than its fair share of our studio time. The song was a leftover from the *High 'n' Dry* sessions. We laboured over it for so long that we ran out of time to get it on *High 'n' Dry*, but Mutt was keen to pick up the thread when we started work on *Pyromania*.

Progress was slow again. We knew we had something there, but it still hadn't gelled. After eight weeks, we'd only managed to record half the song.

One day, when we were working down in the studio in Battle, I was watching TV with Sav and Charlie and Russ, our two crew members.

We could hear the others playing in the studio and then suddenly we heard this amazing intro. All of us immediately ran into the control room. Mutt stood there grinning, 'Well, if it's got your attention, it must be OK.' That was when 'Photograph' was reborn and reinvented. It was the kind of song we'd been trying to write since 1977 and we finally nailed it.

PHIL COLLEN: 'Photograph' did feel like our gateway to the States. With it we looked more like Duran Duran than we did Iron Maiden. It was a huge hit and it actually sounded different from other rock bands.

---

62 PYROMANIA
Def Leppard
Mercury

THE ALBUM TOOK A YEAR TO RECORD AND had to sell 1 million copies just to break even. But Def Leppard's 1983 chart torcher *Pyromania* was worth the time and expense: It sold more than 9 million copies and, with its radio-ready blend of melodic savvy and stadium wallop, defined the mainstream metal sound of the Eighties, for better and worse. For worse because *Pyromania* unleashed a plague of cheap imitators (Poison, Winger and White Lion). For better because the Leppards and their producer, hard-rock auteur Robert John "Mutt" Lange, set precedents for commercially astute songwriting and sheer studio ambition (the massive yet airy vocal harmonies, philharmonic layers of guitar) without compromising the basic thump.

"We gave Mutt songwriting credits because this time he actually helped us structure the songs," singer Joe Elliott said in 1985. "They weren't written songs that he changed. He sat down with us as a sixth member of the band and participated in the whole thing."

Lange and the Leppards worked for months on riffs and choruses, trying different combinations and then sewing them up when they made melodic and commercial sense. But the writing wasn't all so academic. "Photograph" was a song with a good chorus, a hot bridge but a flabby verse riff until guitarist Steve Clark started noodling around on his guitar one night while the rest of the band was watching World Cup soccer.

"The announcer suddenly got quiet," Elliott said, "and we heard this guitar blasting from the room next door. It sounded great, so we got up and ran over to see what was going on. Steve sat there beaming, saying, 'I fixed it.' And that was it. 'Photograph' was born."

Pyromania was a hard-rock temple built brick by brick. To get a sound that combined metal muscle with studio precision, Lange recorded each member of the band individually, starting with bassist Rick Savage. A single guitar riff overdubbed with clean harmonies, funky distortion and screaming feedback might take up to three weeks to record, often one string at a time. When the band members later went to do background vocals, they discovered all of the guitars were slightly out of tune. It was too late to re-record them, so the guitars were put through an electronic harmonizer to cover up the bum notes.

Lange's obsessiveness with the smallest sonic details had a big downside: It was hard to tell, from day to day, whether *any* progress at all was being made on the record. After an all-night session, Lange would often play work tapes for Leppard comanager Peter Mensch, who lived a short drive from Battery Studios. "Mutt would come in and say, 'Listen to what we did tonight' – and three more words would be added to a vocal," says Mensch. "It got to a point where I'd keep listening to these tapes and I couldn't tell what was there and what was missing."

There were personal complications, too. Founding rhythm guitarist Pete Willis was fired midway through the sessions because of a debilitating alcohol problem; within forty-eight hours, his replacement, Phil Collen of the London glam-rock band Girl, had cut the solo for "Stagefright."

That was nothing compared to the calamity of recording the next LP, *Hysteria*. That album took three years to record; drummer Rick Allen also lost his left arm in an auto accident. Fortunately, it takes more than a little trauma to keep a good Leppard down, as *Pyromania* so ably proved. "There was always that feeling there, that we have to do it right," Rick Savage said a couple of years ago. "Or we don't do it at all."

Producer: Robert John "Mutt" Lange. Released: January 1983. Highest chart position: Number Two.

63 ENTERTAINMENT!
Gang of Four
Warner Bros.

"THEY OFFER CUT-UP SITUATIONAL ACcounts of the paradoxes of leisure as oppression, identity as product, home as factory, resident as tourist, sex as politics, history as ruling-class private joke," wrote Greil Marcus in ROLLING STONE of the Gang of Four in 1980. But as the

---

PolyGram Records

Memo

To: The Promotion Staff

From: Drew
Date: 6/1/83
Subject: Def Leppard--BACK TO NUMBER ONE!

AOR /ALBUMS
Continued From the Back Page

This chart comp reporting station of listeners aged

June 3, 1983   **169 REPORTERS**

❶ DEF LEPPARD/Pyromania (Mercury/PolyGram)   "Ages" (134) "Too Late" (82) "Photograph" (42) 152+ 136+

THAT'S why there is no better promo team on the street.....

You are the BEST! Now, lets keep it there!

• What New England state has the purple finch as its state bird and the purple lilac as its state flower?

• What album did Def Leppard contribute to 1983's biggest sellers?

• What country did Peugeot and Citroen cars originate in?

• Who did The Three Blind Mice run after?

• What two colors of feathers do male cardinals have?

• What's a series of 180s called in skateboarding?

687

Kodak
Video
Cassette

DEF LEPPARD.

JOE ELLIOTT: *Pyromania* came out in January 1983, just a month after we'd delivered it. 'Photograph', the lead single, went ballistic in America. It even got some play in the UK, on BBC Radio 1, but peaked at 41 so it just missed being played on the Sunday top 40 show, which might have helped it take off. Consequently, in our home market we were still preaching to the converted. The album got great reviews, but that doesn't necessarily convert to sales.

DEF LEPPARD: Pyromania. Def Leppard (vocals and instrumentals). *Rock! Rock! Till You Drop!; Photograph; Stagefright; Rock of Ages; Too Late for Love;* and five others. MERCURY 810 308-1 M-1 $8.98.

Performance: **Incendiary**
Recording: **Good**

Def Leppard's aptly named "Pyromania" is a little like a building going up in flames: it doesn't shed much useful light, but there's something about its blistering intensity that makes you stand and gawk despite your better instincts. The music is straight, unapologetic heavy-metal that makes absolutely no demands either on the cast-iron formula or on your intelligence. But it is played with more skill and written with somewhat more wit and less pretension than this burned-out form usually gets. Thundering power chords spill from Phil Collen's rhythm guitar like gasoline splashing over dried floor-boards, and Steve Clark's searing lead guitar dances and crackles like flames leaping from beam to beam. If you're a heavy-metal maniac, this one's for you.
                                              M.P.

PolyGram Records
* *

January, 1983

Dear Music Person:

Enclosed you will find the cassette of the brand new DEF LEPPARD album, "Pyromania". The vinyl version of this masterpiece will be on your desks and your turntables on Tuesday morning - January 18th!!

We all know that the eighties is the so-called age of uncertainties and that there is not much you really can count on! The whole Rock Department believes that there are two things you can all count on without any doubt in 1983:

    1. It will be hot in Arizona
    2. The new DEF LEPPARD album, "Pyromania",
        will be one of the biggest albums of the decade!

In case there is anybody who does not know the history of this band, let us briefly explain - "Pyromania" is the band's third album. The first album, "On Through The Night", which was released in 1980, now stands at 400,000 sold. The second album, "High and Dry", which was released in the summer of '81 now stands at 600,000 sold and incidentally is still selling between 10-15,000 weekly. This leads us to the conclusion that this new album is bound to be <u>the</u> enormous breakthrough album for DEF LEPPARD. The entire <u>LP</u> is full of absolutely superb metal magic and the production by Robert "Mutt" Lange is impeccable as usual! The Rock Department advises that "Photograh" (The first single !?) and "Rock Of Ages" should be the first two tracks on the air - followed closely by the rest of the album!

Listen and enjoy one of the new true superstar bands of the '80's !!

Sincerely,

The Rock Department. !!!

Jerry Jaffe, Jim Sotet, Derek Shulman, Drew Murray, Linda Walker, Francesca DeFeo

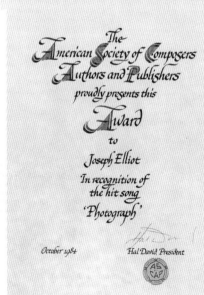

PYROMANIA
DEF LEPPARD
Mercury
★★★½

Just when it seemed like synthesizers had taken over the airwaves, along comes Def Leppard with *Pyromania*, a heavy-metal album full of brawling guitars and boasting state-of-the-radio production. Steve Clark and new member Phil Collen's fat fuzz riffs and power chords are more emotionally charged than most of the synthesized disco that passes for "modern music," and Robert John "Mutt" Lange's work behind the board brings singer Joe Elliott's screaming vocals into focus.

"Action! Not words," crows Elliott in the track of the same name, and that *modus operandi* holds true for most of the album. Rick Allen's crack-shot drumming, the thick layers of guitars and the enveloping echo of Lange's artfully busy mix more than cover up the street-corner rhyming of these tales of Tarzan sexuality and macho party exploits. But this young band (the average age is twenty-one) demonstrates surprising sophistication as it manipulates old heavy-metal tricks into tight, invigorating songs while holding epic pretensions in check. Both "Comin' under Fire" and "Photograph" combine the kaboom of AC/DC with slick choruses and brassy vocal harmonies that sound like a gassed-up Boston. Def Leppard may not be highly original, but they mean what they play, and *Pyromania* puts some much-needed fire back on the radio.
                                      —DAVID FRICKE

The *American Society of Composers Authors and Publishers* proudly presents this *Award* to *Joseph Elliot* In recognition of the hit song *'Photograph'*

October 1984   *Hal David President*

This side faces forward   Do not touch the tape inside   VHS

VHS
PAL SECAM
HITACHI

VIDEO CASSETTE
60 MINUTE RECORDING AND PLAYBACK
THIS SIDE IN   E-60

DEF LEPPARD

Photoghaph music
video only
Fine grain
BERIDOX   13

*'Photograph' video shoot,
December 1982, for which
Joe bought his famous
Union Jack T-shirt (see
p.114)*

JOE ELLIOTT: We eventually came back up to London to finish off 'Photograph' and I went back to the dingy little basement apartment I was renting in Isleworth. Above the toilet there was a hole punched in the wall, which I had covered with a poster of Marilyn Monroe (a bit like in *The Shawshank Redemption*, except that this hole wasn't an escape tunnel). Mutt had the 'photograph' idea for the song, so we were singing that and I probably came up with the response, 'I don't want your photograph. I don't need your photograph.' I remember suggesting to Mutt that the song should be about a photograph of the ultimate woman that you can never have, because she's no longer alive.

'Photograph' isn't specifically about Marilyn Monroe. There's no mention of her in the song. But when we made the video, we incorporated an image of her. It's not 'Candle in the Wind: Part Two', but there was still that connection.

PHIL COLLEN: Our videos at Battersea were directed by David Mallet, who had a fantastic reputation. He had created some of the most interesting and ground-breaking videos of all time – a slew of them for Bowie, as well as for the Boomtown Rats, Blondie and many others. When we arrived at Battersea to film for 'Photograph', we were very impressed with the dramatic set that David had created for us. The song was cranked out over and over through giant speakers and we simply lip-synched along, striking poses throughout.

PHIL COLLEN: We hired a Marilyn Monroe lookalike to act out a bit of the storyline. There are two versions of the video. The uncensored version includes a brief knife scene at the beginning, which got banned from British TV.

JOE ELLIOTT: Def Leppard were quicker than many bands to understand the power of promo videos. We had made three for *High 'n' Dry* – 'Bringin' On the Heartbreak', 'Let It Go' and 'High 'n' Dry' – and so when MTV America launched in a few cities in August 1981 we were well placed to benefit.

Over the next year, MTV started spreading across the country as more and more cable companies picked up the option. And then our tracks started getting requested on the radio because people were seeing the videos. And then *High 'n' Dry* started selling again. An album that had peaked at about a quarter of a million copies in 1981 all of a sudden had gone gold by Christmas 1982.

STEVE CLARK: It's very difficult because you can never tell if it's a song that's selling a record or the look of the video. I personally don't like making promos. It's two days' work for a three-minute video. But I think they're a necessity now.

JOE ELLIOTT: MTV played a huge part in the success we would achieve in 1983. But none of that could have happened without a good album and an insane tour. We had to go out there and perspire.

Drum Beat

by Carmine Appice

Rick Allen's drumming on "Photograph"

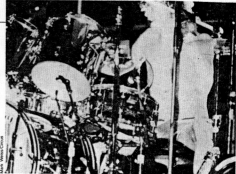

On "Photograph," Rick Allen changes his drumming throughout, but always keeps it steady and simple.

JUST AS THE members of Def Leppard often call attention to the fact that they are not just a heavy-metal band, so is their drummer, Rick Allen, not just a typical hard-rock player. Allen joined the group in 1979, just before it recorded its debut, *On Through the Night*. Although he's still just 19, he plays with the finesse of a pro twice his age.

With their third LP, *Pyromania*, Leppard have become one of rock & roll's most popular groups, and the song in particular that launched them is "Photograph," the track to be discussed here.

Allen plays with a very simple approach, especially on the verses.

For most of the song, he hits the snare on 2 and 4, playing only occasional fills. Here is the approach taken on the verses (see Exercise 1):

NEXT MONTH: A look at the style of Police-man Stewart Copeland.

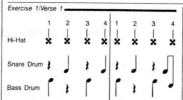

Exercise 1/Verse 1

As you can see, the hi-hat is on quarter notes. You can also play eighth notes on the hi-hat throughout the song.

On the second verse, the bass drum pattern that goes around every other measure on Verse No. 1 now happens every measure (see Exercise 2).

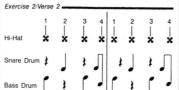

Exercise 2/Verse 2

The next pattern change is what is called the "pass" to the chorus. A cowbell is put into the pass, playing quarter notes. The bass drum now plays along with the rhythm guitar, and, together with the cowbell change, gives a nice rhythm change for the pass (see Exercise 3).

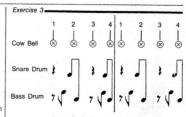

Exercise 3

Now go to the song's chorus. Once again the pattern changes a little; different drum parts for each section of the song. The pattern for the chorus is (see Example 4).

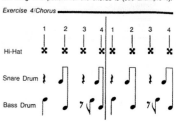

Exercise 4/Chorus

This chorus pattern completes the three different patterns for the three parts of the song.

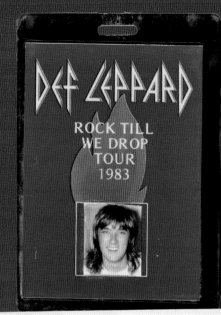
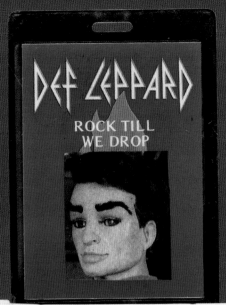

R.G. Allen.

DEF LEPPARD

"Rock Till We Drop"

Tour 1983

Itinerary

DEF LEPPARD

"Rock Till We Drop" Tour

February 1983

Fri	4th	Load Trucks			
Sat	5th	Load-In	Bray Studios		
Sun	6th	Rehearsals	Bray Studios		
Mon	7th	Rehearsals	Bray Studios		
Tue	8th	Rehearsals	Bray Studios		
Wed	9th	Marquee Club	London	U.K.	600
Thu	10th	Day Off			
Fri	11th	TV Club	Dublin	Eire	1200
Sat	12th	Ulster Hall	Belfast	N.Ireland	2000
Sun	13th	Day Off			
Mon	14th	Day Off			
Tue	15th	Parc Expositions	Annecy	France	2500
Wed	16th	Salle Europa	Metz	France	1500
Thu	17th	Exo 7	Rouen	France	1200
Fri	18th	Paradiso	Amsterdam	Holland	1200
Sat	19th	Muecke Elyde	Poperinge	Belgium	1700
Sun	20th	Day Off			
Mon	21st	Apollo Theatre	Manchester	U.K.	2645
Tue	22nd	Playhouse	Edinburgh	U.K.	3053
Wed	23rd	Day Off			
Thu	24th	City Hall	Sheffield	U.K.	2292
Fri	25th	Mayfair	Newcastle	U.K.	2500
Sat	26th	Royal Court	Liverpool	U.K.	1500
Sun	27th	Colston Hall	Bristol	U.K.	1800
Mon	28th	Day Off			

March 1983

Tue	1st	Rock City	Nottingham	U.K.	1700
Wed	2nd	Odeon	Birmingham	U.K	2579
Thu	3rd	Apollo Theatre	Oxford	U.K.	1693
Fri	4th	Hammersmith Odeon	London	U.K.	3883
Sat	5th	Day Off			
Sun	6th	Hall Tivoli	Strasbourg	France	3000
Mon	7th	Day Off			
Tue	8th	Bataclan	Paris	France	1500
Wed	9th	Salle Du Baron	Orleans	France	1200
Thu	10th	Salle Des Fetes de Thonex	Geneva	Switzerland	1100
Fri	11th	Alp Expo	Grenoble	France	2500
Sat	12th	Grand Odeon	Montpellier	France	1200
Sun	13th	Day Off			
Mon	14th	Palais d'Hiver	Lyon	France	2500
Tue	15th	Salle Des Fetes	Melun	France	2000
Wed	16th	Load Out			

DEF LEPPARD :

" Rock Till We Drop Tour "

Tour Manifest

BAND:	Richard Allen	
	Steve Clark	
	Phil Collen	
	Joe Elliott	
	Richard Savage	
MANAGER:	Peter Mensch	Tel:(01) 603 0921
TOUR MANAGER:	Robert Allen	Tel: (0246) 412684
LIGHTING ENGINEER:	Phay MacMahon	
SOUND ENGINEER:	Steve Cox	
DEF LEPPARD CREW:	Russell Major	
	Malvin Mortimer	
	Mike Rogers	
SOUND CREW:	Ian Black	
	Pete Varcoe	
LIGHTING CREW:	John Mallard	
	Tony Austin	
	Simon Thomsett	(U.K. Only)
TRUCK DRIVERS:	Keith Griffin	
	Sandy Flat	(U.K. Only)
BUS DRIVER:	Bob Collins	

JOE ELLIOTT: The first gig of the Pyromania tour – and Phil's first ever with us – was in London at the Marquee on 9 February 1983. An audience of 800 people. Brian Robertson of Thin Lizzy got up on stage with us for the encore, something I'd completely forgotten until I listened to a bootleg of the gig a few years later. When one of your teenage heroes joins you on stage and you don't remember it, some magnificent stuff must have been happening in your career at the time.

PHIL COLLEN: I felt like I'd been playing with these guys my whole life. The chemistry, the timing and the camaraderie were so natural and effortless. Especially between Steve and me, there seemed to be something really magical on stage.

JOE ELLIOTT: By mid-March we were in America. For the first three or four weeks we were opening for Billy Squier, but it was us that everyone had come to see. You could tell by the T-shirt sales. When we played Seattle, Billy Squier sold $12,000 worth of merchandise. We sold $92,000.

Then the promoters started booking shows with us as headliners, starting with Odessa, Texas on 29 April 1983. We got there a day or two early to rehearse and somebody broke into Phil's hotel room and stole his suitcase, so he literally had nothing to wear. When you see these really cool pictures of Phil on stage with no shirt and camouflaged pants with braces on them, that's what he bought from an army surplus shop with the $30 we rustled up for him. They became his stage wear for a while.

JOE ELLIOTT: For the first few weeks, sales weren't that great – there'd be maybe 5,000 or 6,000 people in a 12,000-seater arena – but we gathered momentum and by June, with 'Rock of Ages' riding high in the charts, we were the hottest ticket in the country. At the end of August, our two shows at the Joe Louis Arena in Detroit sold out faster than Led Zeppelin's had on their last tour. We'd get out of cars and girls would faint, which was hilarious because we weren't exactly David Cassidy in the looks department. Unlike most rock bands, we had as many women as men at our gigs. It was like we were Duran Duran!

The rest of the US tour just got bigger and bigger. I think we were one of the few British bands since Zeppelin and Deep Purple to sell out the LA Forum and Oakland Coliseum Arena. We sold out everywhere.

RICK SAVAGE: We're not the type of band that strives for total musical perfection when we play live. If you do that, you might as well put five cardboard cutouts on stage and play the album through the speakers. Our attitude is that we've done our perfecting in the studio and now we're going to go out there and create something visual. We're not just there to play music, our job is to entertain and that means getting the crowd involved. As long as people go home happy that's all that matters.

AFTER
SHOW
ACCESS

V.I.P.

Backstage at the LA Forum
September 1983

Top row: Phil Collen, Rick Allen,
Rick Savage, Joe Elliott
Middle row: Ken Savage, Geoff Allen,
Kath Allen, Joe Elliott, Sr., Steve Clark
Bottom row: Connie Collen, Sally Savage,
Cindy Elliott, Barrie Clark, Beryl Clark

Opposite top (left to right): Brian May,
Denise Dakin, David Lee Roth, Connie Collen,
Phil Collen

RICK SAVAGE: When Phil joined the band in 1983, it immediately became obvious that he'd had the same support systems as we had. We've often talked about this. We know a lot of school friends who went through a difficult adolescent period where they despised their parents and had endless arguments with them. The opposite could not be more true of us. Maybe that had something to do with our connections together and our longevity.

We all had parents that took genuine interest in what we were doing, gave us constant encouragement and helped us out in many ways, including financially.

It was just wonderful for them to come and actually witness their boys playing in front of 20,000 people. It showed them what we could do and it was proof that we actually had made it. For them to see that, with their own eyes, was fantastic.

I remember it with such fondness, because it was a nice experience for them. It wasn't just about seeing their son, it was the camaraderie within the group. They formed friendships because of our band and that would never have happened otherwise. Stuff like that is priceless.

PHIL COLLEN: In 1983, we brought our parents out to Los Angeles. Well, most of them. My dad didn't make it on that particular trip, but my mum was there. She hadn't been out of the UK so it was an absolute culture shock. She was seeing her little boy as a rock star for the first time. She was so proud and so gushing and beaming.

All our parents got on with each other and they had so much in common. Their kids had done well and they'd helped them get there. Coming from working class east London or Sheffield or wherever, we all had an identical value system that our parents had instilled in us. They were World War II survivors. They'd had to go down to the air-raid shelters. I can't even imagine what that would have been like, but they just got on with it. To this day, there's a work ethic that we all appreciate and it came from them. So, this was us saying thanks.

RICK ALLEN: To bring our parents over en masse to America was so special. It was amazing for them to finally share in this phenomenon called Def Leppard, for them to see us play in front of a giant crowd and how people responded to that.

JOE ELLIOTT: When we heard that Brian May wanted to play with us at the Forum, we thought, 'You've got to be fucking kidding? You're waiting for an answer? Of course you can play with us!' So, Brian turned up for soundcheck with his little Vox amp and his guitar. He plugged in and immediately started playing the riff to 'Photograph'. To hear this man, who had been such an enormous influence on every member of Def Leppard, playing one of our songs really brought it home to us how far we'd come.

Song

DEF LEPPARD ISN'T SPOTLESS BUT SHOWS SOME HEAVY METTLE

We are not talking musical elegance or social consciousness. Nobody is likely to mistake the rock quintet Def Leppard for the London Symphony or even The Who. Admits Joe Elliott, Leppard's lead singer and lyricist, "I've got political opinions, but why should I force them on everybody else? I don't like to hear Pete Townshend's views on the Labor Party. I'd rather write about women and beer."

On the other hand, as heavy metal bands go—which is usually way too far—Def Leppard is relatively sophisticated, musically and otherwise. "Compared to Black Sabbath and Ozzy Osbourne," wrote one New York critic recently, "Def Leppard sounds like the last outpost of civilization."

The Leppards also have proved that a heavy metal band doesn't have to put one in mind of Attila the Hun to succeed commercially. The group's current LP, Pyromania, has sold four million copies and reached No. 4 on the American charts, and a single, Rock of Ages, has hit No. 19. They're now winding up an eight-month U.S. and Canadian tour, at the end of which more than a million people will have seen them live. True, drummer Rick Allen has taken to mooning the audience as a curtain call, but Elliott sums up Leppard's basic appeal this way: "We're all young, none of us is particularly ugly and the songs are good."

Elliott, 23, co-founded the band in 1977, but he had come up with its name earlier. As a high school boy in Sheffield, England, he studied mainly the two R's—rock 'n' roll. In art class, he designed posters for imaginary rock concerts, many involving the then imaginary group "Deaf Leopard." (The later spelling change was in emulation of Led Zeppelin.) For homework he turned in reviews of their "shows." When teachers asked what he planned to do, "I always told them, 'I'm going to be a pop star,' " Elliott says.

Rock was, in any case, an alternative to working in the Sheffield steel mills. Founded by Elliott, bassist Rick Savage and guitarists Steve Clark and Pete Willis, the band rehearsed at night in an abandoned spoon factory. By day Elliott drove a van for an iron foundry, Willis was a draftsman, Savage an apprentice British Rail technician and Clark a lathe operator.

Elliott finally borrowed £150 (about $300 at the time) from his father so the group could make a record. The Def Leppard EP sold more than 24,000 copies in 1979 and led to a major record deal. Allen, son of a Sheffield insurance broker, joined up soon after—he's still only 19—and Phil Collen, 23, last year replaced Willis, who quit even though the Leppards were landing opening gigs for such hit groups as AC/DC and Billy Squier. Collen proved the needed lift for a band exhausted by too much touring.

"It's an entertainment business," Elliott occasionally has to remind his fellow Leppards, "and we're in it as much to entertain ourselves as other peo-

The Queen might not approve but Def Leppard—from left, Rick Allen (with wrapped ribs

from a soccer injury), Steve Clark, Phil Collen, Rick Savage and Joe Elliott—shows the flag in Hollywood, Fla.

ple," Elliott himself still is a rock fan. He owns four copies of Love Gun by Kiss, and on the tour bus the group is often glued to the TV, watching videos by AC/DC or the Stones.

The band can get serious, too. There is a morning roll call and a dollar-a-minute fine for getting on the bus late. Fines are deducted out of a strict $30 per diem. (The rest of the band's income goes into an escrow account until the end of the tour.) There are the usual road temptations—girls, booze, chemicals. But Geoffrey Allen, 44, says of son Rick, "In many ways, he's mature for his age. We hope we educated our kids to behave responsibly."

The group members all have girlfriends in England, except Allen, whose squeeze lives on Long Island. The musicians have also learned to distinguish between groupies and fans. Says Savage, "A lot of girls just want to give us presents, not jump into bed with us." One girl in Houston gave Savage a notebook in which "I love Sav" was written 20,000 times.

The Leppards also say they exercise restraint with drugs and alcohol. "This is the most exciting part of my life," says Clark, 22. "I don't want to miss it." Adds Elliott, "I'd hate in three years to have Steve turn to me and say, 'We had a great time in Seattle that year,' and for me to say, 'Really? What happened?' "

—DAVID FRICKE

JOE ELLIOTT: When we shot the video for 'Photograph' I was given a budget of £25 to buy some stage clothes. I went down the King's Road to what used to be Malcolm McLaren's shop but it had changed hands and was now more like a punk surplus store. I bought these plastic faux-leather trousers that finished at the shins because I've got really long legs. So, I bought some red leg warmers to cover the gap from my trousers to my Adidas basketball boots. After buying a leather belt with handcuff buckle, I had £8 left for my top half. I spotted this Union Jack T-shirt for £7.99. So, that would leave me a penny change out of my £25. I only bought that T-shirt because it was within my budget, but it became iconic. We printed up a version with Def Leppard written on the front, and it was the most popular shirt we sold.

For the American Pyromania shows, I'd come out for the encore still wearing the Union Jack shirt but with a Stars and Stripes shirt hidden underneath. Rick would lay down this booming drum beat that went on forever. I'd be making some small talk with the audience and then Phil would take the mic off me and ask them, 'Do you want to see him take his shirt off?' And all the girls would scream. Then Rick would get more intense on the drums and I would yank off the Union Jack shirt to reveal the Stars and Stripes. The place would go bonkers.

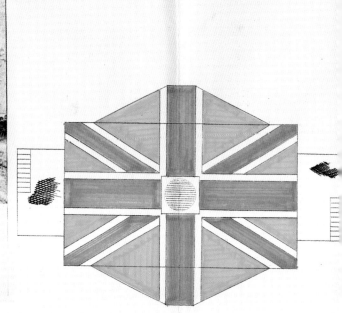

DEF LEPPARD © C. KAIL
SET PROPOSAL – FLORESCENT (U/V) FLOORING.

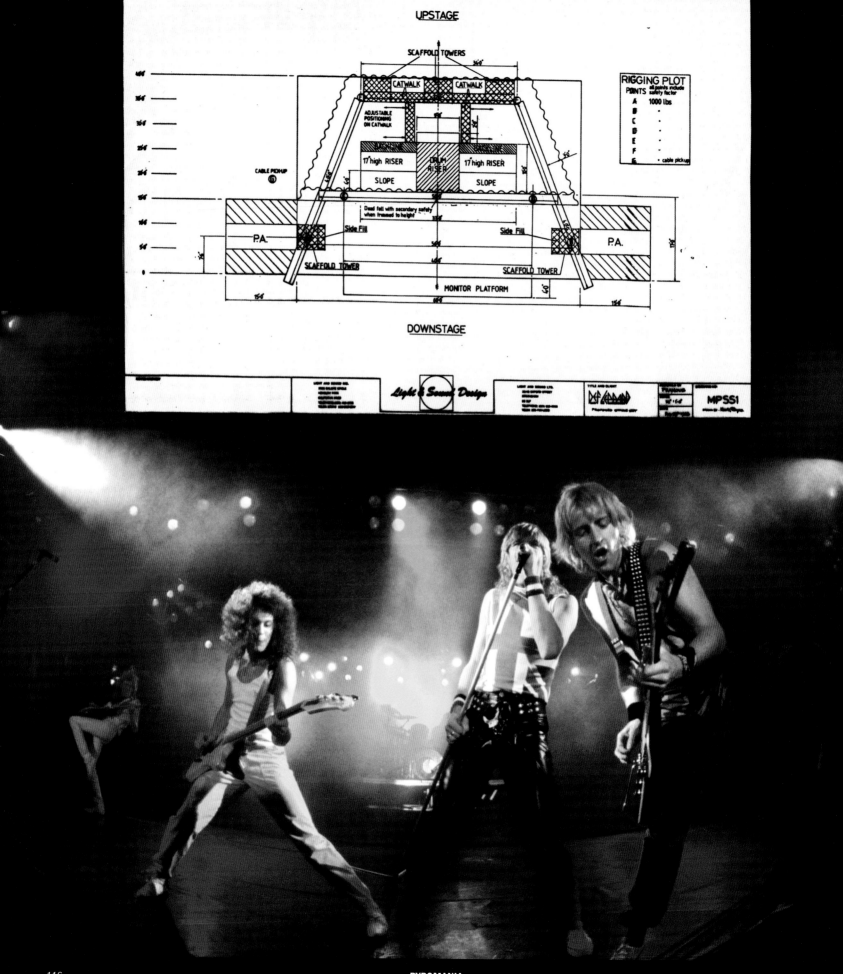

PYROMANIA

Def Leppard concert will be postponed

Times-Union

Def Leppard, the hard-rocking British band which sold out next week's Rochester performance weeks ago, has postponed its show because of illness in the group.

The band, along with Krokus and Gary Moore, were to play at 7:30 p.m. Wednesday in the War Memorial. The show has been rescheduled for Aug. 25 because Def Leppard lead singer Joe Elliott "blew his voice out" in the midst of the band's current American tour, according to a spokesman for John Scher Presents, the show's promoter.

Tickets for Wednesday's date will be honored at the Aug. 25 show. Persons wishing refunds should return the tickets to the outlet where they were purchased.

JOE ELLIOTT: It wasn't all plain sailing. As headliners, we had to get used to playing an hour and 40 minutes, six shows a week, for the first time. I'd never done any vocal training and I started to lose my voice. We had to reschedule some shows while I hunkered down on Long Island with my girlfriend, Denise, who was working for a family there as an au pair. The family kindly let me stay with her and I just sat by their pool with my Sony Walkman on and my mouth shut, letting my voice heal. It made me realise that I had a responsibility to look after myself. Not many shows get cancelled because the guitarist catches a cold, but they do if the singer does (although, to this day, we've never actually cancelled a gig; we've only ever postponed them).

Steve Clark, Rick Savage, Joe Elliott, Rick Allen and Phil Collen sing together before a charity football match against the Allentown Z-95 radio team at the J. Birney Crum Stadium, Allentown, PA, June 1983. It was a 3-2 Def Leppard victory, with Joe scoring all three goals.

JOE ELLIOTT: Our last mainland show of the US tour was at Jack Murphy Stadium in San Diego on 17 September. It was our first stadium gig as headliners – we played to 55,000 people. Straight after that, we treated ourselves and the crew to a ten-day holiday in Hawaii built around two shows in Honolulu. We'd earned it.

JOE ELLIOTT: Shortly before the European tour, Phil and I were sent to Japan to do some promo ahead of a few dates we were going to play there in December. As we went from one TV studio to the next we kept running into John and Roger Taylor from Duran Duran, who were on the same round of interviews as us. We arranged to meet them after work at the Lexington Queen nightclub, where all the models used to hang out. You'd think that two members of Duran Duran would have nothing in common with two members of Def Leppard, but both bands had become phenomenally successful in America that year, so we bonded over that. At three in the morning, when we realised that we had a singer, a guitarist, a drummer and a bass player, we made a drunken plan to find a recording studio and record 'All the Young Dudes'. We were deadly serious. And then back to our rooms at six only for Cliff Burnstein to wake us up two hours later to get the bullet train to Kyoto for a day of sightseeing. I've never felt so ill in my life.

Joe-3101
Phil-3103

Keio Plaza Hotel
2-1 Nishi-Shinjuku 2-Chome,
Shinjuku-ku
011-81-3-344-0111
Telex J26874

PROMOTION SCHEDULE FOR DEF LEPPARD

Sept. 26 (Mon.)	11.30	Arrival in Japan. *Alex- help w/ travel plans*
27 (Tue.)	13:00-14:00	An interview with "Yomiuri Shimbun", a national newspaper (Joe Elliott only).
		An interview with "Young Guitar", a music magazine (Phil Collen only).
	14:00-15:00	An interview with "Jiji News Agency", a news agency (Joe).
		An interview with "Player", a music magazine (Phil).
	15:00-16:00	An interview with "Asahi Shimbun", a national newspaper (Joe).
		An interveiw with "Sankei Sports", a sport paper (Phil). *CANCEL*
	16:30-18:30	An interview with "Music Life", a music magazine, at its offices and an autograph session at "Rock Za", a shop owned by Music Life (Joe and Phil).
	19:00-21:00	A radio interview with "Miss DJ Request Parade", a highly rated program JOQR, at dinner (Joe and Phil).
28 (Wed.)	13:00-14:00	An interview with "Goro", a non-specialized magazine (Joe and Phil).
	14:00-15:00	An interview with "Rock Show", a music magazine (Joe).
		An interview with "Guitar Magazine", a music magazine (Phil). *Asahi Shimbun*
	15:00-17:00	An out-door photo session with "FM Recopal", an FM magazine (Joe and Phil).
	17:00-19:00	Videotaping of a tv interview with "Funky Tomato", a popular variety show on TVK (Joe and Phil). *Dinner (subj. to Mr. Udo)*
29 (Thu.)	13:00-14:00	An interview with "FM Station", an FM magazine (Joe and Phil).
	14:00-15:00	An interview with "Pia", a non-specialized magazine (Joe).
		An interview with "Rockin' f", a music magazine (Phil).

Joe-3101 (handwritten notes on left margin: *sorted w/ Guitar Magazine (Joe + Phil)*)

	15:00-16:00	An interview with "Ongaku Senka", a music magazine (Joe).
		An interview with "City Road", a non-specialized magazine (Phil).
	17:00-19:00	A live tv interview with "Kochira Jyohobu", a highly rated news show on NHK - the public tv station, at its studios (Joe and Phil).
	20:30-21:30	Videotaping of a tv interview with "Best Hit USA", a highly rated music show on ANB, at its studios (Joe and Phil).
30 (Fri.)		Departure from Japan.

Notes:

1) Unless specified, all interviews will be done at the hotel.
2) Photos will be taken at all press interviews.
3) Pick-up times will be notified duly.

WE WISH YOU A VERY PLEASANT STAY IN JAPAN!!

TADAO SEKIGUCHI (Phonogram) 479-3713 ALEX --- 479-3713
HIRO NAKAMURA (") "
TACK (UDO) 402-7581×4
AKI MORISHITA (APRIL) 583-5050
NAMIHIKO SASAKI (") "
ALEX ABRAMOFF (Phonogram)

200 pins + 200 T-shirts for M. Sekiguchi for April + Udo - 80-Phonogram
Fan club   60-April
*   60-Udo &*
*   100-Medium*
*   80-Small*
*   20-Large*
*   Mixture of ...*
*   (inc sleeves...)*

Japan promo visit
September 1983

```
+++++++++++++++++++++++++++++
V E N U E  -  CONTACT SHEET
+++++++++++++++++++++++++++++


DEF LEPPARD - EUROPEAN TOUR 1983
=================================

OCT  7  -  STOCKHOLM  -  DRAKEN THEATRE .. .. ..   010 468 51 20 48
     8  -  OFF
     9  -  LUND  -  OLYMPEN   .. .. .. .. ..        010 4646 126 210
    10  -  COPENHAGEN  -  SALTLAGARET .. .. ..      010 45 115 27 01
    11  -  OFF
    12  -  KOLN  -  SARTORYSALLE .. .. .. ..        010 49 221 134 813
    13  -  OFFENBACH  -  STADTHALLE .. .. ..        010 49 611 806 52824
    14  -  HAMBURG  -  MARKTHALLE .. .. ..          010 49 40 339491
    15  -  OFF
    16  -  ERLANGEN  -  STADTHALLE (NUREMBERG) ..   010 49 9131 86486
    17  -  MUNICH  -  LOEWENBRAUKELLER .. .. ..     010 49 89 526 021
    18  -  ZURICH  -  VOLKSHAUS .. .. .. ..         010 411 241 6404
    19  -  OFF
    20  -  MILANO  -  ROLLING STONE CLUB  .. ..     010 392 738 100
    21  -  BRESCIA  -  TEATRO TENDA  .. .. ..       010 3930 348 888
    22  -  BOLOGNA  -  TEATRO TENDA  .. .. ..       010 3951  323 200
    23  -  OFF
    24  -  HYERES  -  LE GYMNASE  .. .. .. ..       010 33 94574 301
    25  -  MONTPELLIER  -  SALLE VICTOIRE .. ..     010 33 67 644 831
    26  -  OFF
    27  -  BARCELONA  -  PALAKIO DE DEPORTES .. ..  010 343 224 2776
    28  -  VALENCIA  -  SALA BONI  .. .. .. ..      010 346 155 0773
    29  -  MADRID  -  PABELLON DEL REAL MADRID  ..  010 341 215 0046
    30  -  SAN SEBASTIAN  -  VUAPLON ANOETA .. ..   010 344 346 1011
    31  -  OFF

NOV  1  -  OFF
     2  -  BORDEAUX  -  SALLE DU GRAND PARC  ..     010 33 56 501 985
     3  -  CLERMONT FERRAND  -  MAISON DES SPORTS   010 33 73 921 705
     4  -  LE MANS  -  LA ROTONDE  .. .. .. ..      010 33 43  840 050
     5  -  ORLEANS  -  HALL PRESTIGE  .. .. ..      010 33 38   662 820
     6  -  OFF
     7  -  RENNES  -  SALLE DE LA CITE .. .. ..     010 33 99  791 066
     8  -  BREST  -  PETIT PENFELD .. .. .. ..      010 33 98   033 808
     9  -  PARIS  -  ESPACE BALARD .. .. .. ..      010 33 1 557 2403/2335
    10  -  LYON - PARIS D'HIVER  .. .. .. ..        010 33 7 894 6515
    11  -  OFF
    12  -  OFF
    13  -  CAMBRAI  -  PALAIS DES GROTTES .. ..     010 33 27  839 051
    14  -  STRASBOURG  -  HALL TIVOLI  .. .. ..     010 33 88  366 078
    15  -  METZ  -  SALLE EUROPA  .. .. .. ..       010 33 87  625 473
    16  -  ANTWERP  -  HOF TER LOO .. .. .. ..      010 323 235 08 93

              -----------------------
```

JOE ELLIOTT: Back in Europe in October we came down to earth with a thud. Having just done 55,000 in San Diego, now we were in Stockholm in front of 1,200 again. From a long-term point of view it was character-building, but at the time it was depressing as hell. We did do a couple of 4,000- or 5,000-seaters around France and Germany. I remember the German shows being fantastic because they were full of Americans GIs. US army radio was playing as much Def Leppard as normal American radio, so we had this amazing micro-climate of American fans in Germany.

'Terror Twins' T-shirt made by a fan for Steve

PHIL COLLEN: After the American Pyromania tour, where we'd been packing out arenas, we got back to Europe and we were back to playing clubs and half-full theatres. This was before we actually started banking any money at all. Along with that came sharing rooms in budget accommodation and travelling in two cars instead of having a tour bus. Rick was driving one and his brother Robert was driving the other. It was shit. You would never do that now.

Steve and I used to share a room. We were called the 'terror twins'. We were having a great time but things just kept happening, most of which we didn't remember at all. One time when we were in France on the Pyromania tour, Steve and I were in our room and Robert knocked on the door, looked at Steve and me and handed me my shoes. We had no idea why he had them. Robert said, 'You two were fighting each other in the lift, and that was the last we saw of you.' We didn't remember any of it.

These blackouts kept happening and that's why I eventually gave up drinking. The thing that swung it was when we were in Dublin and I borrowed Joe's car while he was asleep. Steve and I got fucked up and I drove back and, when I woke up, I had a Rolex on my wrist and another ear piercing. Then Joe came in and he was off with me because I'd left his car running with the radio on and the door open. I had no memory of any of it. I realised it was time to knock it on the head. And I was able to do it. Sadly, Steve wasn't, although we did keep talking about it.

Opposite: Hammersmith Odeon, London 5 December 1983

Channel 4 Supersonic Christmas show recording London 6 December 1983

PYROMANIA

JOE ELLIOTT: Word of our success in America was getting back to the UK, so there was a positive vibe about our three shows in Birmingham, Nottingham and London at the beginning of December. One of the reviews that we got in London was brilliant. It kept referring to Phil and Steve as Phil Duran and Steve Duran, because of the way they were dressed. You could see that as taking the piss if you wanted, but we saw it as evidence that finally we were managing to shed the heavy metal tag.

RICK SAVAGE: I wouldn't call Def Leppard a heavy metal band. But I struggle to find another term that actually suits us. A melodic hard rock band is what I'd call us. We get described as heavy metal, but I don't think we're quite the same as Iron Maiden. We're good friends with them and we know that they don't take any of it seriously. It's just one way that people pick up on you. We'd rather dress like Duran Duran than Motörhead.

PHIL COLLEN: Heavy metal gets a bad rap. It's perceived as being not very intelligent and only appealing to kids with acne. So, when we get lumped into that genre we feel slightly insulted. That's why we end up spending so much time trying to explain why we're not that.

I think the problem was that they didn't have a category for us when our albums were selling three or four times more than any other rock act. We should have been in the pop category because of all the hits we were having, but we never got Grammys for any of them because they couldn't categorise us.

STEVE CLARK: Why can't we, as a rock group, sell records to an Elton John fan or a Michael Jackson fan without losing our original market? It's just good rock music and we'd like to appeal to everybody.

JOE ELLIOTT of DEF LEPPARD

JOE ELLIOTT: Finally, we were able to clear our enormous debt to the record company and by the end of the year our accountants started divvying out some proper money to us. I bought a place in Cobham in Surrey, which coincidentally was ten minutes from Brian May's house. But, as things were to turn out, I should never have bought that house because I never got a chance to spend any time in it.

PHIL COLLEN: Steve and I bought a place in Paris. When we had a little bit of time off, we would float around the city having a blast with our girlfriends.

We were both very working class, but all of a sudden we had models as girlfriends, we were living in Paris and everything changed. Our eyes and minds started opening up to culture and travel. Seeing different places and meeting different people takes away your blinkers.

We'd be sitting in a brasserie where Picasso used to sit, and it was a great vibe. Seeing this growth in my best friend that I was also experiencing was really cool. We would have these wonderful conversations that would go on for hours. We'd just be sitting in a bar – I'd be drinking water by this point and he'd be nursing a drink, but not getting fucked up – and we'd talk and talk and talk. It was an amazing time.

January 1984

9 Monday
(54) You ARE DOOMED - TO A LIFE OF TAX EXILE. GET OUT! PARIS (PHIL).

10 Tuesday
(55)

11 Wednesday
(56)

12 Thursday
(57)

January 1984

16 Monday
(61)

17 Tuesday
(62) days.

18 Wednesday
Week of Prayer for Christian Unity
Japan Leave for Japan From Paris. Interviews.

19 Thursday

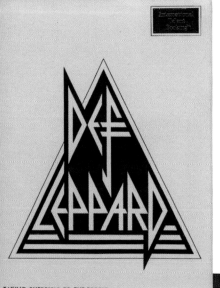

TAKING SHEFFIELD TO THE PEOPLE

DEF LEPPARD - S.E. ASIA & AUSTRALIA 1984

JAN 24	-	TOKYO SHIBUYA KOKAIDO
25	-	OSAKA KOSEI NENKIN HALL
26	-	TOKYO SUN PLAZA
27	-	DEPART TOKYO
28	-	ARRIVE SYDNEY
29	-	NARARA FESTIVAL
30	-	OFF
31	-	OFF
FEB 1	-	OFF
2	-	DEPART SYDNEY FOR MELBOURNE
3	-	MELBOURNE, THE VENUE
4	-	SYDNEY, SELINAS
5	-	DEPART SYDNEY FOR BANGKOK
6	-	OFF
7	-	HUA MARK STADIUM
8	-	DEPART BANGKOK

JOE ELLIOTT: We went back out to Japan with the rest of the band to play the three dates Phil and I had been promoting. Then we went on to Australia, where we did a club in Melbourne and a club in Sydney. We also played the Narara Festival where it rained like you wouldn't believe. The first thing I did when we came out for the encore was pour a bucket of rainwater over my head. I said, 'If you lot can get wet, so can we,' and we went down a storm. Playing to the peanut gallery, I suppose, but I was 24 years old and having the time of my life, so I didn't really care.

DEF LEPPARD Vol. 2

VISA APPLICATION FORM TO ENTER JAPAN

Name in full _____
(Surname)
_____
(Given and middle name)
Different name used, if any ____ stage name
(Photo)
approx. 45 mm x 45 mm
Sex ____ Marital status ____ married ____ single ____
Nationality or citizenship _____
Former nationality, if any _____
Date and place of birth _____
(Day) (Month) (Year) (City) (Province) (Country)
Criminal record, if any _____
Home address _____
Tel. _____
Profession or occupation _____
Name and address of firm or organization to which applicant belongs ____ This should be the Artists' American
based (contractual) company.
Tel. _____
Post or rank held at present _____
Principal former positions _____
Passport (Refugee or stateless should note the title of Travel Document)_____
No. ____ Diplomatic, Official, Ordinary Issued at ____ relevant office
Issuing authority British Passport Authority ____ (or whatever)
Purpose of journey to Japan ____ Promotional
Length of stay in Japan intended _____
Route of present journey : Name of ship or airline _____
Port of entry into Japan ____ Probable date of entry____
Address of hotels or names and addresses of persons with whom applicant intends to stay
to be arranged by Japanese Agent
Dates and duration of previous stays in Japan _____
Guarantor or reference in Japan : Name ____ UDO Artists
Address _____
Relationship to applicant ____ none ____ Tel. ____
Persons accompanying applicant
and included in his passport ____ Name ____ Relationship ____ Birthdate

I hereby declare that the statement given above is true and correct. Also, I understand that immigration status and period of stay
to be granted are decided by the Japanese immigration authorities upon my arrival.
Date of application _____
Signature of applicant _____
(FORM No. 1-C)

(LETTER OF GUARANTEE)

氏 名(NAME)

国 籍(NATIONALITY)

上記の者本邦在留に関し、下記事項について保証致します。
1. 滞在費の負担
2. 帰国旅費の負担
3. 本人が日本国法律を遵守すること
4. 滞日期限内に帰国せしめること
上記確かに相違ありません。
保証人住所 東京都渋谷区千駄ケ谷3-11-2
コーポ南202号
比 名 音楽舎
秦 慎一郎
被保証人との関係 雇主

JOE ELLIOTT: We finished the tour in Bangkok on 7 February 1984, almost exactly a year after we'd kicked off at the Marquee. The funny thing was we sold out an arena in Bangkok despite never having released a record there. Everybody bought the bootlegs for 20 pence, so we thought we might as well get back some of the money we'd lost on record sales by playing a gig there. If somebody had said to me three years earlier when we were still playing in pubs, 'In 1984 you're going to be in Thailand playing to 6,000 people,' I'd have just laughed at them.

Bangkok, February 1984

M C K

BLACK LINE AROUND
ILLUSTRATION
DOES NOT PRINT
THE INSIDE OF
THE LINE
INDICATES WHERE
THE TRANSPARENCY
STOPS AND THE
BACKGROUND
BEGINS

THE BLACK
SHOULD BE
MATCHED IN
DENSITY TO THE
DARKEST BLACK ON
THE ILLUSTRATION

FAX TO : LINDA WALKER
AND POLYGRAM
NEW YORK ..... 29.1.88.
FROM : ANDIE AIRFIX .... SATORI.

MATCHED
BLACK
TO BLEED.

WHERE THE ILLUSTRATION ENDS IS SHOWN
ON THE OVERLAY AS A KEYLINE. AT
THIS POINT THE ILLUSTRATION BECOMES
THE BACKGROUND OF MATCHED BLACK
KEYLINE DOES NOT PRINT

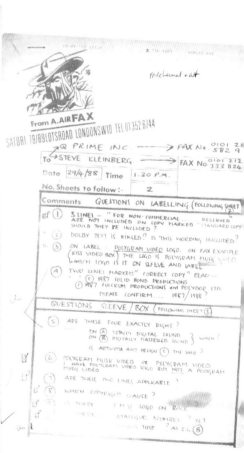

Hysteria
Recorded: 1984–1987
Released: 3 August 1987

HYSTERIA

JOE ELLIOTT: *When it came to doing the Hysteria cover, my God, did we go round the houses!*

Andie Airfix flew back and forth from London to Holland about half a dozen times to show us different concepts. The cost of the flights alone was more than we'd spend on an album cover these days.

The beginning of the idea that ended up as the final cover was this freaky-looking head that had two faces, like it was a pair of twins mashed together in a womb and come out as one person. We thought it looked a bit like a planet so we suggested turning it into a cross between a head and a spinning planet. And then, because it was the Eighties, the Tron-style lettering around the border became a big part of it as well. In fact, I think that's the most striking part of all. The triangle over the top referred back to the original triangular logo, which had been used on the first album. Then we had the yellow and red logo, which had now become well established.

So, there were all these very strong elements, each of which was recognisable in its own right. Eventually they came together, but it took a hell of a long time.

February 1984

6 Monday

7 Tuesday

8 Wednesday

Go to Dublin, ~~rehersals~~.
write for new album.

9 Thursday

JOE ELLIOTT: When the Pyromania tour finished, we went straight into *not* being on tour. We decided to relocate to Dublin, Ireland and rented a big house in an area called Booterstown. My lucky run of drawing lots for bedrooms that had seen me get John Lennon's room at Startling Studios continued here: I got the biggest room and everybody hated me for it!

We settled ourselves in. It was hard to get our head round the fact that we were actually going to be taking our clothes out of a wardrobe and not a suitcase.

The first ten days we spent just drinking ourselves to oblivion. It was the first time we'd had a chance to celebrate everything we'd achieved over the previous year. I started saving all the empties to see how much we'd actually drunk. I put them all in a corner and took a Polaroid (now long lost). There were about 150 empty vodka and whiskey bottles and 400 Heineken cans. Things did calm down after a while.

Peter Mensch was very clever. He got Denis Desmond, our Irish promoter, to line up a chaperone for us, someone to tell us where to go and where not to go and generally help us find our feet. The first thing we had to do was buy some furniture. We went to the cheapest furniture shop we could find, the Big Red Corner Shop, and we bought five beds, two couches, a coffee table and a TV. We set all the gear up in the back room, which became our studio. Steve started brewing his own beer. It was like being in *The Young Ones*.

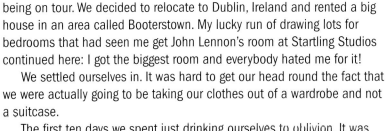
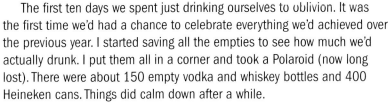

Additionally, when we return the contract to the estate agent in Dublin, we will be sending them a booking advance of Irish pounds 250.00. The total amount to be paid for the first three month's rental and deposit (including the booking fee) will Irish pounds 3,400.00. That is a deposit of I£1,000 plus I£800.00 a month rent. We will not hand over the balance of the funds until we are satisfied with the property.

At home in Booterstown, including bottom left (left to right): Steve Clark, Lorelei Shellist, Denise Dakin, Joe Elliott, Phil Collen, Valerie Claire, Rick Savage

JOE ELLIOTT: Denis was looking after us well – we were being taken to places, introduced to people, put on the guest list for shows, we were having a great time. We went to see Simple Minds at the SFX and we were hanging out with them in their dressing room after the show when this bloke came over and said, 'I heard you guys were in town.' He got a pen out, wrote his phone number down and said, 'If you need anything, give me a ring.' And that was Bono.

I had lived in London for three years and nothing like that had ever happened. I'd been in Dublin for three weeks, and I already had Bono's phone number in my back pocket. We were playing football with Stockton's Wing, a traditional Irish band who were great people, hanging out with Clannad, also fantastic people, going to pubs where nobody bothered us, and finding the best clubs downtown. By March, I was looking for an apartment there. One way or another, I've been living in Ireland ever since (officially resident since 1989).

```
Def Leppard in Dublin:
  House Rental: 6 months .....................$ 5670.00
  Phonogram money (float, rehearsal etc)      $16800.00
  Airfares (for band, crew)                   $ 1529.00
  Airfares (Lange, Mensch)                    $ 3500.00
  PD's Lange                                  $ 1680.00
  Miscellaneous (utilities - who knows?)      $ 7500.00
                                              ----------
TOTAL.......................................$36679.00
(Our salaries are being paid out of our corporations,one could
theoretically add these in also.)
```

O'Connell Bridge and Street, Dublin, Ireland.

Shellist
2000 Broadway
NYC. 10023
NY.
AIRMAIL

Wisseloord Studios
Steve Clark - Def Leppard
Cat Van Renneslaan 1217CX10
Hilversum Holland

JOE ELLIOTT: It was great to be hanging out with U2 while they were making *The Joshua Tree*. And there were other bands doing what we were doing, so we would go down to the Pink Elephant, which was *the* club in Dublin, and have a drink on the VIP floor with Spandau Ballet, Frankie Goes to Hollywood or Terence Trent D'Arby. I'm still really close friends with Gary Kemp. Sav and I teamed up with John Keeble and Steve Norman from Spandau and a couple of guys from our gym to form a five-a-side team, which played in tournaments. For the first time in ages, we actually had a life outside music and it was amazing.

We probably wouldn't have got to know these people if we'd met them in London. But in Dublin it was us against the world. Gary Kemp even sang backing vocals on 'Animal', because he just happened to pop into the studio while we were all standing round the mic screaming the chorus. I've often said to Gary that the Spandau track 'Through the Barricades' is a rock song. They'd been spending too much time with us!

That first six months in Dublin was all about writing and demoing material for the next album. We came up with about six or seven songs, including most of 'Gods of War' and 'Women' and an early version of 'Animal'. Then in August 1984 we moved to Holland to start recording at Wisseloord Studios in Hilversum and stayed there until the following February. Our hotel was in a nearby village called Loosdrecht and we had the place to ourselves – it was a bit like *The Shining*.

Apart from six weeks in Paris in summer 1985, which was fun but not very productive and way too expensive, all we ever did was go from Dublin to Holland, Holland to Dublin, six months here, six months there, until 1987.

JOE ELLIOTT: With each new album we wanted to make a leap of songwriting, performance and production, but this time we were going to have to do it without the guidance of the phenomenal Mutt Lange. While we were in Dublin Mutt dropped the bombshell that, having been working non-stop since 1976, he now needed to take a break. He said he'd help us with pre-production and sit in on the songwriting sessions but he wouldn't do the recording itself.

Our management talked us into having Jim Steinman produce the album. Jim was an odd choice because *Bat Out of Hell*, the album for which he was best known (and which half of us didn't particularly like), was actually produced by Todd Rundgren. Jim's role on that album was as the writer. We didn't need Jim to help us write the songs and his dramatic style wouldn't have fitted with Def Leppard anyway. We didn't really follow the logic but we went along with it.

Def Leppard in Amsterdam:

```
    Accomodation (6 rooms 14 weeks)..........$15400.00
    Flights (9 or the equivalent; Mike back 2)$ 3150.00
    Float (petrol 2 cars, food, maid etc)    $ 9800.00 ($750 per week)
    Salaries (since we could very easily take our salary money
    from P&F and transfer in Dublin, that is what we did. However,
    in Holland it is a pain to do this so I propose that we pay
    ourselves via the recording budget the Dutch equivalent of £400.00
    a month. Needless to say, you can increase it if you want)
                                             $ 9800.00
                                             ----------
    TOTAL....................................-....$38150.00
```

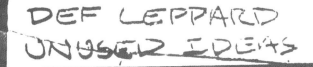

Explanation of "Steinman Budget"

Dublin: Time Period - 8 July - 28 July
    21 Days Hotel (Steinman, Jansen)....... $ 3000.00
    21 Days Per Diem ($50 per day; 2 people) $ 2100.00
    Airfares (Steinman 1st, Jansen Bus Class)$ 4500.00

Something I forgot in the early Grand Total for the "Steinman
Budget" is that Neil Dorfsman and John Jansen will be flying to
Wisseloord for the day in early July. Those airfares, plus hotels
etc. will bring Steinman from $299,000 to $300,000.

Amsterdam: Time Period 6 August - 21 November (1 week break)
Here I assume that if we don't use the studio or rooms, they can
be rented. I know the studio can be.
    14 weeks Studio rental................. $ 84000.00
    14 weeks Outboard gear.(this is high)... $ 28000.00
    Tape $ 7500.00
    PD's (3 people St, JJ, ND)($50 per day) $ 14700.00
    Accomodation (3 people) $ 9200.00
    Car (so far, we will rent 1 car) $ 3500.00
    Engineer's fee (we think $2000 a week) $ 28000.00
    Airfares (2 trips each person; start and
             break) $ 12000.00

**If we have to pay for the additional week car and hotel rental
for Steinman and us, please add the following.$ 2750.00

New York: Time Period: 21 November - 25 December (5 weeks)
Steinman says 5 weeks (5 a day a week) mix is no problem. Any
mix is quicker than the last one.
    Power Station ($3300 a day @ 25 days) $ 82500.00
    Engineer $ 10000.00
    Outboard $ 7500.00
    Misc $ 2500.00

Steinman is currently checking 2 studios which are cheaper than
the Power Station. Also it is possible that the Power Station rate
will come down. At those rates it is frightening to contemplate
what Springsteen's lps cost!!

I think I covered everything cost-wise. If you see any glaring
omissions, please let me know.

                ADDITIONAL NOTES: PAGE 4

JOE ELLIOTT: After three or four weeks it became blatantly obvious that we were getting nowhere with Jim. He had no clue about guitar sounds and no respect for our work ethic. One of the problems was that he was staying up all night in his hotel room writing *Bat Out of Hell II*. We'd turn up at the studio wanting to make a start at 11 a.m., but Jim would leave us waiting for another three or four hours. What the fuck? He had the carpet changed in his hotel room because he didn't like the colour. When we ate in the studio restaurant, he'd order one portion of everything so every meal became a banquet. And all this was on our tab! The other bands who were recording there would wait for us to leave the table, then rush in for our leftovers. We fed Mink DeVille for six weeks.

When it got to six weeks in and we hadn't even started doing vocals, we had a band meeting and decided to get rid of Jim. We had to pay him off, a serious amount of money. I know you shouldn't speak ill of the dead, but let's just say Jim really didn't work out well for us.

Neil Dorfsman, Jim Steinman's engineer, stayed with us for a little while and then Nigel Green came over. Nigel had worked as engineer on *High 'n' Dry* and *Pyromania*, so he knew us, he knew Mutt's way of working and he knew how to get sounds. All of a sudden, it started to sound like Def Leppard again. The only problem was that it also sounded like *Pyromania*, which is exactly what we didn't want.

We took a break for Christmas. I went to my house in Cobham and my mum and dad came down from Sheffield; Sav and Rick went back to Sheffield; and Phil and Steve went to Paris. Everybody was having a jolly time and the plan was to get back together in the first week of January.

RICK ALLEN: Having got used to working with Mutt, we realised Jim's standards weren't quite up to ours. I liked Jim. The work that he did with Meat Loaf and other significant artists was really influential. But I'm not sure he was the right choice for us.

JOE ELLIOTT: At about 4 p.m. on New Year's Eve I got a call from Peter Mensch. The first thing he said was, 'Are you sitting down?', so I knew it was going to be really bad news. I said, 'Who died?' And he said, 'Nobody died, but your drummer's just lost his arm.'

It was unimaginable. I'd never known anybody who had lost an arm. I couldn't get my head around it. Then I got on the phone with everybody and we tried to work out what the hell we were going to do.

For two or three hours, we assumed that Rick would have to leave the band. Because there's no such thing as a one-armed drummer. But then your thoughts settle down and you begin to see things more rationally.

I drove up to Sheffield the next day and went to see Rick in hospital. He was in an induced coma and they'd reattached his arm. His brother kept grabbing my hand and saying, 'Feel his hand, it's warm.'

RICK ALLEN: I was in a coma for about three weeks. During that time, they put my arm back on and then took it off again because it had got infected and I didn't know a thing about it.

When I came round and started to get an idea of what had actually happened to me, I remember thinking that I didn't want to do this, I didn't want to be here anymore. I just wanted to disappear. I felt way too self-conscious, and I didn't want to be around anybody. I just felt completely defeated. My brother Robert was really supportive – he actually slept in a chair in my hospital room and was there pretty much all the time. Without my brother, I really don't know if I would have gotten through this.

Mutt came to see me in hospital and arranged for a Hare Krishna couple to come up from Watford to cook proper vegetarian food for me. The entire ward smelled like an Indian restaurant. He also helped me to see past the situation I found myself in, to realise that yes, I could play drums again.

JOE ELLIOTT: Rick got a piece of foam for the bottom of his bed so he could push himself upright and tap at it with his feet and make beats and sounds with his one arm and two feet. Within a week or so of the accident he was convinced he could continue.

We realised that moping about wasn't going to do anything to help him so we went back to Holland and worked away on the record. Rick had recorded drum tracks for seven songs and there were loads of overdubs still to be done, so his not being there wasn't going to be a problem for the time being.

We were back at Wisseloord by about 10 January, but the spirit was a bit flat and we weren't really getting anywhere. There were so many doubts in the air – about what would happen to Rick, how we were going to finish the album and whether it was even the right album to be making.

Rick was supposed to be in hospital for six months, but was discharged after four weeks. Then, after a couple of weeks of being at home with his mum and dad, he came over to Holland. He missed playing on the record, so he would sit at the back of the control room listening to whatever we were doing. A guy called Pete Hartley invented an electronic drum kit with foot pedals for him. When that was ready Rick locked himself away in the smallest studio at Wisseloord and relearned how to play the drums.

Richard Allen — How he does it.

Much attention has been focused on the drum kit used by Richard on tour. Surprisingly, it's not that unusual, just standard electronic drums but used in a unique, creative and rather special way. It's really two drum kits combined. One kit is played by electronic foot pedals and the other with sticks on electronic drum pads.

The reason it sounds so good has as much to do with the way it's played as what equipment is used. To understand this, you need to know a few drumming truths. First, it is possible to play some simple rhythms using just feet, if your technique is good enough. Conventionally it's something most drummers don't do. Secondly, as most drummers will tell you, the average drummer's left foot is under-used. It usually just keeps time in a relatively simple way on a pair of Hi Hat cymbals.

But Richard's left-foot technique lets him play complex drum patterns with remarkable ease. It's possible to play very simple rhythms on just the top kit too. But here's the bonus: combine both kits and the playing potential becomes immense. By triggering the same sounds from either kit some 'impossible' drum licks become possible.

The first kit (the 'top' kit) is five small Simmons electronic drum pads. The 'bottom' kit is four specially constructed foot-pedals and a Simmons Bass Drum pad. None of these drums produce sound – only electronic pulses or 'triggers' which are sent to a controller or 'Brain'. It's *this* that produces the sounds.

The 'Brain' is a Simmons SDS7, where sounds are 'sampled' onto a silicon chip, loaded into a brain, and when triggered, reproduces sound like a piece of magnetic tape. Richard is using a blend of SDS7 Library Samples and samples taken from his own recorded drums.

Each drum in each kit sends a trigger to the Brain, five sounds on the top kit and the same five sounds on the bottom kit. Ten triggers, five sounds — Bass Drum, Snare Drum and three Tom Toms.

The system also includes a switching device called Simmons MTM. This switches pads and pedals so that any sound can be triggered from any pad or pedal at the flick of a switch – any pad, any pedal, any kit, any sound.

Suddenly it's no longer an ordinary kit, but a precise and flexible electronic instrument offering incredible versatility. Combine it with a totally original playing technique and you've got DEF LEPPARD's drums.

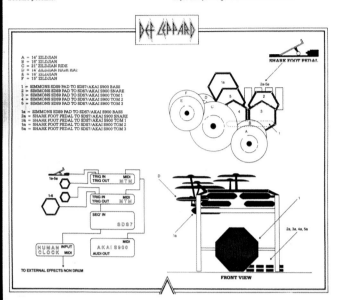

PHIL COLLEN: We asked Rick what he wanted to do and he said he thought he could make it work with these electronic drums that Mutt had talked to him about. So, that was it – we left it up to him. At this point, Rick, Steve and I lived together in Donnybrook, just outside the centre of Dublin, in a house where Spandau Ballet had stayed. It had so much space and Rick was able to lock himself in a wing of the house and just practise from eight in the morning until ten at night. The progression was amazing. At first, he literally couldn't play and it would be really frustrating for him. He'd be going, 'Fuck, fuck, fuck!' As he went on, he'd be a bit out of time and a bit clunky, but then all of a sudden he was able to play perfectly through a whole song. It was fascinating.

RICK ALLEN: The thing the guys did for me that took all the pressure off me was give me time to decide for myself what I wanted to do. Did I want to disappear and blend into the scenery, or did I want to carry on? And with the love of my family and the love of people all over the planet who wrote letters to me, I discovered the power of the human spirit. Once you tap into that you're pretty much unstoppable.

```
White Light, strange city, mad music all around
Midnight street magic crazy people crazy sound
Jack Flash, Rocket man, Sgt. Pepper and the band
Ziggy, Benny and the Jets, take a rocket
We just gotta fly

I can take you thru the centre of the dark
we gonna fly
On a collision course to crash into my heart
I will be your, I will be your, I'll be your

Rocket    yeah    Satellite of Love
Rocket    yeah    Satellite of Love
Rocket    yeah    Satellite of Love
Rocket baby c'man I'll be your
Satellite of love .

Spotlight magnetic razor rhythm lazer love
Guitar, drums, load up, stun!!!

Jet Black, Johnny B, Gene Jenie,
Dizzy Lizzy, Major Tom So C'mon
We just gotta fly

I can take you thru the centre of
we gonna fly
On a collision Course to crash in
I will be your, I will be your,

Rocket    yeah    Satellite of Love
Rocket    yeah    Satellite of Love
Rocket    yeah    Satellite of Love
Rocket    baby    C'mon

We just gotta fly
I can take you thru the centre o
we gonna fly
On a collision course to crash i
I will be year, I will be your,

Rocket    yeah    Satellite of Love
Rocket    yeah    Satellite of Love
Rocket    yeah    Satellite of Love
Rocket    baby

We gonna fly        - Rocket yeah
Satellite of love   - we gonna fly
Rocket yeah         - Satellite of
Rocket              - yeah
```

3 COLOUR SEPARATION.

ARMAGEDDON IT   METAL.

ARMAGEDDON IT   YELLOW

ARMAGEDDON IT   BLACK.

ARMAGEDDON IT!

```
Y'Better come inside when you're ready t'o....
But no chance if you don't wanna dance
You like four letter words when you're ready to...
But then you won't 'cos you know that you can

you got it, but are you gettin' it?

You say that love is won when you get some
But then your finger won't trigger the gun

Y'know you can't stop
so don't rock it
Y'know you got it

Hey! But are you gettin' it?
        Really gettin' it ooh
        come get it from me

Gimme all of your lovin' - every little bit
Gimme all that you got   - every bit of it
Every bit of your lovin' - c'mon and live a bit
Never want it to stop

Hey! but are you gettin' it - Armageddon it!
    really gettin' it - Yes Armageddon it!

You try comin' on when you need some....
But then you don't 'cos you already did
Yeah you jangle your jewels while y'shakin' ya....
And drive the pretty boys outa their heads

you got it, but are you gettin' it?

You flash your bedroom eyes like a jumpin' Jack....
Then play it pretty with a pat on the back

Y'know you can't stop it
So don't rock it
Y'know you got it

Hey! but are you gettin' it?
really gettin' it oh
```

RICK ALLEN: When Mutt came to visit me in the hospital I remember saying, 'Mutt, the guys are really struggling with what I'm going through at the moment. I would really appreciate it if you came back and gave us some help.' Ultimately he did and I'm very grateful for that.

JOE ELLIOTT: About halfway through 1985 we got a call from Mutt, saying he now felt rested and ready to help us. Although still full of beans and enthusiasm, we were directionless – swirling around like water going down a plughole. We were making progress with Nigel, but we were still not where we wanted to be.

Mutt came along and started working the way we'd always worked with him. First, he added guitars to the guitars that we already had, but what we didn't realise was that he was gradually replacing what we'd done. After about three months I said, 'Where are the original guitars?' Mutt laughed and said, 'What original guitars?' Next, he moved on to the drums. He fixed the Steinman-sounding stuff that had been shoehorned in and brought in click tracks and electronic drums, which made sense given that Rick was going to be playing an electronic kit.

All of a sudden, our direction became clear. We tidied up the songs that we knew were keepers, elbowed the ones that weren't and came up with new ones like 'Rocket', 'Excitable' and 'Love and Affection'.

'Rocket' came from a trip I made to the sauna opposite our hotel. Somebody there was playing a track called 'Burundi Black' by Burundi Steiphenson Black, which had a tribal drum rhythm that I found totally mesmerising. I asked if I could borrow the record, took it to the studio and one of the engineers made a loop of the drum part and put it on a 45-minute cassette for me. I used that to come up with a chorus and Mutt loved it. We felt like the Beatles when they were working with George Martin, turning tapes upside down and inside out, and 'Rocket' was us at our most experimental. The middle section sounded like monks chanting with backwards sounds and guitars – *Star Wars* for the ears, we used to call it. We were more or less the only people in rock doing that kind of off the wall stuff with the emerging digital studio technology of the time. It had more in common with what Trevor Horn was doing with Frankie Goes to Hollywood.

Inspired by 'State of Shock', the song the Jacksons did with Mick Jagger, 'Excitable' was our take on a 'funk rock' song. We got to know Mick when he was working on his solo album *Primitive Cool* with Jeff Beck in the studio next door at Wisseloord. When he went away for a while and then came back, I remember him saying, 'Bloody hell, are you still here?'

'Love Bites' was another song we wrote in 1985. That was literally just Mutt, Phil and Steve goofing around on an idea that Mutt had.

With Mutt we were also able to finish songs that had been knocking around since the early days, like 'Gods of War', which I remember thinking was the new 'Kashmir', and 'Don't Shoot Shotgun', for which we did a whole new arrangement at the beginning. We started 'Run Riot' from scratch with Mutt and it sounded so up to date and real.

'Armageddon It' was going nowhere until Steve suggested the T. Rex-style rhythm on the verses. For the chorus we lifted 'Give me all of your lovin'' from ZZ Top just as a placeholder until we could think of something better, but we never did. We didn't think Billy Gibbons was going to sue us, so we left it in and that was that.

RICK SAVAGE: 'Hysteria' is one of my all-time favourite songs. For me it's the highlight of the night when we play it. There's a special bond between the audience and the band on that song. I don't really know why. We just all come together in a kind of mutual appreciation.

I remember coming up with the verse idea, which is just this very simple jangle. We were in Paris recording some of the tracks for the album. I played it to Joe who didn't like it initially. I remember him saying it sounded too much like a Police song and that we shouldn't be going down that route. Then I played it to Phil and he said, 'No, it's fantastic. And by the way I've got this bit that'll fit on to it.' Phil had this idea for the bridge – 'I gotta know tonight' – and it literally just glued right on to the end of this idea that I had.

Now there was too much of a song to be ignored. Soon after that Steve came up with the idea of the chorus chords and the little guitar parts that feature within it. Then we got Mutt involved and he and Joe finished the thing off.

At that point in time the album didn't have a title. But when Mutt and Joe came up with the 'Hysteria' lyric Rick said, 'That's what we should call the album. It's a great album title.' So it all fell into place. The song became the title track of the album and *Hysteria* to me is like a greatest hits album in its own right.

Excitable   X - Citable

Obsession, temptation, frustration
I'm gettin' nervous

let me spit it out, spit it out
I'm gonna rip it up
ain't never gonna (never go down)

This obsession is inviting
it's outrageous it's exciting
ooh babe, you turn on and off again
you take pleasure but give out pain
so loosen up and strut you stuff
you know that once is never enough

you know I get so Excitable
I really get so
I wanna get you. Excitable
so baby let's go
baby don't say no

PHIL COLLEN: Mutt had this clear idea of what the band should sound like. *High 'n' Dry* was one thing, but it was still reminiscent of other bands. When *Pyromania* came out, it only sounded like Def Leppard. And *Hysteria* took things even further. That was down to Mutt bringing in different elements and not being trapped in a rock stereotype. He blurred the boundaries between genres. It was like the Police – my favourite band of all time – who created a hybrid of Sly and Robbie-style reggae and post-punk rock.

When we got to *Hysteria*, it was a bit of Frankie Goes to Hollywood, a bit of Billy Idol, a bit of Prince. Other rock bands wouldn't do that. They'd still only be listening to Judas Priest and AC/DC, so there was never any chance for them to develop. There was an open-mindedness to everything Mutt did. He'd point us to Sixties R&B – Otis Redding, James Brown – and tell us to listen to the rhythm, the backbeat, where the snare falls. Or he'd say, 'Well, let's do a George Jones country bend on the end of this vocal line.' And you'd say, 'Great idea. Who's George Jones?' So, he'd tell you. It was just like going to school.

STEVE CLARK: The group's definitely progressed with every album. We try never to repeat ourselves. The good thing about Def Leppard is you can always do something new and, as long as you don't go totally out of bounds, the fans seem to accept it. It's very good for us as musicians because we don't become stagnant or stale and it's a very creative group to be in. It doesn't feel like we're doing the same thing we did ten years ago.

Opposite: 'Don't Ask' T-shirt and Andie Airfix early draft artwork that never got printed

JOE ELLIOTT: The idea had been to ride on the momentum of *Pyromania* and get the next album out in 1984, or 1985 at the latest. That proved to be unrealistic, so after maybe the fifteenth person said, 'Is it done yet?' we ended up with the 'Don't Ask', 'Not Yet' and 'It's Done' T-shirts. They were just for us. We would wear them around town in Dublin or Hilversum. If anybody wanted to know how we were getting on we would just point at the T-shirt.

1985
WAITING!
1986
WAITING!!
1987
WAITING!!!

It will be released -
We just don't know when
(DEF LEPPARD 1988 - ??)

Listen, the band doesn't even know
(when they're going to start to record...much
less finish it.)
DEF LEPPARD for the 90's?

RICK ALLEN: The album took so long to make and the record company just kept pounding us: 'When are you gonna deliver this thing?' Peter Mensch came up with the idea of making shirts with these little slogans on them. I loved it; it just took off within our circle and it seemed like there was a new slogan every other day. We were all showing a united front. We had so much faith in the record and everybody that was working with us, particularly Mutt. If Mutt said it wasn't finished, then it wasn't finished, and there was nothing we could really do about that because his will is extremely strong. But I think his intuition in making sure that the record was perfect before we released it was the right one.

WINDMILL LANE RECORDING STUDIOS LIMITED
4 WINDMILL LANE, DUBLIN 2, IRELAND. TELEPHONE 01 713444, TELEX 30643.

JOE ELLIOTT: The whole process of making *Hysteria* spanned nearly three years, starting with the first demos we made in Dublin in early 1984.

We were coming towards the end of our last six-month stint in Holland and I was on my own in the studio with Mutt working on the lead vocals for 'Armageddon It'. When that was done, we would have 11 songs and we thought that, finally, the album would be more or less complete.

While Mutt went off for a coffee break, I picked up an acoustic guitar and started playing this three-chord turnaround and singing a chorus to it. Mutt came back in the room and asked me what I was playing – I think he thought it was an old song by the Kinks or the Stones or something – and I told him it was just an idea I'd had for a while, which would now have to wait for the next album. He said, 'No, it can't wait. That's the best hook I've heard in five years. What's it called?' I said, 'Well, I've only got the chorus, so I guess it's called "Pour Some Sugar on Me".'

Mutt immediately took the 'Armageddon It' tape off and replaced it with a blank piece of tape. He programmed the synth bass and drums to a 'We Will Rock You' kind of rhythm to give us something to play along to. Then he plugged in an electric guitar and we banged out some chords and threw down the chorus. Did I have any ideas for lyrics, he asked me. No, I hadn't got that far. What about melodies? I told him that I kept singing it like the meter for 'Come Together' by the Beatles.

So, we each went into different corners of the control room with a micro cassette recorder and started humming it around. Mutt decided we needed to double up the tempo, because 'Come Together' was too slow. Then we started scatting, Cab Calloway style, into our cassette recorders, which is what you always do when you haven't got any words. Next, Mutt suggested that we reinterpret each other's tapes. When I listened to Mutt's tape, I could have sworn he was singing 'love is like a bomb'. He said he wasn't, but we agreed that it was brilliant anyway.

After that, we just started throwing these phrases around: 'come and get it on', 'livin' like a lover with a radar phone', 'lookin' like a tramp, like a video vamp'. We were aware of the Sting song 'Demolition Man', so 'demolition woman, can I be your man' was a tip of the hat – or just plain theft, depending on your point of view. It was all about speed, simplicity and catchiness – 'red light, yellow light, green light, go'. We wanted 'Sugar' to be like all the T. Rex songs that we loved. We got as much of the song down as possible in a rush of excitement and inspiration.

When the rest of the band came back, we thought the last thing they'd want to hear was that we'd got a new song to record. But Mutt could sell ice to the Eskimos. At first Steve rolled his eyes, but 30 seconds into the demo you could see that they were all on board. Mutt said, 'I think we can do this pretty quick.' Our reaction was, 'Just hold up. You don't do pretty quick.' But we recorded the majority of 'Pour Some Sugar on Me' in seven or eight days, which, compared to the rest of the album, was rocket speed.

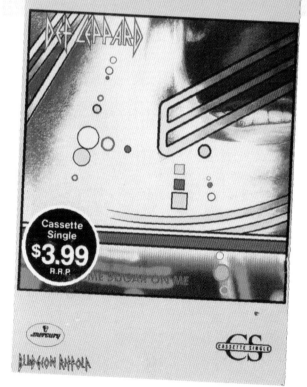

POUR SOME SUGAR ON ME

Step inside, walk this way
you and me babe, hey! hey!

Love is like a bomb baby c'mon get it on
Livin' like a lover with a radar phone
lookin' like a tramp like a video vamp
demolition woman can I be your man

Razzle 'n' Dazzle 'n' flash a little light
Television lover baby go all night
Sometime anytime sugar me sweet
little miss innocent sugar me yeah

C'mon, Take a bottle, shake it up
      Break the bubble, break it up

Pour some sugar on me
Ooh, in the name of love
Pour some sugar on me
C'mon fire me up
Pour your sugar on me
Oh I can't get enough

I'm hot, sticky, sweet
from my head to my feet yeah

Listen! Red light yellow light green light go!
      Crazy little woman on a one man show
      Mirror queen mannequin rhythm of love
      sweet dream saccharine loosen up

You gotta please a little, squeeze a little
            tease a little more
easy operator come a knockin' on my door
sometime anytime sugar me sweet
little miss innocent sugar me yeah
give a little more

Take a bottle, shake it up
break the bubble, break it up

Pour some Sugar on me
Ooh, in the name of love
Pour some sugar on me
C'mon fire me up
Pour some sugar on me
Oh can't get enough

(- continued -)

(- continued -)

I'm hot, sticky sweet
from my head to my feet yeah

You got peaches I got the cream
Sweet to taste saccharine
'Cos I'm hot, say what, sticky sweet
from my head, my head, to my feet

Do you take sugar, one lump or two?

Take a bottle   shake it up
break ~~a bottle~~ shake it up
       the bubble
Pour Some Sugar on me

Pour Some Sugar on me

Pour Some Sugar on me

Pour Some Sugar on me

Pour Some Sugar on me

Pour Some Sugar on me

Pour Some Sugar on me

RICK SAVAGE: It was an 11-track album and then Joe came up with this idea on an acoustic guitar. When Mutt got wind of it and wanted to do something with it, I was like, 'You gotta be kidding me?!' I was back in Dublin thinking the album was just about finished and ready for mixing.

JOE ELLIOTT: By summer 1986, we'd been in the studio for two years and cabin fever had set in. So, when we were offered four Monsters of Rock shows in Europe – one at Donington, one in Sweden and two in Germany – we said yes to all of them.

As a warm-up, we did six Irish club shows with a second drummer called Jeff Rich, who played drums for Status Quo. They were on tour in the UK at the time, so we booked the dates on Quo's days off. Jeff would fly in, rehearse, do a gig, then he'd go off to do a Quo gig and come back for our next gig. We played Cork, Galway, Limerick, Ballybunion, Waterford and Dublin.

We had a great time in Ballybunion. The weather was perfect, we saw dolphins, played football on the beach, got drunk. And the gig was after a roller rink party, so we didn't have to go on stage until midnight. Three years previously we'd stormed America on the Pyromania tour. Now we were playing a show that was being advertised with a photocopied poster stuck up in the local chip shop. It was weird, but we wanted to fly below the radar. Rick needed to make his mistakes in front of a small audience.

RICK ALLEN: The first few warm-up shows in Ireland went really well – I'd play a couple of songs on my own and then Jeff would do the rest of the show with me. But then Jeff got delayed getting to the Ballybunion gig, which meant I ended up playing more than half of the set on my own. The next night, in Waterford, there literally wasn't enough room on stage for two drum kits, so the guys came up to me before we went on and asked me if I'd like to try doing the whole gig on my own. With no hesitation, I just said yes. I did the show, kept it simple, and everybody seemed to love it. Afterwards Jeff came up to me and said, 'Well, I guess I'm going home tomorrow then.' It was a huge vote of confidence.

JOE ELLIOTT: Rick played on his own again at the SFX in Dublin, and again it worked.

Right, third down: Jeff Rich and
Rick Allen, backstage at the
Savoy, Limerick, 7 August 1986

146

Aimcarve Ltd presents **MONSTERS OF ROCK**

DEF LEPPARD

DONINGTON PARK SATURDAY 16th AUGUST

ACCESS ALL AREAS

JOE ELLIOTT: We were third on the bill at Donington, which was perfect for us. We weren't a big band in England, but by 1986 *Pyromania* had sold a respectable number of copies. A lot of the kids out there knew who we were and people were obviously curious to see how this guy was going to play the drums. Brian May, God bless him, had driven all the way from London to lend his support; he hung out with us all day and stood beside the stage watching our performance.

Monsters of Rock
Donington Park, Derbyshire
16 August 1986

JOE ELLIOTT: We'd planned not to make a meal of Rick, but you could see everybody peering through the cymbals and marvelling at what he was doing. We were going down really well, middle of the bill and middle of the day. I leaned into Phil between numbers and said, 'I can't not introduce him.' And he agreed. So before 'Rock of Ages' I said, 'Ladies and gentlemen, I want you to make a lot of noise for a very special person on the drums, Mr Rick Allen.' The roar that came towards us from that crowd was like a hair dryer. You could feel it, never mind hear it. How Rick didn't burst into tears, I don't know. He probably did.

RICK ALLEN: I felt so vulnerable at the prospect of having to play that gig. I've never felt so nervous in my life. I felt like a bit of a freak show. How are people going to react? Are they going to accept me? Are they going to start throwing things? It was very uncertain.

Joe introduced me and it was like taking a cork out of a bottle of champagne. The energy was overwhelming. Right there and then I felt that I had arrived at a new part of myself.

WORTH THE WAIT

Hysteria

6949 Broadway Def Leppard - Worth the Wait   ⊕ FLASH WHITE 86

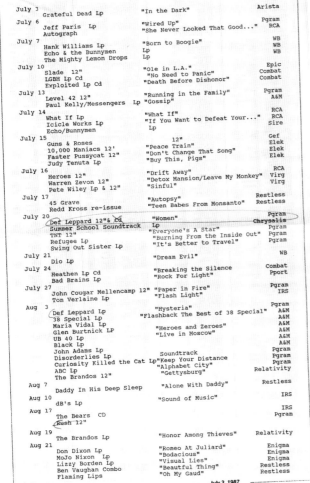

JOE ELLIOTT: Back in the studio two days after Donington, the fire in the band was insane. By the end of September 1986 we had the record pretty much finished, and by the end of the year it was ready for mixing. Like the rest of the album, this was not a quick process: Mutt spent three weeks just on 'Women'. We got together in Holland to start rehearsing the tour and the mixes were coming in thick and fast, but finally in summer 1987 people had a chance to hear what had been keeping us busy for so long.

STEVE CLARK: It's great to know we could take such a long time away and then still come out and get it back again. We definitely didn't fade away. Nobody actually put any pressure on us at all, especially the record company. They were great about it. They didn't even come into the studio and bug us or anything. They just waited until we delivered. And there wasn't any real pressure, because we wanted to make *Hysteria* totally different from *Pyromania*. We didn't want to put out second best. So we just kept on working until we got it right. What made it take so long was all the accidents and bad luck we had along the way.

JOE ELLIOTT: *Hysteria* was released on 3 August 1987. We couldn't have planned a better way to mark the tenth anniversary of the band being formed back in my bedroom in Sheffield.

PolyGram Rocks Radio
★ ★ ★ ★ ★ ★ ★ ★ ★ ★ ★ ★ ★ ★

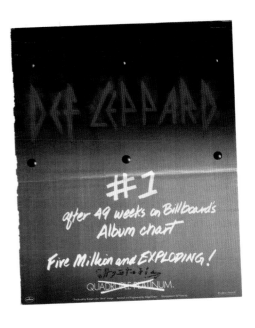

DEF ZEPPARD

87-88

JOE ELLIOTT: The British tour started at the end of August. We played places like the Edinburgh Playhouse and Sheffield City Hall before heading over to America in late September.

After the raging success of the Pyromania tour, we were maybe a little disappointed by how things were going this time round. *Hysteria* was selling OK but not spectacularly, and the ticket sales were a little soft. We were playing to 11,000 people in a 14,000-capacity arena, so the seats at the back were empty. Four years was too long a time to have been off the scene. We weren't coming back to America as conquering heroes; we were on trial again.

JOE ELLIOTT: After ploughing away in America for four and a half months, we embarked on our biggest ever tour of Europe at the beginning of March 1988. The first show was in Stockholm, where we got to see Prince play the same venue the night before us. Steve, who was the biggest ABBA fan ever, lost his lunch because he was standing next to Agnetha Fältskog in the VIP area. He couldn't get his breath. *Hysteria* by now was picking up momentum. We sold more tickets in that arena than ABBA did. The contrast with the 1983 European tour was incredible. All of a sudden we were selling out major venues like the Bercy in Paris, Wembley Arena, the NEC in Birmingham.

While we were on this insane tour in Europe, 'Pour Some Sugar on Me' was doing the business for us in America. I wouldn't say that we knew 'Sugar' was going to be a massive hit. We knew that it had a shot but, at the same time, we saw it as just one of 12 great songs on the album. It was never in contention to be the first single: 'Animal' was released first in the UK (where it became our first ever top ten hit) and 'Women' was chosen for America.

In America, we initially put 'Sugar' to rock radio and it absolutely bombed because it wasn't heavy enough. We had made a concept video in Ireland featuring 'demolition women' with sledgehammers and a wrecking ball. Then we put out a new live video shot in Denver in February 1988, which started to work well on MTV when 'Sugar' was released in the US in April.

What really broke the song, though, was that it started getting played in strip clubs in Florida and then it spread like wildfire across the nation. Requests for 'Sugar' in strip clubs turned into requests on radio. Soon it went through the roof. We were hearing that the single was top five on the Billboard chart, and then it peaked at number two.

We were absolutely flying. When we came back to the States at the end of May, the arenas were full and we had a song that you couldn't get away from on the radio. That summer we shifted four million copies of the album in the US alone; at its peak it was selling at a rate of 100,000 copies a day. When we released 'Love Bites' in July, it went to number one. We were outselling U2, Michael Jackson, Guns N' Roses ... For about six weeks we were the biggest band in the world.

HYSTERIA

153

DEF LEPPARD
Hysteria tour
HOUSE ACCESS

SUPPORT
DEF LEPPARD
ACT   GUEST
Hysteria
WORLD TOUR

ON MAY 13, 1983 WE GAVE YOU THE THIRD HIGHEST NET GROSS ON YOUR TOUR TO DATE

ON SEPTEMBER 10, 1988 YOU HAVE GIVING US OUR FASTEST SOLDOUT CONCERT TO DATE

Thank you
The Most
MS Gold Album

FASTER THAN   Come Back Soon!!
ELO

THE WHO   RUSH   AC/DC
EAGLES   VAN HALEN   BOB SEGER HEART
DOOBIE BROTHERS DAVID LEE ROTH   STYX   Mly Crue
JOURNEY   FOREIGNER   POLICE Bon Jovi

WELCOME TO LA
DEF
LEPPARD
8789 Sun

FRESCO
LEAGUE
55
Original Sportswear

PHIL COLLEN: We were on tour when 'Love Bites' went to number one on the Billboard charts, and we'd never played it as a band. I'd only ever played sections of it in the studio. I'd go and play a bridge, and then two days later I'd be playing something on the chorus. Then a few months later, we'd move studios and I'd play another section.

We had to get a rehearsal room in Vancouver for two days and work it all out. I had to learn how to sing the chorus while I was playing the guitar part, which I didn't think I'd be able to do. I practised it over and over and over again until I got it right. That particular song caught us with our trousers down.

9

Love Bites

When you make love
do you look in your mirror
who do you think of
do they look like me
do you tell lies
and say that it's forever
do you think twice
just touchin' 'n' see

When I'm with you?
do you let go
are you wild and willing
or is it just for show
ooh babe

I don't wanna touch you too much babe
'cos making love to you could drive me crazy
I know you think that love is the way you make
So I don't wanna be there when you decide to
break it

No! Love bites Love bleeds
it's bringin' me to my knees
Love lives love dies
It's no surprise
Love begs love bleeds
It's what I need.

When I'm with you
are you somewhere else
Am I gettin' thru'
or do you please yourself.
when I wake up
will you walk out
It can't be love
If you throw it about

LOVE BITES

If you've got love in you sights
watch out, love bites

When you make love, do you look in your mirror
Who do you think of, does he look like me?
Do you tell lies and say that it's forever
Do you think twice or just touch 'n' see
ooh' babe oh yeah

When you're alone do you let go
are you wild 'n' willin' or is it just for show
ooh c'mon .

I don't wanna touch you too much baby
'cos makin' love to you might drive me crazy
I know you think that love is the way you make it
So I don't wanna be there when you decide to break it
No!

Love Bites Love Bleeds - It's bringin' me to me knees
Love lives Love dies   - It's no surprise
Love Begs Love Pleads - It's what I need

When I'm with you are you somewhere else
Am I gettin' thru or do you please yourself
When you wake up will you walk out
It can't be love if you throw it about
Ooh babe

I don't wanna touch you too much baby
'cos makin' love to you might drive me crazy

Love Bite, Love Bleeds - It's bringin' me to my knees
Love Lives, Love Dies - It's no surprise
Love Begs, Love Pleads - It's what I need

I don't wanna touch you too much baby
'Cos makin' love to you might drive me crazy
I know you think that love is the way you make
So I don't wanna be here when you decide to break it
No!

Love Bites Love Bleeds - It's bringin' me to my knees
Love Lives Love Dies
Love Bites Love Bleeds - It's bringin' me to my knees
Love Lives Love Dies   - It's no surprise
Love Begs Love Pleads - It's what I need

If you've got love in your sights
watch out, love Bites

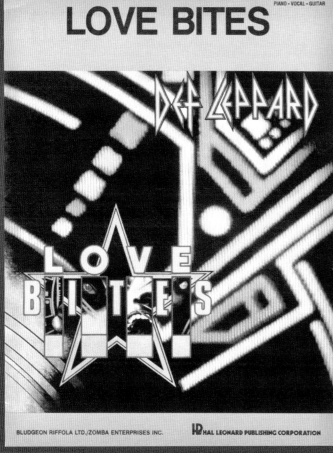

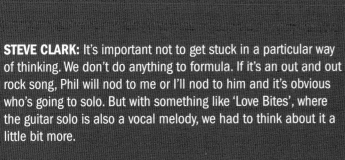

STEVE CLARK: It's important not to get stuck in a particular way of thinking. We don't do anything to formula. If it's an out and out rock song, Phil will nod to me or I'll nod to him and it's obvious who's going to solo. But with something like 'Love Bites', where the guitar solo is also a vocal melody, we had to think about it a little bit more.

JOE ELLIOTT: The 'in the round' stage setup we used for the Hysteria tour wasn't completely new but we were the first band to take it into arenas.

When we were in Holland rehearsing the tour, Peter Mensch brought along a model of the stage he had had made. It was a three-foot cube and looked a bit like a wedding cake, with little Subbuteo men for the band. The main PA was just below the stage, behind the barriers, and the lighting rig and the upper PA were hung from the ceiling. You really got the sense that this was going to be something special. All we'd ever known was playing at one end of a room to a number of people all looking in the same direction. What we were about to do was display our backsides to half of the audience for half of the show.

RICK SAVAGE: It came about from the success of the Pyromania tour and Peter Mensch was trying to think of a way to get more people in to see us. One of the obvious answers was to play in the middle of the arena, which would open up where the staging and the backstage areas usually are. So it started as a commercial venture, and then we became absolutely captivated by the artistic possibilities it gave us.

STEVE CLARK: We noticed on the last tour that it was great for the kids down the front, but for the ones in the nose bleeds at the back you're just a speck on the horizon. Putting the stage in the middle makes things much more intimate. There's four front rows, the sound's much better, and it gives everybody in the band the chance to be a front man.

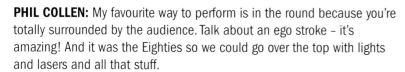

PHIL COLLEN: My favourite way to perform is in the round because you're totally surrounded by the audience. Talk about an ego stroke – it's amazing! And it was the Eighties so we could go over the top with lights and lasers and all that stuff.

JOE ELLIOTT: We had sets of backing vocal mics on opposite sides of the stage. The guys would swap sides at random – almost like dodgems. I can't count the number of times that someone would run from one side to the other and nearly smash into somebody else, but that was the fun of it.

RICK ALLEN: I think I had the best seat in the house as the whole riser would rotate. I had a T-shirt with a giant picture of my face on the back so if somebody was looking at my back, at least they were looking at a picture of my face.

JOE ELLIOTT: Before the show the stage was hidden by four giant kabuki screens with the album cover painted on them. It all added to the sense of anticipation, because everyone was waiting for this thing to erupt. As it got closer to nine o'clock the intro music would get a little louder and then, just before we went on, we would drop the kabuki.

The next part of the puzzle was how to get to the stage without being seen. We didn't really want to spend two and a half hours hiding under the stage before the gig, so we decided to smuggle ourselves in shortly before the show, in laundry baskets. The second the support band finished, we'd have roadies pushing empty laundry baskets back and forth. At first, the kids would get excited and think we were in there – but we weren't. After seeing these baskets going back and forth for a while, everyone would lose interest. And that would be when the roadies would push us through to the stage and nobody would be any the wiser.

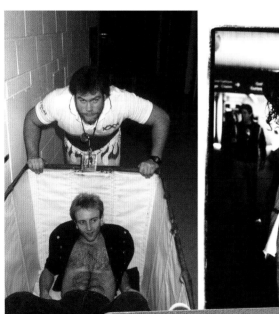

JOE ELLIOTT: Steve was completely claustrophobic so he hated it. Phil and Sav went in one basket, Steve and I were in another, and Rick went out before us disguised as a roadie. We did around 180 shows in the round on that tour and I think Rick got busted twice. Most people were looking towards the stage, so he would breeze past them and all they would see would be his back.

RICK ALLEN: I'd wear this silly brown wig, a baseball hat sitting too high on my head and I'd stuff a mannequin arm into the pocket of a crew jacket and carry a huge plastic cup in my hand. I'd wander out to the stage with the disguise on, putting the cup up to my mouth when I thought somebody caught my eye.

I remember going out one night and I got about 10 feet from the stage and somebody just said, 'Rick Allen, man!' How was that possible? It was such a good disguise. When I took my jacket off, I found a sticker on my back that said, 'I am Rick Allen.' Then I realised how it had got there: as I was leaving the dressing room Steve had come up to me and given me a big pat on the back and said, 'Hey, have a good one tonight.' He had a really wicked sense of humour.

JOE ELLIOTT: When Robert Plant came to see us in Chicago, we bet him £10 that he couldn't push Steve and me to the stage in our laundry basket without being recognised. Robert being Robert accepted the bet. He disguised himself with a pirate bandana on his head, a pair of shades, and a cushion shoved up his shirt so he looked like a big, fat roadie. As he got closer to the stage with nobody recognising him, it began to piss him off. So, he started stripping the veneer away so people would see who he was. Although he failed to stay undercover, we gave him his tenner anyway.

PHIL COLLEN: Steve was a very shy person. But put him on stage and he was like the Tasmanian Devil. He'd be running around like someone had lit a fire under his arse. It was a completely different persona.

OCTOBER • NOVEMBER 1987

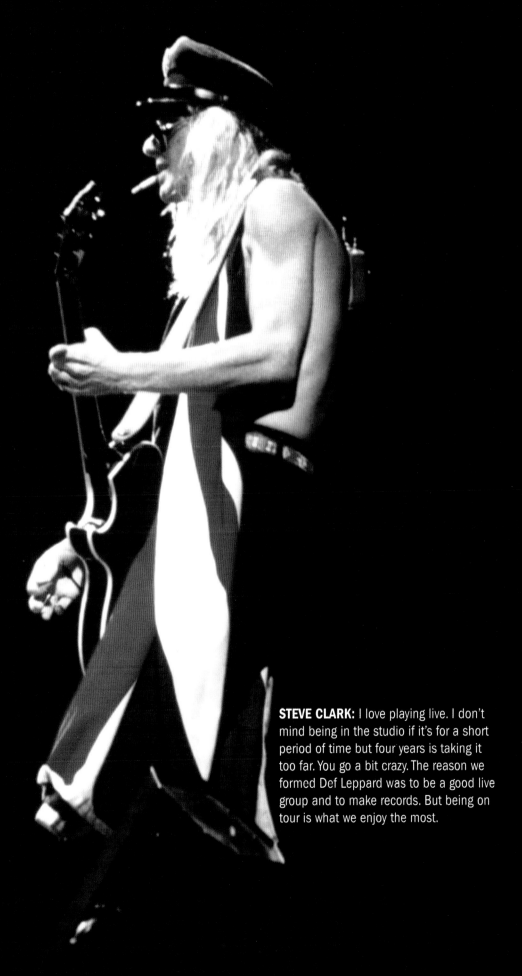

STEVE CLARK: I love playing live. I don't mind being in the studio if it's for a short period of time but four years is taking it too far. You go a bit crazy. The reason we formed Def Leppard was to be a good live group and to make records. But being on tour is what we enjoy the most.

JOE ELLIOTT: After 14 months the Hysteria tour finished at the Tacoma Dome on 27 October 1988. When we played the same venue in late 1987 before *Hysteria* had really kicked into top gear, 11,000 people came. If the capacity had been 11,000 – or even 15,000 – we would have seen that as a decent crowd, but the building held more than 25,000 people and so it looked kind of sad.

So, when we added 27 gigs to the end of the tour, I insisted that we finish at the Tacoma Dome. Everybody looked at me as if I had two heads, but I wanted to overwrite the bad memory of the last time we had been there. Anyway, lo and behold, it sold out at 27,000.

And that was Steve Clark's last gig with Def Leppard.

STEVE CLARK: You're only as good as your last record. You shouldn't take anything for granted and always keep your feet on the ground. Everything was going so smoothly after *Pyromania*, but we didn't know what fate had in store for us. You just have to be humble and accept whatever happens. Don't expect anything and don't get big-headed. That way you get a second chance sometimes.

Attn: Linda
From: Rachel

ATTN: LINDA WALKER

C D LABEL
(WITH PRODUCTION CREDITS)

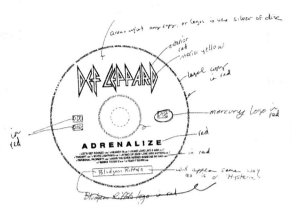

To
John Mazzacco

Here's Andie's final
CD label for UK + elsewhere
X U.S. — lettering is red + yellow
so let's keep ours red + yellow too.
(Passed a logo + LP/song titles on single
art now + all future single art. titles
will always be red re yellow me). So
forget blue + white CD label. Thanks, LW

FROM: ANDIE

TOTAL P.01

PDO   CONFIDENTIAL   Revised

15' long?

032 RED

BLACK PDO

WHITE OVERSIZE/BACK

ADRENALIZE

RICK SAVAGE: *I wanted to call the album Dementia. I liked the idea of having a trilogy of albums ending in '-ia'. Phil thought it was cool but wondered if it was a little contrived, like we were running out of good '-ia' words. Joe hated it with a passion. After two and a half hours of discussion, he was so pissed off that we were still talking about this one word that he just turned around and said, 'Well, as far as I'm concerned, you might as well call the album Bob!'*

JOE ELLIOTT: *Adrenalize got fantastic reviews and was our biggest album by a country mile in Europe. It went to number one in 23 countries and it has outsold Hysteria in Scandinavia, Germany and France by about three to one. It wasn't as big in the States, but still shifted five and a half million copies there.*

Adrenalize
Recorded: 1988–1992
Released: 31 March 1992

1) Intro Tape
2) Let's Get Rocked
3) Tear It Down
4) Women
5) Another Hit and Run
6) Too Late For Love
7) Hysteria
8) Make Love Like a Man
9) Phil Collen Solo

JOE ELLIOTT: Everybody went home to get over the tour and prepare for the next record. Phil was living in America now, Sav and I were in Ireland and Steve was in London, so we weren't the same band that had rented a house together in Dublin to record *Hysteria*.

The fact that we were living in different places didn't really hinder us, though. This was the beginning of a whole new way of working. People were starting to write songs on their own. Phil would write a track and then say, 'Have you got any words for this?', the way most bands do. We just weren't doing it in the same room. The band broke down into sub-groups, if you like. Phil and Steve used to go to Mutt's house in Guildford to work on songs; in Dublin Sav and I made some 16-track recordings. Sav came up with 'Tonight' and we wrote 'When Love & Hate Collide' together (although this wasn't released until 1995). The whole group would assemble now and again to share what we'd been getting up to and through this process we ended up with seven new songs for *Adrenalize*. Another track was going to be a re-recording of 'Tear It Down', a B side of one of the *Hysteria* singles which had had a lot of airplay in America.

Most of my focus and energy, though, was going into building a studio at my house in Dublin. I figured that we could get together to write there and we wouldn't be paying someone else five grand a week for the privilege. We could treat the studio like a rehearsal room and if we happened to come up with something good, we'd have it on tape. It really would be the best of both worlds.

ːruary 15 - 28

ˌck Allen returns to Holland Wednesday and begins the search for a 24 trk Mid
pe studio utilizing all of his friends and anyone else who is in Holland Sʰi
                                                                            1

ˌe Elliott returns to Holland and begins singing Tear it Down.

ˌst of band returns throughout the weekend or whatever with a view toward working
ˌ the remaining 5 tracks in a compositional sense (Touch,Slow E, Emotion, BLJ
ˌd the Clark/Elliott song.

ˌey all continue to work and use Wisseloord until the Mutt day(s).

ˌ will be asking Bart to get rid of the studio time working backwards from March 13
ˌith a view towards keeping the studio through Monday Feb 27.

ˌtch

ˌirst week of March various and sundry members go to Mutt's house to play and
ˌork on as many songs as we need to and Mutt will let us.

ˌhe rest of the month is off provided we get rid of the studio time which we should
ˌse somehow for something, *if we Con't*

ˌpril

ˌe start Monday April 10 in the Dutch 24 trk demo studio. When you find the studio
ˌou should discuss amongst yourselves and decide how many weeks we will use to get the
ˌcmaining 5 songs recordable. Assuming 5 weeks, we end this time on Sunday May 14.

ˌlark, Collen and maybe Savage (Check this with Shipley) as well as Shipley and Woodruff
ˌtake a week off and then begin tracking gtrs/basses/backing vocals in Toronto for the
ˌnext 3 weeks with a week on hold. The starting date will be :

May
The Canadian studio starts on Monday May 22 and goes for 3-4 weeks through June 18
(shouˌd we use all 4 weeks)

June

Shipley and the tapes go to Dublin and begin doing vocals with the singer as soon as
he can. Let's call it mid-week starting on June 21 for vocals. Joe is to stay in contact
with the rest of the band and decide when to book his vocal time. Joe should talk to
Shipley about the studio as I gather that Mike has some thoughts about dealing with too
many studios.

Then after this is all done, we see how well the system works. The only catch I can see
is what happens if Joe's voice is screwed and there is nothing else to do with the vocal
studio time. ANy thoughts? or do you all have the answer?
IT IS IMPORTANT FOR EVEYONE TO Rˌˌ THIS AND DISCUSS THAT I KNOW WHAT TYPE OF STUDIOS TO BOOK
AND WHERE. ALSO MAKE SURE THAT MIKE AGREES WITH THE STUDIOS YOU WANT. WHAT KIND OF STUDIO
IN TORONTO FOR THE 4 WEEKS AND IF IT IS OK TO DO VOCALS IN EIREAND WHERE, ˌˌ

sorry about the typos - p'gram typewriters stink.

JOE ELLIOTT: During that whole period, it became blatantly obvious that Steve wasn't in good shape. His drinking was nothing new, but previously he had always managed to bounce back. That was no longer the case; he went in and out of rehab three or four times in 1989 and 1990.

As part of Steve's therapy, we all flew out to his treatment centre in America, including Mutt. We each had to write a letter to him and then read it out while everyone else was sitting listening. It felt like we were being sent back to school.

We were all in tears listening to each other's eulogies. Talk about group therapy! Yet the one person in the group who didn't seem affected was Steve himself. He was so far away from understanding what the problem was. It was so frustrating; you wanted him to burst into tears and say sorry, but instead he said, 'Oh. Yeah, I guess it's a bit of a problem.' The understatement of the century.

We didn't know how to handle it. The rest of us, other than Phil, still drank, so how could we tell Steve not to? Our argument was, 'But we don't get fucked up like you do. We have a couple of beers and then go to bed. You drink until 6 a.m. and open a bottle of whiskey for breakfast.'

RICK SAVAGE: Steve would begin to hate the things he loved most because he felt tied to them. He was always the one who wanted to get out of the studio and on the road. But when we were in Glens Falls, New York, rehearsing for the big American tour, the one that he'd always wanted, he tried to smash his hand in the bathroom of his hotel room because he didn't want to do it.

JOE ELLIOTT: Steve's problems definitely interfered with the making of *Adrenalize*. We'd gone through it with Rick and his accident and now we were going through it with Steve and his drinking. We decided to give him six months off from the band to try to get himself together.

RICK ALLEN: I was facing my own problems with drugs and alcohol. Whenever I tried to talk to Steve about his situation, he'd come back at me with 'What about you?' I found it difficult to get through that barrier. The last thing I wanted to say to him was, 'I lost my arm. I got through all that. I conquered it.' Because I wouldn't have been honest. At that time I don't think I really had conquered it. I found out about Steve a bit too late to help him in the way he deserved.

PHIL COLLEN: We were in England discussing the forthcoming album, *Adrenalize*, and we got a phone call. Steve was in Minneapolis and had passed out, foaming at the mouth. He'd drunk six quadruple brandies in half an hour, then fallen over and now they were taking him to hospital. When we went to the facility, they explained that Steve had reached a point of extreme alcoholism and what that could mean for him. If he fell off the wagon there was a good chance he would die – and people with alcoholism literally die from falling over. Steve was on painkillers when he died, as he had fallen off a pavement and cracked a rib. His girlfriend at the time wasn't helping because she was a former addict, and they were taking all sorts of shit along with the drinking.

We treated Steve the same way we had treated Rick when he had his accident. We told him to take some time off to get himself well and we would take care of the rest. Rick used his time to relearn the drums, but Steve didn't have that kind of goal. It was just free time. So, he and his girlfriend would get fucked up and it just got worse and worse. He was in and out of rehab.

You think about what you could have done differently. I remember wondering whether I should put Steve up in my spare room and keep an eye on him. But he was a grown man with his own girlfriend. I couldn't say, 'You're living with me now.' Maybe I should have done ...

RICK SAVAGE: It really drives you mad to the point of desperation, because he was such a nice person. We tried to protect him and look after him. It was only after he died that I realised how much energy we spent worrying about him. I understood what it must be like to be married to an alcoholic, to have that co-dependency. It consumes everything you do.

Steve Clark, guitarist for Def Leppard, dead

By TIMOTHY McDARRAH

The guitarist for the British heavy-metal rock band Def Leppard was found dead yesterday in his London home, police there said.

Steve Clark, 30, was found by his girlfriend on the living room floor of his fashionable Chelsea district apartment.

CLARK

There were no obvious injuries and no suspicion of foul play, Scotland Yard reported. An autopsy was conducted last night, but results were not immediately available.

The band has been riddled with personal and professional tragedies before.

> **There were no obvious injuries and no suspicion of foul play.**

In the four years following its "Pyromania" album — which sold 8 million copies — the group suffered several setbacks that might have ended the careers of less determined musicians.

Just after "Pyromania" album was released, a knee injury sidelined the group's producer, Robert "Mutt" Lange. And the band's lead singer, Joe Elliot, mysteriously lost his voice for several months before regaining it.

Then, drummer Rick Allen lost his left arm in a car accident. But with Clark leading the way, the band played on.

Allen augmented his drumming with a sophisticted computer system that he operated with his feet as well as his arm.

The band's next album, "Hysteria," hit the top of the U.S. charts in 1988 after spending 49 weeks on the Billboard charts.

The popular quintet started out in a garage in Sheffield, in northern England, in the mid-1970s. They got a record contract from Polygram in 1979. Their debut album in 1980, "On Through the Night," launched their career on the back of the hit teen anthem, "Rock Brigade."

Ten years and six albums later, a 1989 survey said the band was reputed to earn $28 million a year.

Alcohol-and-drugs binge killed rocker

LONDON (AP) — Steve Clark, guitarist with the heavy metal band Def Leppard, died of a lethal combination of alcohol and drugs after a night of heavy drinking, a London coroner ruled yesterday.

Westminster Coroner Paul Knapp said Clark "was a very heavy drinker who seemingly had abused drugs and regrettably paid the final price."

The 30-year-old guitarist was found dead the morning of Jan. 8 at his London home.

Daniel Van Alphen, Clark's drinking companion the night before, testified that the two went to the local pub and returned to the guitarist's home at midnight to watch a video.

Van Alphen said Clark drank a triple vodka, a quadruple vodka and a double brandy within 30 minutes. When Clark passed out on the couch, Van Alphen said he left.

Clark, who reportedly earned $28 million a year according to a 1989 American survey, was found dead in his home in London's upscale Chelsea neighborhood by his girlfriend Janie Dean.

Dr. Iain West, the pathologist

STEVE CLARK
Def Leppard guitarist.

who performed the autopsy, testified that Clark's blood alcohol level was three times the British legal driving limit and an antidepressant drug and a painkiller were both found at levels exceeding normal therapeutic doses. He said valium was detected at normal levels.

GUITARIST DIES: Steve Clark, 30-year-old guitarist for the heavy metal rock group Def Leppard, was found dead at his London home Tuesday. There were no obvious injuries or signs of foul play. An autopsy will be conducted today, Scotland Yard says. "He was the master of riffs; he wrote some of the best we've ever done," said lead singer Joe Elliott. Tragedy isn't new to the band. Drummer Rick Allen lost his left arm in a 1984 New Year's Eve car accident. The band rebounded with 1987's *Hysteria*, one of the most popular heavy metal albums ever, selling more than 9.5 million copies.

RICK ALLEN: Steve was such a beautiful person. It's just so sad that he didn't make it through a difficult part of his life. Even though he's not here physically, he's definitely here in spirit and inspires us to be better.

We were all so young when we started out and we spent so much time with each other that we literally grew up together. You think people are going to be around forever, and they're not. It's the illusion of permanence.

RICK SAVAGE: I remember the first time I met Steve just being in awe of his style and his image. He looked like we all wanted to look like back in the day, and he carried that through pretty much all of his life. I would say he wore his guitar just as well as he played it.

JOE ELLIOTT: Everything about him was rock star. Way more than the rest of us were.

TOUR STAFF

NO MORE HAMPER!

ACCESS ALL AREAS

RICK SAVAGE: Steve was a very gentle soul, easily influenced by both the good and the bad in this world.

RICK ALLEN: All my memories of Steve are good ones. He had a beautiful sense of friendship and love. I really enjoyed being around Steve. He was always very encouraging. If he came up with any new riffs, he would always play them to me and refer to John Bonham. It felt as though he wanted to really include me in the process. I'm forever grateful for him being that person.

VIVIAN CAMPBELL: I met Steve very briefly. All I know about him is through his music and through the records and videos. Steve had very melodic solos that weren't blisteringly technical, but they fitted the song perfectly.

PHIL COLLEN: Every riff had almost a lyrical meaning to it, with both melodic and rhythmic value. It wasn't just some guy playing guitar, it was so much deeper.

A note from Steve

JOE ELLIOTT: After getting over the initial shock of Steve's passing, we had some serious issues to confront. First, were we even going to continue as a band? Perhaps in the immediate aftermath we wondered whether we wanted to carry on – that's a natural emotional reaction to such a devastating event. But I don't think I ever really felt we would break up, because we were so deep into the album and, besides, Def Leppard was our livelihood.

RICK SAVAGE: At one time or another everyone in the band has said, 'This is nonsense. It isn't worth it. I'm leaving.' The one thing we're fortunate about is that no two or more members have said it at the same time.

JOE ELLIOTT: The next question was how were we going to finish the record? Well, that decision came pretty quickly. We were going to do it as a four piece. We had already been working on the album as a four piece while Steve was on his break, leaving gaps for him to fill when he came back. We certainly weren't going to start looking for another guitarist. It was too soon to be thinking about that.

PHIL COLLEN: We just got on with it. And that was something we learned from Rick's accident – not to dwell on it, not to get depressed about it. Of course, Rick had a great attitude: 'OK, no left arm. So what? I've still got a left foot.' We used that as a yardstick and carried on.

JOE ELLIOTT: We made a feeble attempt to carry on making the album while we were still mourning, but it was horrible. Although we were finishing *Adrenalize* as a four piece we still wanted to sound like a five piece, which meant double guitar duties for Phil. He had to play the parts of the ghost of Steve Clark, his best friend. Not an easy task.

What made things even stranger was that it was actually a very uplifting album. The songs, which had mostly been written before Steve died, had a feel-good theme to them, yet we were feeling really bad. But we just ploughed on, doing what we had to do to get the record done.

PHIL COLLEN: The time we spent making *Adrenalize* was the worst case of déjà vu. I remember sitting in this room for 15 hours, playing this one guitar riff over and over again. The other guys just stood outside. They thought I was mad.

RICK SAVAGE: I'm sure when we spent two and a half years in the studio, people thought we must have done a couple of hours a day and taken weeks off. But when we did *Adrenalize* there was one of us in the studio every day for 12 hours a day. We only took weekends off.

When we went in to record *Pyromania*, in April 1982, I was 21. I was 31 when we finished *Adrenalize*. I basically missed my twenties.

Concept art for the animated Flynn character in the 'Let's Get Rocked' video

ADRENALIZE

DEF LEPPARD

"LET'S GET ROCKED"

PRELIGHT

TUESDAY, JANUARY 21 1992

SHOOT DAYS

WEDNESDAY, JANUARY 22 1992
THURSDAY, JANUARY 23 1992

Hollywood
6904 Lexington Avenue Los Angeles California 90038 (213) 464 3808 Fax (213) 464 3709
London
3 Bramley Road London W10 5HB (071) 255 3939 Fax (071) 436 4334
Video: 32 D'Arblay Street London W1V 3FH (071) 439 0467 Fax (071) 437 2055

JOE ELLIOTT: 'White Lightning' was one of two songs on the album that we wrote after Steve's death to give ourselves a kick up the backside. The title was a reference to Steve, who used to wear a white suit on stage and run around like a loony. It was written as a tribute to Steve, but we kept it slightly vague. The idea was that the song could be about anybody with an addiction to the 'sweetness' of the world, whatever form that might take.

Working on that song was very draining so, as a counterbalance, every day around dinner time we'd plonk ourselves in front of the TV and watch *The Simpsons*. We fell in love with Bart, seeing him as the kind of cheeky, anti-establishment kid that we had all been once. It wasn't a deliberate psychological plan, but it did help to lighten our mood. I think it was being in that frame of mind that enabled us to write 'Let's Get Rocked', a song that was the polar opposite of 'White Lightning'. It was our take on Prince's 'Let's Go Crazy', with a funky, glam groove, silly lyrics, and me taking on the character of an 'average, ordinary, everyday kid'.

So, that gave us the ten songs we needed for the album. We always thought that *Hysteria* was two songs too long. It worked out fine in the end, of course, but we weren't going to do it again. We should have held back 'Love and Affection' for *Adrenalize*. Then we could have released the album in 1990, rather than two years later when we were going head-to-head with Nirvana, and it would have been a massive hit – maybe even bigger than *Hysteria*.

KODAK 5054 TMZ   KODAK 5054 TMZ   KODAK 5054 TMZ   KODAK 5054 TMZ   KODAK 5054 TMZ   KODAK 5054 TMZ

KODAK 5054 TMZ   KODAK 5054 TMZ   KODAK 5054 TMZ   KODAK 5054 TMZ   KODAK 5054 TMZ   KODAK 5054 TMZ

JOE ELLIOTT: We always knew that eventually we were going to have to find another guitarist, as a lot of our songs don't work with one guitarist. But we didn't start looking properly until early 1992, a year after Steve died, when we were preparing to take *Adrenalize* out on the road. It wasn't a case of replacing him, it was finding someone to become the fifth member of the band.

The first time I properly met Vivian Campbell was in about 1990, at the house of my son's godfather, the band's promoter, Denis Desmond, who lives in Dublin about 15 minutes from me. He'd invited Vivian down from Belfast, who was there visiting his folks having come over from his home in LA. I went round and we hung out, played pool and just shot the shit about the state of the music industry, football and God knows what else.

VIVIAN CAMPBELL: Joe was actually the only one that I knew prior to joining the band. We had a lot of mutual friends in Dublin, so every time I was in town I'd see him. And when Joe came to LA, I was his football connection – he'd call me to get a pickup game on a Sunday morning. So, we knew each other socially but we'd never played music together – although obviously he knew I could play guitar. He knew I'd been in Dio and Whitesnake and Riverdogs.

JOE ELLIOTT: When we started talking about people that might work I brought up Vivian, but we also talked about John Sykes, who'd originally come to everybody's attention in Tygers of Pan Tang and then he'd joined Thin Lizzy followed by Whitesnake.

John came over to Dublin to work with us over a long weekend. He didn't do any guitars – we already knew he could play – but he added some backing vocals on a song called 'Heaven Is' off *Adrenalize*, which showed us what a great singer he was.

Halfway through his visit, we all disappeared over to Sheffield for the wedding of our tour manager, Malvin Mortimer, and left John at the studio with Mike Shipley, the producer of the album. When we got back, Mike was very quiet. He said, 'Get this guy out of here. He keeps suggesting all these changes. It's like he's trying to take over the project.' So, we thanked him very much and that was that.

We didn't really consider anybody else until we got to Mates rehearsal rooms in Los Angeles. There were three people on our shortlist: Adrian Smith, who had left Iron Maiden two years previously; a young kid from Birmingham called Huwey Lucas; and, at my suggestion, Vivian.

VIVIAN CAMPBELL: Joe called me up and said that he was coming over to LA with the band. He explained that they'd finished the *Adrenalize* record with just Phil playing guitar, but that for the tour they wanted to get another guitar player so they could go back to being a five-piece band. He said, 'I put your name forward. We're talking to a couple of other guys, but I think you're the guy for the band.' I immediately agreed with him. I said, 'Yes, I am totally the guy for the band.'

I knew that Joe was a real salt of the earth, friendly, easy-going guy. And he knew me and he thought that I'd fit in, but the other guys didn't know me and I didn't know them. In the back of my mind, there was a part of me that was thinking, 'I've been in Dio, I've gotten fired. I've been in Whitesnake, I've gotten fired …'

JOE ELLIOTT: Adrian, Huwey and Vivian were all fine musicians. We played with each of them and then chewed over our decision for a few days. We came to the conclusion that, much as we really liked Adrian, there was something about his playing that just wasn't right for our sound.

So, then it went to the wire between Huwey and Vivian. We had one of those classic band meetings where we went around for hours upon hours.

RICK SAVAGE: We've had some band meetings on far more trivial matters that have gone on forever, to the point where I mentally will just leave the meeting. I'll sit back and let my mind wander and when I come back they're still talking about the same thing.

JOE ELLIOTT: It ended up on a swing vote, which was Sav. He spent about 20 minutes talking about how great Huwey was before uttering the immortal word, 'but …', at which point I jumped in and said, 'Oh, oh, oh! I think Vivian and here's why …' And I reeled off all my reasons. Then everybody else said, 'OK, fine.'

It came down to singing ability. Huwey was a great player but his voice was not quite strong enough. Vivian could really belt it out.

VIVIAN CAMPBELL: What they didn't know was that I'd been working on my vocals for years. Even back when I was with Dio, I wanted to sing because I always admired singers. I'd be listening to Ronnie Dio thinking, 'Wow, this guy could sing the phone book.' I asked Ronnie if I could sing background vocals, but he refused. He said, 'Ritchie Blackmore didn't sing. Tony Iommi didn't sing. You're not singing.' Ronnie was always laying down the law like that. But then, when I was with Whitesnake, David Coverdale was really encouraging of my singing. He gave me lots of tips and fixed me up with his vocal coach, which really worked for me.

So, when I went into the rehearsal room to play with Def Leppard for the first time, they were all pretty surprised that I could sing as strongly as I could. They knew I could play guitar, but this was a little something extra.

It was less like an audition and more like a courtship. We hung out and got to know each other. Leppard is such a unique band that it wasn't just about playing or singing or songwriting, it really had to be a personality fit. And, for me, after many bad experiences with bands, I wanted to make sure that this was somewhere I could really have a home.

174

VIVIAN CAMPBELL: Seeing Marc Bolan on *Top of the Pops* one night in 1971 was what set me on my path (I later found out that it was the same for Joe). I grew my hair and kept pestering my folks for a guitar, until eventually my dad brought home a ukulele. That led to an acoustic guitar and then some cheap electric thing.

After Bolan, Rory Gallagher was my next big influence. His 1972 album *Live! In Europe* was the first album I owned and he was the first person I saw live (but then nobody else really came to Belfast in the Seventies). By then I was beginning to figure stuff out on my electric guitar – I'm self-taught.

Even though I didn't grow up in the same area as the rest of the guys in the band, we all grew up in the same era and fed on the same musical diet: *Top of the Pops*, Alan Freeman, *The Friday Rock Show*, *Sounds*, *NME*, *Kerrang!* While we actually have very different musical influences, there are still certain areas where our tastes overlap. I think that's what makes it possible for us to work together.

When I was in my first band, Sweet Savage, back in Belfast in 1979/1980, I used to read all about Def Leppard. I heard them when they first got played on John Peel's show on Radio 1. As a band that had made it, Leppard were our idols and we wanted to learn from the steps that they had taken. I always thought that they were head and shoulders above every other hard rock band in terms of songwriting and ambition and vocal prowess. Right from the start, I was a huge fan.

That's why when Joe called me and said I'd be perfect for Def Leppard, I was so quick to agree with him.

JOE ELLIOTT: We rehearsed with Vivian at Mates for quite a while and then went over to Dublin and carried on at the Factory, which was the go-to place for everybody from Hothouse Flowers to U2. He didn't take too long to learn the songs, because he'd already been playing along with the records.

VIVIAN CAMPBELL: I most definitely noticed from day one that the work ethic within Def Leppard was ingrained into every single aspect of what the band does. While we don't take ourselves seriously, we do take our work very seriously.

JOE ELLIOTT: The myth is that Vivian's first gig with us was the Freddie Mercury Tribute Concert, but it was actually the Wednesday before at McGonagle's in Dublin, a tiny little club gig with about 300 people. We hadn't played live since October 1988 and it was now April 1992, so we needed a warm-up.

After McGonagle's, we flew over to London and rehearsed with Queen in studios in Ascot. I was going to be doing 'Tie Your Mother Down' with Queen – Brian May singing the first verse, me singing the rest of it – and we were all going to be performing 'Now I'm Here' with Brian.

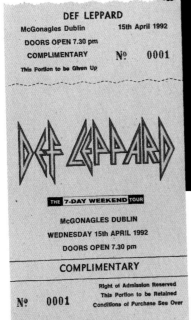

VIVIAN CAMPBELL: I didn't actually find it that intimidating to make my full debut at such a big show. For me, the bigger the gig the easier it is to do. When you play at a small venue, people are right in front of you and you can see the whites of their eyes. Now, that's really intimidating. I was used to being in big bands and playing big world tours. Plus, I was used to stepping into different situations and working with new people.

I can't say for sure, but I think the other four guys were actually more nervous than I was. For the first time ever, they were looking to their right and seeing someone who wasn't Steve Clark. And it was a hectic sort of a show. We only did four songs and there was a big technical issue with Rick's kit and the show was going out live to a billion people around the world. So, there wasn't a lot of margin for error.

JOE ELLIOTT: The immediate lead up to our set was terrifying because you don't get a proper soundcheck when there are 90,000 people already in the venue. Because of union rules, we weren't even allowed to have our guy plug in Rick's electronic drum kit. When he came to hit his pedals, he found out that some things had been plugged in backwards and upside down. He'd hit his bass drum pedal and get a snare sound and vice versa. This all happened 45 seconds before we were due to start playing. So, then there was some insane speed-merchant, off-the-fly reconfiguration of his kit. We got it right just in time.

There were so many highlights that day. From a selfish point of view, the best moment of my career took place during that gig when I sang backing vocals with Phil on 'All the Young Dudes', which was performed by Queen, David Bowie, Mick Ronson and Ian Hunter. That was my entire childhood in four minutes up there.

I only realised it recently, but I was the first person to sing with Queen after Fred died, as 'Tie Your Mother Down' was the opening song of their set. Another immense highlight was being introduced by Roger Taylor, somebody who had been a hero of ours since we were kids: 'They're number one all over the world and they're British, please welcome Def Leppard.'

Right: Joe Elliott rehearsing with Queen for the Freddie Mercury Tribute Concert

THE
FREDDIE MERCURY
TRIBUTE

CONCERT FOR AIDS AWARENESS

ARTIST
3

Freddie Mercury Tribute Concert
Wembley Stadium, 20 April 1992

Above: Backstage with Mick Ronson

JOE ELLIOTT: The sights and sounds that we saw and heard backstage were quite extraordinary. Elton John came storming into our dressing room and said, 'Who the fuck does bloody Axl Rose think he is? I'm supposed to be doing a duet with him in four hours, but the security guard keeps saying he's asleep. I said, "Fucking well wake him up then." He said, "I can't do that."' He was not a happy bunny.

Also backstage was Mick Ronson, who was fighting liver cancer but brave and strong enough to come and give what would be his last major live performance. He was in good spirits, but he was very gaunt and spent half the time asleep on a couch. He died a year later.

You'd see people and nod; you wouldn't have to be great fans of each other, but there was a mutual appreciation society backstage. You'd bump into Elizabeth Taylor coming out of the bathroom and then be interviewed by Cindy Crawford for MTV. It was pure theatre, which totally suited what the day was all about.

I didn't see much of the concert until the encore, when we all got up for 'We Are the Champions'. Liza Minnelli was doing her thing and we were all ushered on to the stage, trying to hide in the background because we didn't want to make a fuss. Somehow, we ended up close to Brian. As the last note sounded and he started to walk off like he would at any other gig, I grabbed hold of him and shouted, 'Brian! Stop! Turn around and have a good look at this. You'll never see the likes of this again. Soak it up.' Luckily it turned out I was full of shit, because Queen have done a ton of massive gigs since then.

There was a big do somewhere afterwards. I remember talking to John Deacon. He was a lovely guy and had plenty of time for me; he didn't try to fob me off so he could go and talk to somebody more famous. The funny thing was that day I was wearing a jacket over a T-shirt of a woman diving into a swimming pool. Well, it was John Deacon's shirt. At Queen's Slane Castle gig in 1986 I was wearing my legendary T-shirt with the 'Freddie Starr Ate My Hamster' headline from the *Sun*. Deacon saw it and said, 'I've got to have that T-shirt. I'll give you mine if you give me yours.' I said, 'Deal.' So, during rehearsals for the Freddie Mercury gig, I thought it would be fun for me to wear his T-shirt. I bounded on to the rehearsal stage with my back to him and then spun around and stood in front of him with my arms out going, 'Ta-da!' He looked at me with a 'Holy shit! That's my shirt' kind of expression on his face. I ended up wearing it at the actual gig – probably a joke agreement between the two of us! That was another great memory, one of a lifetime's worth we made that day.

RECORDED LIVE ON MAY 29,
1992 in Bonn Germany

1. Hysteria
   (Clark/Collen/Elliott/Lange/Savage)
2. .Photograph
   (Clark/ willis/Savage /.Elliott/Lange)
3. Pour SOme Sugar On Me
   (Clark/coll en/ Elliott/Lange/savage)
4. Let's Get roc ked
   (Collen/elliot/Lange/ savage)

NO OVERDUBS!
NO REMIXES
NO BULLSHIT!

studio/ mixdown an d produc tion
mobile engineer : Pete woodroffe/ Pete woodroffe

BLUDGEON RIFFOLA

℗ 1993 PHONOGRAM LTD (LONDON). ALL RIGHTS RESERVED.
UNAUTHORISED COPYING, REPRODUCTION, HIRING, LENDING, PUBLIC
PERFORMANCE AND BROADCASTING PROHIBITED.
© 1993 BLUDGEON RIFFOLA LTD
Manufactured and Distributed by Nippon Phonogram Co., Ltd, Tokyo. Made in Japan. JASRAC.
PHCR-16002

🔵 COMPACT
disc
DIGITAL AUDIO

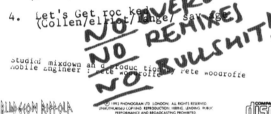

JOE ELLIOTT: The day after the Freddie Mercury concert, we flew to Ibiza for a month to rehearse for the Adrenalize tour.

We got a really good deal for a rehearsal space in a closed-down nightclub owned by Phil Carson, the head of Atlantic Records in London, and then we paid a homeless guy to sleep in there overnight so nobody would break in and steal our gear. It didn't occur to us that he might steal the gear himself, but fortunately he didn't.

When Vivian joined Def Leppard, one of the most important things he brought to the band was a vocals culture. He told us that we should meet his voice coach, Roger Love. I was reluctant at first because I don't like suddenly changing the way I do things. But then Vivian explained that Roger didn't teach you to sing, he taught you not to lose your voice. That caught my interest.

When you're headlining you're doing up to six gigs a week at 90 minutes or more and there isn't enough recovery time. The older you get, the more you feel it. I'd lost my voice many times on tour through not warming up properly. This was going to be another long tour and we needed all the help we could get to strengthen us up.

So, Roger came out to Ibiza and gave us individual half-hour singing sessions in the mornings before we went down to the rehearsal room. It made an enormous difference. After one of my very first sessions with him, I started singing 'Photograph' and managed to hit all the high notes at the end. I remember our sound engineer peeping his head around from behind the monitors and saying, 'Fucking hell, is that really you, Joe?'

JOE ELLIOTT: First we did a few club dates in Europe as a warm-up for the main part of the tour. At the show in Bonn, Germany we recorded the four tracks that featured on a little bonus EP that came with certain releases of *Adrenalize*. We called the EP *In the Clubs, In Your Face*, referring back to our *In the Round, In Your Face* live video from 1989.

I remember one of the shows in Germany where, literally seconds after we'd come off stage, Rudolf Schenker of the Scorpions burst into our dressing room, nearly kicking the door off its hinges. 'What's happened to your voice?' he asked me. 'It's amazing. Who did this for you?' And so we hooked the Scorps up with Roger.

What Roger also did was make cassettes of warm-up routines tailored for each band member. Everybody would go to a different corner of the dressing room with headphones on and do their warm-ups. But that became impractical, so eventually they all started joining in with mine because it was close enough to theirs.

We'd put my tape on and all four of us (Rick didn't sing) would be wandering around the dressing room, shaving, drying hair, deciding what to wear, but 'gugging', as we call it, at the same time. So, 'gug, gug, gug, gug, gug, gug, gug' – putting the 'guh', the hard 'g', on the front of a phrase stretches your vocal cords more than, say, 'jug'. The soft vowels are important, but it's the hard ones that really kick the phlegm off everything. We've been doing it ever since.

We can't thank Vivian enough for bringing Roger on board. In my opinion, this guy is the best there is, an absolute genius. There's no way on earth I'd want to work with anybody else.

DAILY ITINERARY

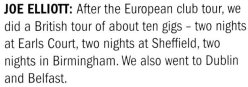

THURSDAY	JULY 9	Def Leppard arrive in Perth
FRIDAY	JULY 10	Pre - Rig Day
SATURDAY	JULY 11	PERTH ENTERTAINMENT CENTRE
SUNDAY	JULY 12	Travel Perth / Adelaide
MONDAY	JULY 13	Pre - Rig Day
TUESDAY	JULY 14	ADELAIDE - ENTERTAINMENT CENTRE
WEDNESDAY	JULY 15	Travel Adelaide / Brisbane
THURSDAY	JULY 16	Pre - Rig day
FRIDAY	JULY 17	BRISBANE - ENTERTAINMENT CENTRE
SATURDAY	JULY 18	Travel Brisbane / Melbourne
SUNDAY	JULY 19	MELBOURNE - FLINDERS PARK
MONDAY	JULY 20	MELBOURNE - FLINDERS PARK
TUESDAY	JULY 21	Travel Melbourne / Sydney
WEDNESDAY	JULY 22	SYDNEY - ENTERTAINMENT CENTRE
THURSDAY	JULY 23	SYDNEY - ENTERTAINMENT CENTRE
FRIDAY	JULY 24	N.Z. Tour Party Travel Sydney / Auckland
		Remainder of Crew Party Travel Sydney / Home
SATURDAY	JULY 25	AUCKLAND - THE SUPERTOP
SUNDAY	JULY 26	AUCKLAND - THE SUPERTOP
MONDAY	JULY 27	Band Travel Auckland / Tokyo
		Remainder of Crew Travel Auckland / Home

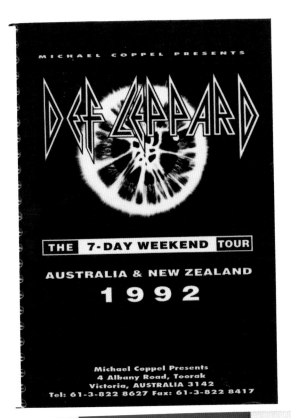

JOE ELLIOTT: After the European club tour, we did a British tour of about ten gigs – two nights at Earls Court, two nights at Sheffield, two nights in Birmingham. We also went to Dublin and Belfast.

Then we went to Australia in July. We had been supposed to go to there for some standalone dates in 1989, because *Hysteria* had taken longer to catch on in Australia: it took two years to get to number one. But by that point we were already busy doing *Adrenalize*, so we had to say no. Going down there first thing after Britain just seemed like the right thing to do having lost the opportunity three years previously.

I don't know if it was a mix of only just waking up and having drunk too much at altitude, but when our tour manager, Malvin, got us off the plane after the 18-hour flight and put us on the bus he left Vivian at the airport. When we finally realised and went back to get him, Vivian didn't throw a wobbly. He was just like, 'Yeah, yeah, I get it. I'm the new guy.'

We did two nights everywhere, and the ticket sales were really good. We did the rounds of the great music TV shows they have down there, like Molly Meldrum and all that crowd. Australia was great.

NEC, Birmingham
29 June 1992

How to get fired from the
DEF LEPPARD CREW?

1. Show up @ 3:00 pm
2. ~~Not load truck~~
3. Show up @ 4:00 pm
4. Miss the gig
5. ~~Flush plane ticket down toilet~~
6. ~~Rent red convertible mustang on corporate band credit card~~ (priceless)
7. Miss ~~lobby call repeatedly~~
8. Punch drummer @ ~~airport~~
9. ~~Show up @ 5:00 pm~~
10. ~~Get speeding ticket in said above convertible~~
11. Bus driving with hot flashes
12. Heroin addiction
13. ~~Miss bus call repeatedly~~
14. ~~Not show up for rehearsals~~
15. Urinate in blender
16. Substitute "Joh!" for "Umpta-Gifenta-Glompta"

SCHLEP WITH LEP FLORIDA TOUR JAN FEB 93 UNLIMITED MILEAGE ALLOWANCE

JOE ELLIOTT: In August 1992 we went over to America, starting with a charity show at Madison Square Garden with Bryan Adams and Richard Marx, our first US gig since the Tacoma Dome in October 1988. After that, we were off doing our tour of the States. To begin with, it wasn't as successful as we'd hoped. We couldn't understand why, because the album had spent five weeks at number one. But we were used to our US tours starting slowly.

RICK SAVAGE: Our set list went as far back as 1981. We always played one song off *High 'n' Dry* but mostly it was made up of *Hysteria*, *Pyromania* and probably four or five songs off *Adrenalize*.

We were bringing new singles out as we went along so they were the obvious ones to add in, but there was a limit to the number of songs we could play. It was a high-energy rock show, so we couldn't really go much beyond two and a half hours. We tried to keep a fair balance of the old favourites, new songs and nostalgic songs that were never big hits but people still liked to hear.

VIVIAN CAMPBELL: Our music is very high energy, which requires a high-energy performance from us to go along with that. We're not like the Eagles, we don't just sit up there on five stools and play our greatest hits. It is a very intense, dynamic rock show.

USA / CANADA SUMMER TOUR 1992

JOE ELLIOTT: For the Adrenalize tour we were back 'in the round', with a bigger stage than we had on the Hysteria tour. We were comfortable with the format, having done it before, but that also meant it wasn't as much fun as it had been the first time.

RICK SAVAGE: We were surprised that not many other bands were playing in the round. We thought that more people would pick up on the idea. We were basically on the move all the time, because you knew that wherever you were on stage you had your back to some part of the audience. It worked out pretty well and it kept everybody fit.

RICK ALLEN: The scariest part of the show was during the middle section of 'Rocket' when the whole riser would start to go up about 30 feet above the deck. Sav was standing behind me looking out, and I would be standing or sitting, looking into my kit. As the riser went up, Sav would start to push into me because he was obviously a little afraid of heights. The higher we got the more he would crowd me and it became quite challenging to play, but I didn't want to push him back because it would have been disastrous if he'd fallen off.

JOE ELLIOTT: The show still had its moments. It wasn't treading water, by any means, but it wasn't breaking new ground either. To be fair, most band tours end up being quite formulaic anyway. You can dress the stage up a certain way, but it still ends up being a drum kit in the middle, a big long ramp out the front for the singer to walk down, a load of amps, and a big screen behind you.

USA / CANADA TOUR SUMMER 1993

"......JERKEY IS BACK.......WHERE'S EVIL BOY"

April 1993
DEF LEPPARD EUROPE / UK / JAPAN TOUR 1993

Sunday	Monday	Tuesday	Wednesday	Thursday	Friday	Saturday
				1	2	3
4	5	6	7	8	9	10
11	12	13	14	15	16	17
18	19	20	21	22	23	24 STOCKHOLM, SWEDEN TRAVEL DAY
25 STOCKHOLM, SWEDEN DAY OFF	26 STOCKHOLM, SWEDEN DAY OFF	27 STOCKHOLM, SWEDEN LOAD IN	28 STOCKHOLM, SWEDEN LOAD IN LIGHTING QUE DAY	29 STOCKHOLM, SWEDEN BAND REHEARSAL DAY	30 STOCKHOLM, SWEDEN SHOW DAY	

May 1993
DEF LEPPARD EUROPE / UK / JAPAN TOUR 1993

Sunday	Monday	Tuesday	Wednesday	Thursday	Friday	Saturday
						1 GOTHENBERG, SWEDEN SHOW DAY
2 OSLO, NORWAY SHOW DAY	3 HELSINKI, FINLAND TRAVEL DAY	4 HELSINKI, FINLAND SHOW DAY	5 COPENHAGEN, DENMARK TRAVEL / DAY OFF	6 COPENHAGEN, DENMARK SHOW DAY	7 HAMBURG, GERMANY SHOW DAY	8 WURZBERG, GERMANY TRAVEL / DAY OFF
9 WURZBERG, GERMANY SHOW DAY	10 ZURICH, SWITZERLAND SHOW DAY	11 LAUSANNE, SWITZERLAND SHOW DAY	12 BRUSSELS, BELGIUM TRAVEL DAY	13 BRUSSELS, BELGIUM SHOW DAY	14 PARIS, FRANCE SHOW DAY	15 TOULOUSE, FRANCE DAY OFF
16 TOULOUSE, FRANCE SHOW DAY	17 BARCELONA, SPAIN SHOW DAY	18 LISBON, PORTUGAL TRAVEL DAY	19 LISBON, PORTUGAL TRAVEL / DAY OFF	20 LISBON, PORTUGAL SHOW DAY	21 SAN SEBASTIAN, SPAIN TRAVEL DAY	22 SAN SEBASTIAN, SPAIN SHOW DAY
23 GRENOBLE, FRANCE TRAVEL DAY	24 GRENOBLE, FRANCE SHOW DAY	25 MILAN, ITALY SHOW DAY	26 MUNICH, GERMANY TRAVEL / DAY OFF	27 MUNICH, GERMANY SHOW DAY	28 VIENNA, AUSTRIA TRAVEL / DAY OFF	29 VIENNA, AUSTRIA SHOW DAY
30 NURNBURG, GERMANY SHOW DAY	31 SHEFFIELD, ENGLAND TRAVEL / DAY OFF					

June 1993
DEF LEPPARD EUROPE / UK / JAPAN TOUR 1993

Sunday	Monday	Tuesday	Wednesday	Thursday	Friday	Saturday
		1 SHEFFIELD, ENGLAND STEEL BUILD DAY	2 SHEFFIELD, ENGLAND STEEL BUILD DAY	3 SHEFFIELD, ENGLAND STEEL BUILD DAY	4 SHEFFIELD, ENGLAND PRODUCTION LOAD IN	5 SHEFFIELD, ENGLAND SOUNDCHECK REHEARSAL
6 SHEFFIELD, ENGLAND SHOW DAY	7 TRAVEL TO USA	8	9 OFF	10	11	12
13 TRAVEL DAY TO JAPAN	14 TOKYO, JAPAN TRAVEL / DAY OFF	15 SENDAI, JAPAN SHOW DAY	16 YOKOHAMA, JAPAN SHOW DAY	17 OSAKA, JAPAN SHOW DAY	18 OSAKA, JAPAN SHOW DAY	19 HIROSHIMA, JAPAN SHOW DAY
20 TOKYO, JAPAN TRAVEL / DAY OFF	21 TOKYO, JAPAN SHOW DAY	22 TOKYO, JAPAN SHOW DAY	23 TOKYO, JAPAN SHOW DAY	24 TRAVEL TO USA	25	26
27	28	29	30			

PAGE # 25

TUESDAY MAY 18, 1993		TRAVEL	LISBON, PORTUGAL
NY IS 6 HOURS FROM PORTUGAL			COUNTRY CODE 351

TRAVEL	BAND		CREW
	FLY TO LISBON		TO LISBON

HOTEL :	BAND		CREW
	SHERATON HOTEL		SHERATON HOTEL
	RUA LATINO COELHO 1		RUA LATINO COAELHO
	P-1097 LISBON		P-1097 LISBON
	PORTUGAL		PORTUGAL
PHONE :	01-57-5757		01-57-5757
FAX :	01-57-5073		01-57-5073
FEATURES :	GYM, TURKISH BATH, SAUNA		GYM, TURKISH BATH, SAUNA
CONTACT :	ON DUTY MANAGER		ON DUTY MANAGER
ROOM SERV :	24 HOURS		24 HOURS
HOTEL REST :	6:30AM-10:00PM		6:30AM-10:00PM
LOUNGE :	10:00AM-2:00AM		10:00AM-2:00AM
TO VENUE :	10 MINUTES		10 MINUTES
TO AIRPORT :	15 MINUTES		15 MINUTES

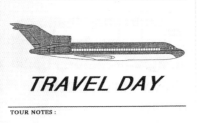

TRAVEL DAY

TOUR NOTES :

PAGE # 26

WEDNESDAY MAY 19, 1993		DAY OFF	LISBON, PORTUGAL
NY IS 6 HOURS BEHIND PORTUGAL			COUNTRY CODE 351

TRAVEL :	BAND		CREW
	IN LISBON		TO LISBON

HOTEL :	BAND		CREW
	SHERATON HOTEL		SHERATON HOTEL
	RUA LATINO COELHO 1		RUA LATINO COELHO
	P-1097 LISBON		P-1097 LISBON
	PORTUGAL		PORTUGAL
PHONE :	01-57-5757		01-57-5757
FAX :	01-57-5073		01-57-5073
FEATURES :	GYM, TURKISH BATH, SAUNA		GYM, TURKISH BATH, SAUNA
CONTACT :	ON DUTY MANAGER		ON DUTY MANAGER
RM SERV :	24 HOURS		24 HOURS
HOTEL REST :	6:30AM-10:00PM		6:30AM-10:00PM
LOUNGE :	10:00AM-2:00AM		10:00AM-2:00AM
LAUNDRY :	VALET		VALET
TO VENUE :	10 MINUTES		10 MINUTES
TO AIRPORT :	15 MINUTES		15 MINUTES

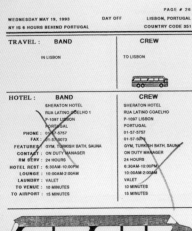

TRAVEL / DAY OFF

TOUR NOTES :

JOE ELLIOTT: Grunge hadn't come on the radar when we were making *Adrenalize*. It only really kicked off four or five months after the album was released and then it started running parallel to what we were doing. Everybody was telling us that grunge was going to kill us. But the thing about grunge was, the people who got into it were people who didn't like us in the first place. So, it didn't poach our fans. There was, obviously, some crossover. We had kids in our audience with Nirvana shirts on, but also ones with Wham! shirts on. People who liked us might also like Michael Jackson, INXS, U2, Simple Minds, Depeche Mode or Duran Duran. We crossed over with all kinds of acts.

There's no doubt that the music industry was changing. We were expected to accept we'd gone into relic mode, but we weren't prepared to do that. It's true that a lot of bands of our type fell by the wayside, but we – and Bon Jovi – were too big for that to happen. Bon Jovi adapted in their way, and we adapted in our way.

VIVIAN CAMPBELL: I think if *Adrenalize* had come out two years earlier, in 1990, it might have been OK. But by 1992, the music industry was changing. Grunge was being born, Nirvana came along and end of story. That's what happens when you spend four years making a record.

RICK SAVAGE: We were fortunate to sell out our gigs as the music business had hit hard times and we would hear stories of other bands not doing so well. We figured, provided people were still wanting to see us we'd just keep adding shows and see where it took us.

JOE ELLIOTT: *Adrenalize* was one of the top selling albums of the Nineties, even though we supposedly got our asses kicked by grunge. We didn't really get a kicking until 1996, when we released *Slang*. By then we expected it, so it didn't hurt. It was like being in a plane that's going down – you know what's about to happen.

The Adrenalize tour was really successful in Europe, really successful in America for the most part, and we did even more shows than we had for the Hysteria tour. It felt never-ending. At the end of the tour we vowed never to do anything as massive as that again. We got through it, but we all went home exhausted. Not many bands these days would attempt a 241-date world tour.

VIVIAN CAMPBELL: It was a strange time. When we started the Adrenalize tour grunge hadn't happened yet, but by the time we finished the tour a year and a half later grunge was really big. So, we all started to grow goatees and cut our hair.

PHIL COLLEN: Grunge was basically America's punk. They'd had New Wave but they'd never really had a musical movement that was a kind of social protest like punk had been in the UK. Mental health was addressed in grunge, so there was a whole new aspect to it that was way more important than bands just writing pop-rock songs.

Any genre of music gets paler the more you dilute it. Say, boy bands: you had Backstreet Boys, NSYNC, and then it went down to 98 Degrees, and it didn't get any better after that. With punk, it was the Pistols, the Clash, the Damned, and then things got watered down.

The same thing happened with rock in the Eighties. There was us, Bon Jovi, Mötley Crüe, Guns N' Roses, and after that it got really lame. People were ready to hear something different. *Adrenalize* was the third in a trilogy following on from *Pyromania* and *Hysteria* but by then we had overstayed our welcome. We could feel it while we were out there playing live, and we wanted a change as much as the audience did.

RING OF FIRE

Thunder - youre tempting me

A feast of spice in the night

Is what I need

Ohh I'm-a-ready to roar

I'm-a-ready for more

And I'm-a-ready to burn

Like a light into the dawn

Oh I gotta see the fire in me

Turning into ecstacy

So stick around and settle down

Enjoy the mystery

A voice in the wilderness

There's something in the air

A hidden love, forbidden pleasure

Suffer secret pain

Thunder (are you ready, ready to burn now)

Feels like fire (are you ready, ready to burn now)

Ring of fire

heartless - so indiscreet

Y' stealing up from behind

A raging heat

Staring into the sun

Staring into a gun

Stirring up a storm

Turn it on and let it burn

Oh I gotta see the fire in me

Turning into ecstacy

So stick around and settle down

Enjoy the mystery

A voice in the wilderness

There's something in the air
A hidden love, forbidden pleasure

Suffer secret pain

Thunder (are you ready, ready to burn)

Feels like fire (are you ready, ready to burn)

Ring of Fire (are you ready, ready to burn)

Feels like fire (are you ready, ready to burn)

Ring of Fire

RING OF FIRE - 3

Instrumental

Thunder - you tempted me you cut me up

Like a knife so tenderly

Oh I gotta see the fire in me

Burning up my ecstacy

A hidden love, forbidden pleasure

Suffer secretly

Thunder (are you ready, ready to burn)

Feels like fire (are you ready, ready to burn)

Ring of fire (are you ready, ready to burn)

Feels like fire (are ready, ready to burn)

Ring of fire

DEF LEPPARD '87/'88

1. Tear it down
2. I wanna be your hero
3. Ring of fire *1
4. Tonight
5. Please, release me...
6. Ride into the sun
7. Ring of fire *2

LIVE
1. Women
2. Love 'n affection
3. Billy's gotta gun
4. Rock of ages

EQ [

JOE ELLIOTT: *Retro Active* was in many senses a new record because, although some of the songs were old to us, much of the record had never been heard by anybody else. There were some B sides from the *Adrenalize* singles that got remixed – for example, our covers of Mick Ronson's 'Only After Dark' and Sweet's 'Action' – but quite a lot of the tracks were genuinely out of the vault. These included songs that were left over from *Hysteria*, like 'Desert Song' and 'Fractured Love', which were two of the last things that Steve played on so it was important for us to get them out there.

We also had songs that were on the original draft for *Hysteria* but didn't make it to the album, like 'I Wanna Be Your Hero', which was originally called 'Love Bites'. We stole the title and moved it to a different song and then had to come up with a different chorus for the original song. 'Ring of Fire' was another that had fallen by the wayside. We re-recorded 'Ride into the Sun' with Phil on guitar because he didn't play on the original.

Because half the songs had been started and just needed finishing off, we were able to make the album while we were on tour. It was a two-day break here and there. We were even recording backstage sometimes.

We finished 'Fractured Love' just before the Don Valley gig in Sheffield in June 1993. I'd lent out all the gear from my own studio to a studio called Bow Lane in downtown Dublin. I was playing percussion over the intro drums, with my bare hands on a flight case, to the point where my fingers swelled up so much I had to cut a ring off with a pair of pliers, otherwise I think I would have needed an amputation. I was doing that until 6 a.m. and then had to catch an 8 a.m. flight over to Sheffield for the soundcheck the day before the gig.

During two days off before a gig in Cascais in Portugal, where we were staying in a castle on the beach, I wrote the lyrics for 'Desert Song'. Then the next break we had, I got home and recorded the vocals, so that was another song ticked off. That's how the album was built. It was crazy how we got it done, but it worked out really well.

JOE ELLIOTT: Hugh Syme's cover for *Retro Active* immediately appealed to me. It's based on a surreal picture from the nineteenth century that looks like one thing until you blur your eyes and then it becomes something else. I thought that was a really cool way to represent what was our basement tapes album, our odds and sods. The record was a total hybrid of then and now, as it was our last to feature Steve and our first to feature Vivian, and the image reflected that. It was like closing one chapter and opening another. It's a great cover.

Retro Active
Recorded: 1984–1993
Released: 5 October 1993

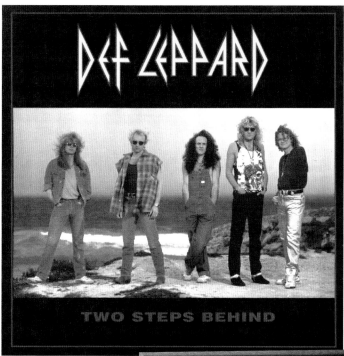

JOE ELLIOTT: 'Two Steps Behind' had been sitting around as a B side of one of the *Adrenalize* singles for a year. It was straightforward – two or three guitars, lead vocals and backing vocals, recorded in about an hour and a half and done, at Phil's suggestion, as an acoustic song. I'd also done a full-on electric demo of the song.

While we were on tour, when we were getting rough mixes of all the *Retro Active* songs together, we had a call from Michael Kamen, who was creating the soundtrack for the Arnold Schwarzenegger movie *Last Action Hero*. He wanted to know if we had anything that hadn't been released, so we sent him a cassette of the 12 songs.

He listened to them all but didn't home in on any particular one. Then one of the girls in his office took the cassette home and played it. When he came back in to work on the Monday, she was whistling 'Two Steps Behind'. Michael vaguely recognised the melody, having heard it a few days earlier, and asked her what it was. She told him that it was a Def Leppard song from the cassette. When he listened to it again in isolation he went, 'Oh my God. Yes.' He contacted us and asked if he could put a string arrangement on it and of course we agreed. Then Mike Shipley mixed it. The finished version is not a million miles from the original but different enough to take it up a division.

JOE ELLIOTT: Columbia kindly paid for the video for 'Two Steps Behind'. We shot it on the lot at Universal Studios where there were ready-made streets that they used in *Kojak* and *Law and Order*.

The day before the video shoot I'd played football and put my back out really badly. The LA football contingent was a bunch of ex-semi-pros and the odd floating musician – Ian Astbury and Billy Duffy from the Cult, Steve Jones from the Sex Pistols, me and Vivian.

In parts of the video it looks like I'm walking forwards towards the camera and mouthing the words of the song the right way while everybody who is walking or cycling past me is travelling backwards. But in fact to shoot it, I had to walk backwards and mime the song backwards and then they ran the film backwards. That was the plan, but I couldn't even walk forwards properly, let alone backwards. We had chiropractors on the set.

Eventually I said I couldn't do it unless they got me a bottle of brandy. I drank three quarters of it and after that I was still in pain, but I didn't care anymore. We managed to pull it off because we had shot the bits where I'm playing acoustic guitar on the back of a truck the previous day before I injured myself. And because I was walking backwards it looked weird anyway so you can't really tell.

The video was a big hit and adding the song to our live set not only sustained the tour, which by the summer of 1993 was promoting an album that was essentially a year old, but was a great way to shine a light on the new album. Despite it being a pieced together, odds and sods record, *Retro Active* sold two and a half million copies. We couldn't believe it.

A SONG WHICH EVOKES THE MEMORY OF GUITARIST STEVE CLARK, WHO DIED IN 1991. THE DRIVING BEAT OF "WORK IT OUT" IS POWERED BY THE BRILLIANT DRUMMING OF RICK ALLEN, PLAYING AN ACOUSTIC DRUM KIT FOR THE FIRST TIME SINCE LOSING AN ARM IN A CAR CRASH IN 1984. IN CONTRAST IS THE GENTLE, ACOUSTIC TOUCH OF "WHERE DOES LOVE GO WHEN IT DIES."

SLANG CLOSES WITH THE SPARKLING, PSYCHEDELIC "PEARL OF EUPHORIA," AN EPIC FINALE WHICH SOUNDS DECEPTIVELY LIKE THE RESULT OF PAINSTAKING WORK IN THE MOST HI-TECH STUDIO SETTING. "IT'S AMAZING, BECAUSE WE GOT THAT SOUND IN A HOUSE," LAUGHS JOE. "THERE WAS NO FANCY STUDIO, IT WAS JUST RECORDED ON A LITTLE CHEAP DESK IN A HOUSE IN MARBELLA."

ESCHEWING THE USUAL STATE-OF-THE-ART TRAPPINGS OF CORPORATE ROCK, THE BAND COBBLED TOGETHER A 32-TRACK STUDIO USING FOUR 8-TRACK DIGITAL VHS MACHINES AND A COUPLE OF CHEAP DESKS, AND GOT DOWN TO THE SERIOUS BUSINESS OF MAKING A GREAT RECORD.

"IT WAS LIKE GOING TO SUMMER SCHOOL," RECALLS JOE. "IT WAS LIKE BOYS TOGETHER OUTRAGEOUSLY. WE GOT ON WITH DOING THE JOB. WE DIDN'T HAVE TO CLOCK-WATCH. WE COULD LOOK OUT THE WINDOW AND SEE THE OCEAN. WE WEREN'T STUCK IN SOME POXY STUDIO SOME-WHERE, AND THE CLOCK'S TICKING AWAY AND YOU DON'T KNOW WHETHER IT'S RAINING OR SNOWING OR THERE'S A RIOT GOING ON OUTSIDE. WE WERE JUST IN OUR OWN NON-CORPORATE WORLD. WE WANTED TO DO A SIMILAR THING TO WHAT ZEPPELIN AND BANDS LIKE THAT DID IN THE '70S, WHEN THEY WENT INTO A HOUSE AND JUST CREATED THEIR OWN.

AND THAT'S EXACTLY WHAT WE DID. IT WAS SO RELAXING THAT IT GAVE US MORE ENERGY TO BE AS NOISY AS WE WERE ON 'PEARL OF EUPHORIA' OR 'FLESH', AND WHEN WE DID ACOUSTIC GUITARS ON 'WHERE DOES LOVE GO WHEN IT DIES,' THEY WERE ACTUALLY RECORDED OUTSIDE AT MID-NIGHT WITH INCENSE, CANDLES, DOGS BARKING, CARS GOING PAST - IT'S ALL ON TAPE."

NOT ONLY HAVE DEF LEPPARD FOUND THEIR OWN VOICE ON SLANG, THEY'VE ALSO NEATLY SIDE-STEPPED THE WEIGHT OF THEIR OWN ENORMOUS SUCCESS. WITH THEIR ALBUMS PYROMANIA AND HYSTERIA, THE LEPS BECAME THE FIRST BAND EVER TO SELL MORE THAN NINE MILLION ALBUMS CONSECUTIVELY IN AMERICA. THEY'VE HAD NO LESS THAN 14 TOP 40 HITS ON THE WAY, AND TO DATE THE BAND'S ALBUMS HAVE COLLECTIVELY SOLD AROUND 40 MILLION COPIES WORLDWIDE. WITH SUCH A TRACK RECORD, YOU'D THINK THEY WOULD BE UNDER IMMENSE PRESSURE TO TOP THEIR LAST ACHIEVEMENT

STREAMLINED. INSTEAD, DEF LEPPARD MADE A DARING DEPARTURE FROM THE FORMULA ROCK BLUE-PRINT, AND HAVE BEGUN TO MAP OUT A NEW ARTISTIC DIRECTION FOR OTHER HARD ROCK BANDS TO FOL-LOW. VAULT CLOSED THE DOOR ON DEF LEPPARD'S FIFTEEN-YEAR REIGN OVER ADOLESCENT HARD ROCK. SLANG SPEAKS A NEW LANGUAGE, ONE WHICH CAN BE UNDERSTOOD EQUAL-LY BY BOTH NEW FANS AND LOYAL FOLLOWERS.

"THE ONE THING THAT ANYBODY IN A BAND HOPES IS THAT THEIR AUDIENCE GROWS WITH THEM," CON-CLUDES JOE. WITH SLANG, DEF LEPPARD HAVE, ONCE AGAIN, PROVED THAT CAN HAPPEN. WITHOUT SACRIFICING INTEGRITY.

SINCE FIRST EXPLODING FROM THE BRITISH METAL SCENE IN 1979, DEF LEPPARD HAVE HELPED DEFINE THE ESSENCE OF MODERN ROCK 'N' ROLL. DURING AN 18-YEAR CAREER WHICH HAS SEEN TRIUMPH WALK HAND IN HAND WITH TRAGEDY, THE LEPS HAVE ENDURED IN THE FICKLE, EVER-CHANGING WORLD OF ROCK, NOT SO MUCH STOMPING ON THE OPPOSITION AS LUMP-HAMMERING THEM INTO THE GROUND. NOW, WITH THEIR BRAND NEW ALBUM, SLANG, DEF LEPPARD HAVE TAKEN THEIR BIGGEST, BRAVEST LEAP FORWARD, AND LANDED SLAP BANG INTO A BRAND NEW PHASE OF THEIR CAREER, WHERE EVERYTHING IS NOT NECESSARILY HARD AND FAST, AND ALMOST ANYTHING IS POSSIBLE.

SLANG SEES DEF LEPPARD'S TRADEMARK HARMONY-FILLED ROCK BLENDING FLUIDLY WITH BLUESY BALLADS, BLACK VEILS OF MELANCHOLY, AND WHITE-OUT PSYCHEDELIA. FROM THE TOUGH BARE-FACED DEFIANCE OF "GIFT OF FLESH" AND THE ETHNIC FLAVORS OF "TURN TO DUST," TO THE ELECTRIC, EMOTIONALLY CHARGED "ALL I WANT IS EVERYTHING," SLANG IS THE SOUND OF DEF LEPPARD EXPANDING ITS VOCABULARY, ADDING NEW INFLECTIONS, UNCOVERING NEW MEANINGS, AND LEARNING TO SPEAK SOFTLY WHILE STILL CARRYING A BIG, BLOCKBUSTING STICK.

PRODUCED BY THE BAND THEMSELVES, WITH PETE WOODROFFE, SLANG IS THE PRODUCT OF A FRUITFUL SOJOURN IN THE IDYLLIC SPANISH RESORT OF MARBELLA, WHERE THE BAND SPENT THE BEST PART OF A YEAR WRITING AND RECORDING THE ALBUM. HAVING CLOSED A GLORIOUS CHAPTER IN THEIR CAREER WITH LAST YEAR'S BEST-SELLING GREATEST HITS ALBUM, VAULT, DEF LEPPARD, (RICK ALLEN, VIVIAN CAMPBELL, PHIL COLLEN, JOE ELLIOTT AND RICK SAVAGE), FOUND THAT MARBELLA PROVIDED THE PERFECT SETTING FOR THE MUSIC TO GROW.

"IT'S THE MOST VIBRANT AND ARTISTICALLY SATISFYING RECORD WE'VE MADE," STATES JOE ELLIOTT. "WE'VE CO-PRODUCED AND WRITTEN THIS RECORD OURSELVES."

THE RESULT IS AN ALBUM WHICH IS INDELIBLY EMBOSSED WITH THE INDIVIDUAL STAMP OF EACH BAND MEMBER, AS THE FIVE DISPARATE ELEMENTS OF DEF LEPPARD FUSE TOGETHER IN A RELAXED, FOCUSED ATMOSPHERE. JOE ELLIOTT'S VOCALS ARE RICH WITH NEW-FOUND RESONANCE, WHILE THE GUITARS OF PHIL COLLEN AND VIV CAMPBELL UNCOVER EVEN DEEPER LAYERS. THE RHYTHM SECTION OF BASSIST RICK SAVAGE AND DRUMMER RICK ALLEN HAVE NEVER SOUNDED MORE TIGHTLY WOVEN, AND THE ORGANIC PRODUCTION ALLOWS THE EMPATHY BETWEEN EACH BAND MEMBER TO SPARK AND TAKE FLAME.

"THE THING WE WERE TRYING TO ACHIEVE WITH THIS RECORD," SAYS JOE, "IS THAT YOU DIDN'T PUT IT ON AND SAY, 'THIS IS A GREAT PRODUCTION,' WHICH IS WHAT PEOPLE JUDGED HYSTERIA AND MAYBE ADRENALIZE ON. THAT WAS A BIG THING FOR US, WE WANTED TO PEEL AWAY THE GROUP RATHER THAN HEAR THE PRODUCTION OF THE RECORD."

DEF LEPPARD FANS WILL BE DELIGHTED BY THE RELENTLESS, DRIVING RIFFS OF "GIFT OF FLESH," "TRUTH?" AND THE ALBUM'S TITLE TRACK, "SLANG," WHICH JOE DESCRIBES AS "POSSIBLY THE MOST OBVIOUS DEF LEPPARD THING ON THE RECORD. WE WANTED TO GET A THING GOING, A CROSS BETWEEN A KINKSY, STONESY ROCK SONG AND A RAP THING."

THE MOST UNTRADITIONAL TRACK ON THE ALBUM HAS TO BE "TURN TO DUST," WITH ITS BLEND OF SWIRLING, EASTERN TRADI-TIONAL SOUNDS AND STRAIGHT-AHEAD WESTERN ROCK. SAYS JOE: "PHIL BASICALLY SCORED THE INDIAN MELODY ON HIS GUITAR, AND WE GOT AN ORCHESTRA TO COME IN AND DO IT."

"BREATHE A SIGH," A SONG ABOUT DENYING ONE'S FEELINGS, IS ANOTHER INTUITIVE DEPARTURE FOR THE BAND, A SOUL-TINGED TUNE WHICH BUILDS UP TO A HEARTLIFTING CLIMAX, AND WHICH FINDS JOE STRETCHING HIS VOCALS AS WELL AS HIS EMOTIONAL RANGE.

DEF LEPPARD BiO

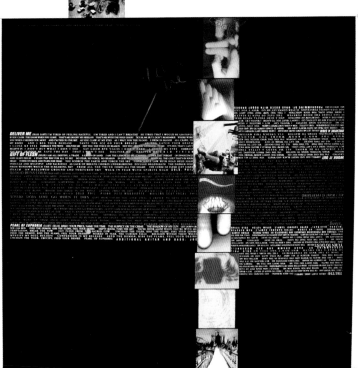

SLANG

JOE ELLIOTT: *We went out of our way to be a completely different band for Slang, and so I really like the fact that the Slang cover is so different from the others. It was designed by a company from Vermont called JDK, who did a lot of adverts for skateboard and surfing magazines. We just fancied a change and they seemed very vibrant and 'now'.*

We'd already eased away from our traditional logo by accident rather than design with Retro Active. It was the same logo, but it was ice blue. And that trend continued with Vault, our first greatest hits album, which came out in late 1995. So, it was less of a leap for us to end up with the Indian-style lettering on the Slang cover than if we'd gone to that straight from Adrenalize. To this day, I still think this is a great album cover.

Slang
Recorded: 1994–1996
Released: 14 May 1996

JOE ELLIOTT: After the Adrenalize tour, we took six months to write the next album and just be at home. Then in April 1994 we went down to Spain to start recording *Slang* in the house where they filmed the second series of *Auf Wiedersehen, Pet*, up in the hills above Puerto Banús. We swam every day in that pool you saw on the TV. We all rented these little blue Renault Twingos.

Recording in the house in Puerto Banús was fun. We were living in apartments that were right on the water and there was plenty to do when we weren't working. There were some clubs where you could literally stay out until six in the morning if you weren't singing the next day. We were working really hard but when we played, we played hard. We'd work Sunday to Friday and then every Friday night we would go hog wild. With a pool right outside the studio, we also knew when to say, 'Let's take a break.' Then you'd go make a coffee, take your shirt off, jump in the pool, have a 20-minute swim, come back out, dry off and get back to work.

PHIL COLLEN: We thought it would be great to make a record in a different fashion – just write the songs, record them and be done with it. Not dwell on things too much. It felt like the right thing to do and I'm really glad we did it. I love *Slang* – it was our album of liberation.

We went to Spain to record the album and it was brilliant. Instead of going to a corporate kind of studio, we rented a villa and made that our studio. I was going through a divorce, so that was pretty hard work. But making the album was a great escape from all the other stuff that was going on.

We had the drums in the living room, with mattresses up against the window. We had some of the guitars out on the balcony, which overlooked the sea and Gibraltar and Africa beyond. There were a couple of songs where we played the backing track as a band, which for us was rare; it was the most real album we'd ever done. Back in the time of the Motown bands and the Beatles and the Stones everyone would go in one room and record together, but people had stopped doing that years ago because you get more control doing things separately. *Slang* was a little bit more like they did it in the Sixties. We'd get the basis of a track and then fiddle around with it afterwards.

It felt like there were no grown-ups, just us bunch of idiots. It was like going on a school vacation or something. We were kicking ourselves that we'd never done it before.

JOE ELLIOTT: *Slang* was a rebirth. We jokingly gave it the working title 'Commercial Suicide' because it was so different from the trilogy of massively produced albums, *Pyromania*, *Hysteria* and *Adrenalize*, that preceded it. We'd hit a ceiling and had nowhere to go, so we figured our next album had to be something totally different. It wasn't that we were trying not to be Def Leppard; we were aiming to sound like we do live but a little more hardcore and edgy.

It was Phil who came up with the final album title and we all thought it sounded good. Slang is the misuse of language. And there's a lot of misuse of language in rock and roll. It just seemed like the perfect title really – loose and funky and streetwise.

VIVIAN CAMPBELL: We were searching for identity when we went into the studio to cut *Slang*, my first album with the band. The only thing we knew for sure was that we couldn't sound like Def Leppard. It was really bizarre but we got through it.

JOE ELLIOTT: All of a sudden, we were in our thirties and we didn't want to write 'Let's Get Rocked' anymore. *Slang* was the first time that this band had collectively and individually gone through big, grown-up experiences like marriage, divorce, parenthood and bereavement, and our songwriting reflected this.

PHIL COLLEN: 'Blood Runs Cold' was about Steve. He was a really funny guy, really warm and lovely, and then all of a sudden things got tragic. But he was still exactly that person. So, the song was about him being this living, breathing fountain of life that wasn't there anymore – that was the idea of blood running cold.

I got as far as I could with the song but I was too deeply involved emotionally, so I talked to Joe about it. He understood what I was aiming for and he was able to finish things off. We had always finished each other's sentences, now we were finishing each other's songs.

RICK SAVAGE: In the past the sound of the lyrics mattered to us as much as their actual meaning. When we wrote *Slang* we put more emphasis on the meaning.

My favourite track is 'Where Does Love Go When It Dies'. It has a very poignant lyric, which is something we weren't renowned for. That song brings out a lot of emotion in people. It's very uplifting, with great hope and faith. Maybe that's why I like it so much.

I guess we've always been softies at heart. But we still know how to crank it out – we can be the tough guys if we want to.

JOE ELLIOTT: Some lyrics sound good but read really badly; others read like beautiful poetry, but when you try to sing them they're just nonsense. You've got to find the middle ground, and I was getting good at that.

I was particularly proud of 'Where Does Love Go When It Dies'. Phil had this two-chord acoustic thing that sounded a bit like U2 or Dave Gilmour, which he thought would be a perfect vehicle for my lyric, and we worked a chorus into it. I still to this day think everything about that song is great.

'All I Want Is Everything' was my first sole writing credit. I'd written songs that were, say, 80 percent down to me, but this was all mine. As soon as I'd written the opening line – 'I don't know how to leave you, but I don't know how to stay. I've got things that I must tell you that I don't know how to say' – I knew it was going to be good.

PHIL COLLEN: Travel is my greatest inspiration for songs. Before being in Girl, I'd never left London. I used to be a motorcycle dispatch rider, then years later I remember walking around London and almost tearing up at the architecture. In all the years growing up and driving around the city I'd never noticed how beautiful it was.

It's only when you start travelling to new places that you begin taking in all these things – not just art and culture but people. I've got this thing on tour where I wake up at six in the morning and get up and explore.

One time when we were in India I heard this amazing music, so I bought the CD. We sampled it and got permission from the artist to put it on the song 'Turn to Dust' on the *Slang* album. Within the caste system in India there's a group called the untouchables, a whole swathe of the country's population who are completely ignored – and that's what the song was about. Going to all these amazing places kicks up so many different influences and themes.

There are so many different ways to write songs and I like using all of them. There's the hack songwriter approach, where you just dial it in as a mathematical process. And then there's a purely artistic approach, where you let an idea flow and grow. Being a guitar player, I sometimes start with a guitar part or bass riff. Or it can be an interesting word or phrase that sparks things off. I'm fascinated by the whole creative process. And the reward for me is being allowed to have that expression. Obviously, it's great to get to do all of the other things, but I wouldn't care if I never went to an awards show again. Getting to live out a childhood fantasy of writing songs, controlling the narrative, that's always been the thing for me.

JOE ELLIOTT: The move towards writing individually that had started with *Adrenalize* developed even further on *Slang*. By now, Rick had moved to California, where Phil and Vivian also lived, which made it even harder for us all to gather in one place. If you were going to write a song on your own you had to be confident enough to follow it through, not just bring along a riff and a couple of verses.

RICK ALLEN: A lot of the songwriting started in our various home studios. Then when we got together in Spain, everybody played their ideas and we picked out what we liked and pieced it all together – 'leppardised' it, as we say.

VIVIAN CAMPBELL: We were taking on board a lot of new music. One album that we listened to more than any other when we were making *Slang* was *Superunknown* by Soundgarden, which I think is the best record of the grunge era. I love the songs and I love the whole sound of that record. It was a big influence on us at the time.

JOE ELLIOTT: Working alone in my studio, I had got used to programming the drums, playing the bass and guitar parts and then singing over the top of all that. My demos were almost like finished recordings, which I could present to the guys so that they could learn the guitar parts if they liked the song. But on this album we would sometimes carry things over unchanged from our demos into the final recording.

For example, when Vivian came in with 'Work It Out' we kept half the stuff from his demo on the finished version. Similarly, the intro guitar part on 'Pearl of Euphoria' is played by me, because once the guys heard my playing over and over on the demo it started to sound like the real thing and not just a demo. I remember Phil saying, 'We should leave Joe's guitar on because he sounds great. Neither Vivian nor I could play that badly.' That was the best left-handed compliment I've ever had.

PHIL COLLEN: We often swap roles in the studio if someone comes up with a good idea. The Stones used to do it. The Beatles used to do it. If it ain't broke, don't fix it.

JOE ELLIOTT: I was struggling to sing a part of 'Blood Runs Cold' and I asked Phil to do it instead. He'd had this idea for a middle section that would be a melodic but wordless yodelling and screaming stream of consciousness – like on Pink Floyd's 'The Great Gig in the Sky'. He sang it to me to show what he meant, but when I went in and tried to do it I couldn't manage it. So, Phil did this whole bit and it was brilliant. We would never have done that five years previously – not because I would have insisted on doing all the singing, but just because we wouldn't have come up with an idea like that.

RICK ALLEN: Making *Slang* was a lot more of a band process. On *Adrenalize* we were going through the motions a little bit, because we were so worried about Steve's situation. With the addition of Vivian, the whole way of recording became so much more of a team effort.

RICK SAVAGE: We didn't see changing musical direction as a challenge. It was something that we'd been wanting to do for a while. It would actually have been a lot harder to try and make the same old records that we'd been making for the previous eight years, because we didn't want to do that anymore. It felt very natural for us to record in a different way and create something that sounded different as a result.

PHIL COLLEN: It was like being in a garage band. The aim wasn't to be loose in the production, we just didn't want to do things the same way as we had in the past. It was a reaction against recording separately and doing everything under a microscope. A lot of the guitar stuff was done in one take. All the effort went into the songs as opposed to getting the right sounds.

RICK ALLEN: It became a lot more convenient, especially after I lost my arm, to use electronic drums. Part of that was also to do with the sounds that we were using throughout the Eighties. But now that we were changing tack with the music, it seemed like the right time to go back to something more earthy. I was starting to miss the physical aspect of playing drums on records anyway. The whole idea of playing acoustic drums set the tone for *Slang* and is a big reason why the record sounds the way it does.

JOE ELLIOTT: In the summer of 1995, we were in LA finishing *Slang* when the record company told us that they wanted to put out a 'Best of' album. We didn't like the sound of this, as a greatest hits album can be like a death knell for a career. We were worried that they would put all their money behind the greatest hits album and neglect our new album.

But we felt better when Howard Berman, the guy who was in charge of the label at the time, came out to see us and told us he wanted to put a new song on the greatest hits album. Sav suggested 'When Love & Hate Collide', an unreleased song that he and I had written in 1989 for *Adrenalize*. When we played Howard the demo his eyes started bulging and he said, 'This is perfect, but I need it in ten days' time.'

We immediately stopped what we were doing on *Slang* and went into complete production mode. The band went into the main room to record drums, bass, guitars, etcetera. Meanwhile, I set up in Phil's walk-in wardrobe with a stool, a microphone and an ADAT machine, which is what we used to record with in those days. I had to sing over the demo because there wasn't time to wait for the backing track to be finished. It was a pretty shambolic way of doing things.

'When Love & Hate Collide' was a fantastic addition to *Vault* because it fitted in musically with our past but was a brand new song. It turned out to be the biggest hit we've ever had in the UK.

JOE ELLIOTT: The *Vault* sleeve was the record company trying too hard to make us look hip. Part of me respects what they were trying to do, and I'm glad that the album was called *Vault* because it tied in nicely with our digital museum, which we gave the same name. I could understand the idea of the lock on the front. They did special promo boxes with an actual lock and you had to find the key to open them, which was a nice idea.

But when I look at this miserable, greeny-grey cover I don't think it does a very good job of representing the celebratory music that's actually on the record. It reminds me of a grim locker room in a prison or a police station. The Def Leppard logo just looks like it's come off the bottom of somebody's shoe, like a footprint.

I think that this cover has worn badly compared to our others. Because we have now reclaimed our place in the industry – as a kind of glam version of the Rolling Stones – everything that we did to become who we are is now OK. Everything that we did to look like Pearl Jam comes over as a bit cheesy.

Vault: Def Leppard Greatest
Hits (1980–1995)
Recorded: 1981–1995
Released: 23 October 1995

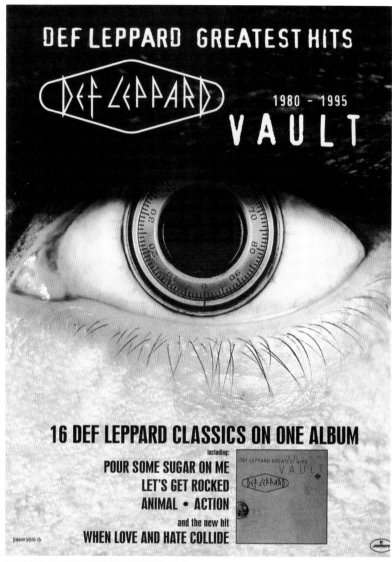

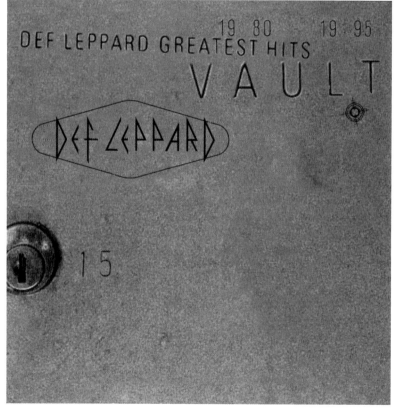

JOE ELLIOTT: To mark the release of *Vault* on 23 October 1995, the record company came up with this brilliant idea of doing gigs in three different continents that day, which we managed with the help of time zones. We chartered a plane and put all the world's rock press on board that were willing to come, so that they could talk to us on the flight and get their interview scoops with free champagne.

First stop was Tangiers in Morocco where we were taken for dinner and camel rides until about 10.30 p.m. and then we did a midnight performance in a cave down near the beach, with all the press watching and a few local people wondering what the hell was going on.

We played a 50-minute acoustic set, then made our way to the airport for a 4.30 a.m. take-off, getting back to Blighty by about 7.30 a.m. When we landed I made the fatal mistake of going to bed. When I woke up, I didn't know where or who I was.

I only vaguely remember the London gig, which took place at around midday. Apparently, I was talking complete gibberish between songs – much to the amusement of everybody on stage, no doubt. I wasn't drunk, just exhausted. Anyway, we got through it.

Then we jumped on a plane to Vancouver and this was great because we were in first class with flatbeds. Once I got that seat down, boom! I was gone. So, I woke up in Canada ten hours later, fully refreshed, went to the hotel, had a shower and felt fine. We played in the Commodore Ballroom and it was a great gig. Afterwards we looked at each other and said, 'Well, we're never doing that again!'

RICK SAVAGE: To top it off we had to travel the following morning from Vancouver to Singapore on a 22-hour flight. It was madness. You wouldn't want to do it every week, but we have fond memories of it. It was a good idea to finish in Canada, because the Canadians have always been very supportive and the audience there is one of the best.

PHIL COLLEN: I'd love us to do four continents in a day next time. Morocco, London, Miami, Bogotá – that would work. We'd just need someone to lend us their private jet ...

JOE ELLIOTT: Either side of the 'three continents in a day' event, we did a series of unplugged dates scattered all over the world to promote *Vault*. These included a show at the Hard Rock in Singapore, which was recorded as a bonus disc to go with *Slang*.

JOE ELLIOTT: After the *Vault* interlude, we went back to working on *Slang* in early 1996, mainly in my studio in Dublin.

By the time we had finished the album, it was really clear just how ground-breaking it was going to be for us. *Slang* was still a very guitar-heavy album, but it didn't have all the big, mad harmonies that the previous records had had, and it certainly didn't have the sugary lyrics or melodies either.

What we learned, though, is that we weren't allowed to change lanes in the way that an artist like David Bowie could. When we released 'Work It Out' on the radio, a DJ in Florida said, 'This is fantastic. I would play it if they changed their name.' That's the kind of thinking we were up against. But we knew that if we'd made another *Hysteria* or *Adrenalize*, we'd just have become part of the machine churning out background noise.

I stand by *Slang*. I think there are some great songs on it, but the album is marmite. Some of my closest friends, who are brutally honest with me, think it's the best thing we've ever done; others think it absolutely is not. I'm proud that we made the record because we dared to try.

VIVIAN CAMPBELL: I have always felt that we took too much of a left turn with *Slang*. I thought we sacrificed the art of songwriting, which is what Leppard is all about. We were too quick to accept the initial song ideas and just record them. But anyway it didn't really matter what we did because anything from the Eighties was deeply resented in the Nineties. The wheel's come full circle now and I think people respect us for having survived all of that.

JOE ELLIOTT: The Slang tour started off in the Far East. In Jakarta we were told that we had to be covered from the neck down to the knees. You weren't allowed to go shirtless. So, Vivian bought a denim dress. There's a photograph of him wearing it in an interview we did for *Q* magazine with the headline, 'Don't fancy yours much'. He found the loophole.

RICK ALLEN: The tour production was a lot more relaxed. It put the emphasis back on the band, as opposed to this huge thing that was getting bigger than the band.

JOE ELLIOTT: We finished our '96 run in South Africa. We'd never been there before but 'Two Steps Behind' had been a number one hit there the previous year. We played to 37,000 people in a football stadium in Johannesburg. The next day somebody came rushing in with a *Johannesburg Tribune* with the headline, 'Def Leppard, better than the Stones'. You don't see that every day.

None More Black

TOUR 1996

DEF LEPPARD

DEF LEPPARD

PEPSI Presents

DEF LEPPARD

LIVE IN BANGKOK

28th MAY 1996
AT INDOOR STADIUM, HUA MARK

DOORS OPEN : 19.00pm.
SHOW TIME : 20.00pm.

TICKET PRICE : 500.-

Conditions : No Cameras or Recording Devices.
This Ticket is Non Refundable.

10% Discount On Food And Beverage
At HENRY J BEANS Until 30 June 1996

CHIVAS REGAL   VOLVO   Thai   AMARI

PolyGram   aura   KLOSTER BIER   TERO

ANOTHER TERO ENTERTAINMENT AND U&I PRODUCTION

DEF LEPPARD
SLANG
JAPAN TOUR '96

ショー

UDO ARTISTS, INC.

RICK SAVAGE: We try to write on the road but very few of the ideas that we come up with actually make it through to the next record. It's very difficult, because you're in a completely different environment that's not necessarily conducive to writing songs. But we're always open to ideas and so if somebody does come up with something we'll always put it down on tape and try to work it into a song if we can.

PHIL COLLEN: Touring and recording act as a tonic for each other. I really enjoy constructing a song in the studio but it can be frustrating; touring is easier because you don't have to think about it. So, going on the road is light relief after the hard work of making an album. But then after a while you start to crave the experience of being creative again.

Opposite:
'Slang' video shoot
Los Angeles, April 1996

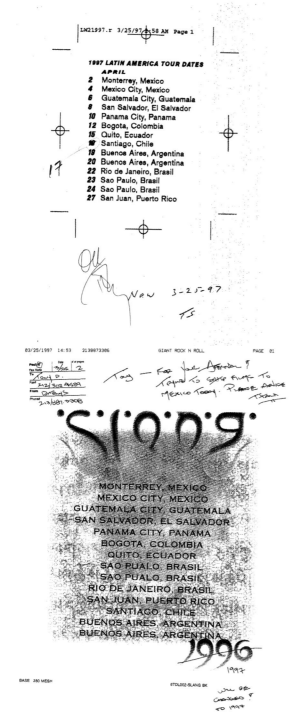

1997 LATIN AMERICA TOUR DATES
APRIL
2   Monterrey, Mexico
4   Mexico City, Mexico
6   Guatemala City, Guatemala
8   San Salvador, El Salvador
10 Panama City, Panama
12 Bogota, Colombia
15 Quito, Ecuador
17 Santiago, Chile
19 Buenos Aires, Argentina
20 Buenos Aires, Argentina
22 Rio de Janeiro, Brasil
23 Sao Paulo, Brasil
24 Sao Paulo, Brasil
27 San Juan, Puerto Rico

03/25/1997 14:53   2138873306   GIANT ROCK N ROLL   PAGE 01

JOE ELLIOTT: We resumed the Slang tour in April 1997 in Mexico and then worked our way down through Central America and into South America. When we got to Panama, the gig was in a field opposite the building where Noriega had been holed up when he was hounded out by the Americans in 1989. It was a big field surrounded with dozens of shipping containers to keep out people who hadn't got tickets. That was the theory anyway. During soundcheck, the locals took us over to the building to show us the bullet holes left in the concrete. They also said we should be proud because when the Americans were trying to drive Noriega mad by blasting out rock music day and night from a PA system set up in front of the building, one of the bands they played the most was Def Leppard.

In Bogotá Sav got on Colombian TV for his football skills. We were playing a charity match on a day off and afterwards I was sitting in my hotel room, just flicking through the channels, when I saw a clip of a beautiful goal he'd scored from 30 yards out. I called to tell him he'd just won Colombia's goal of the month.

We were supposed to play in Santiago, but it got pulled. When we got there we found that the gear was still in Ecuador because we hadn't paid the bribe to get the stuff on the plane. So, we had to hastily arrange a brown envelope to get the gear to the next gig, in Argentina, and cancel the Santiago one.

We met this 13- or 14-year-old kid called Enzo in the hotel. He was absolutely distraught that our gig was off; it was as if someone in his family had died. So, having cleared it with his mum, I offered to fly him to the next show. I arranged for him to sit next to me on the flight and he was chuffed to bits. We got him set up in his room in Buenos Aires and told him to order in some room service. Unfortunately, he also used the hotel phone to call his mum not realising what kind of mark-up hotels put on international calls. When we checked out, we were hit with a 600 quid phone bill. The kid was mortified, but we told him not to worry about it.

Lo and behold, I met Enzo again in 2017 as a grown man in his thirties. He was still a huge Def Leppard fan. We went out and had a drink. Every few months he sends me an email about his life. I always write one back.

VIVIAN CAMPBELL: On the Slang tour we started playing in markets that the band had never been to before. We went to South America for the first time. We did more dates in Asia than ever before. We had to weather the storm in our traditional strongholds.

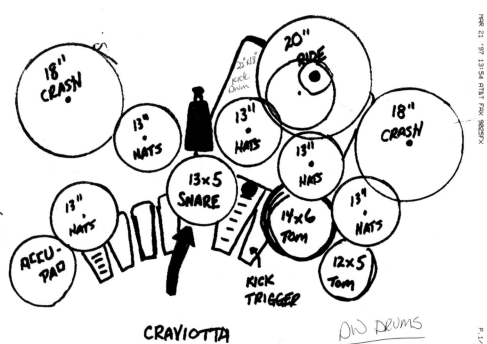

TO: SUE TROPIO   FROM: GARRY.
FAX # 212-302-9389   FAX #

CRAVIOTTA
SNARE

SLANG

VIVIAN CAMPBELL: You can never truly replicate what is on a Def Leppard record in a live situation. You just try and approximate it. On *Slang* 'Where Does Love Go When It Dies' is almost completely acoustic. Phil played mandolin and I played dulcimer. 'Turn to Dust' has an Indian orchestra on it. When we did that live, we tried to play the orchestra parts on guitar. That's where they came from originally, as Phil had scored the song on electric guitar. You just get into the habit of playing quarter notes and such and using a few effects.

JOE ELLIOTT: We didn't have to be as rigid on the Slang tour as we had in the past. On previous tours the lasers were programmed so that if you did the songs in a different order from the night before it was hell for the lighting techs to change things around. This time things were more stripped down, which meant that we could rehearse a song in soundcheck that we hadn't played for a few months and stick it in if we wanted to.

PHIL COLLEN: This tour was very different. Tastes had changed and people weren't as interested in us, so they stopped coming to the shows. That happens to most artists. But we still believed in what we were doing so we carried on.

VIVIAN CAMPBELL: Def Leppard have always had an intense work ethic. After Rick's accident and Steve's death, the band picked up the pieces and kept at it. It was one of the first things I noticed when I joined. Be it songwriting, recording or the live show, the attention to detail is almost mind-numbing. But that kind of resilience and drive are a big reason why the band has endured.

I **2** **3**

THE DESIGNS:

Use the CD's laid out as reference

I. PLAIN GOLD LOGO

Speaks for itself really. Simple and clean with texture added for detail. Will need background adjusting to give the logo more dimension.

2. LOGO REDS AND YELLOWS

Original DEFLEP colours, though graduated to give more depth.

3. LOGO REDS AND GOLDS

A combination of 1) & 2), substituting the gold for the yellow of 2), and adding a little texture and slight embossing as on 1).

4. GOLD LOGO WITH SINGLE FLARE

As 1) but with one flare.
PLEASE NOTE HERE THAT THE LOGO CAN BE DARKENED IMMEDIATELY AROUND THE FLARE SO THE DEFINITION OF COLOURS AND FORM IS RETAINED AS ON 1).

5. GOLD LOGO WITH THREE FLARES

Again logo can be adjusted towards the definition and depth of colour as 1).

6. RED/GOLD LOGO WITH THREE FLARES

As 5) but using the logo of 3)
HERE I HAVE BROUGHT BACK THE DEFINITION OF THE LETTERS MUCH MORE SO THE FLARES ARE NOT SO STRONG. THIS IS WHAT I MEAN BY BRINGING BACK MORE OF THE DEFINITION ON 4) & 5).

7. GOLD LOGO WITH THREE FLARES + REFLECTION

As 5) with reflection. Again more detail can be brought into logo so it is more like 1).

4 **5** **6**

8. RED/GOLD LOGO WITH THREE FLARES + REFLECTION

As 6) with reflection. Again more detail has been brought into logo so it is more like the original plain logo 3).

9, 10 & 11. VERSIONS WITHOUT LETTERING

Exactly the same master designs as 7), 8) & 3) but no lettering.

IF YOU WANT TO LOOK AT ANY OF THE DESIGNS WITHOUT THE TITLE, IN CD CASE 1) IS A STRIP OF BLACK CARD WHICH YOU CAN SLIP INTO EACH CD CASE TO MASK OUT THE LETTERING.

12. LOGO FROM PREVIOUS ROUGHS WITH LETTERING

This is a digital print-out so that you can see the definition and quality of the typeface for 'EUPHORIA''

GENERAL COMMENTS AND PREFERENCES:

My preferences for the album have to be designs with flares or reflections.

Although I think that the plain logos look very stylish I don't think they are weighty enough for an album sleeve.

We will need a single no doubt and maybe the way to go is to use the plain logo for the single art and then follow it through with flares and/or reflections for the album packaging.

It's just that so much more scale and dimension is created with flares and reflections – the logo looks enormous, as on a stage set.

My preference for logo is the red/gold one with texture used on 3), 8) & 10). It kind of takes the sleeve away from the 'best of' or 'greatest hits' vibe. There is still the classiness of the gold without it looking crass or too obvious.

So........... I guess my choices and preferences would be:

    1) Single: No. 3 Album: No. 8 (or No. 10) if there is no title)
    2) Single: No. 3 Album: No. 6
    3) Single: No. 4 Album: No. 7 (or No. 9) if there is no title)
    4) Single: No. 1 Album: No. 7 (or No. 9) if there is no title)
    5) Single: No. 1 Album No. 5

The only variation I have not done which may be worth a try is give a plain logo a reflection (as in 7) & 8)) BUT WITH NO FLARES. This again would give the logo dimension and scale.

That's it. I think some of these look fantastic – I hope you do too.

7 **8**

Euphoria
Recorded: May
1998–March 1999
Released: 8 June 1999

216

EUPHORIA

JOE ELLIOTT: *We got the logo wrong on Euphoria. The Def Leppard lettering should be yellow with a red border, but on Euphoria it's the other way round. It had been seven years since we had last used the traditional logo, on Adrenalize in 1992, and we took our eye off the ball. Satori, which is Andie Airfix's company, did the album cover. He may have got it wrong or he may have deliberately swapped it round. Maybe they had too many red ink cartridges. Who knows?*

PHIL COLLEN: Every failure stings a little bit. We'd had *Adrenalize*, which people didn't generally like, even though it went to number one for six weeks in America and sold more than five million copies there. But we were deemed uncool and there was a bit of a backlash. Then with *Slang* we got to express ourselves artistically and I loved how that turned out, but it didn't sell very well, so that was the other side of the coin.

With *Euphoria*, we knew exactly what we wanted to achieve. The format was defined by the greatest hits album we had just released, which had gone through the roof. When you listen to anyone's greatest hits, whether it's James Taylor's or James Brown's, they always have a thread. You can imagine the songs having been made the same week, even though they've often been done over decades. It was something we noticed on our greatest hits album too.

So, for *Euphoria* the aim was to have that kind of thread running through it. We brought in elements of all the *Hysteria*-type songs, but with a little more knowledge. Every time you go out, you have more expertise – not just as a songwriter but as a producer, singer and player. It's still not always easy, but sometimes it just flows. You know what to add to make things different and better.

RICK ALLEN: Everyone around us wanted a classic sounding Def Leppard album again. We basically used *Pyromania*, *Hysteria* and elements of several other records as a blueprint, and that's how we came up with *Euphoria*.

Working with Mutt Lange again was a huge education. It was like a refresher course to remind us how we used to do it.

VIVIAN CAMPBELL: With *Euphoria* we felt it was OK to return to the classic sound and go to the extreme opposite of what *Slang* was. Our motivation was the same as it had been with *Slang*: to give people what we thought they wanted. This time we thought they wanted a traditional sounding Def Leppard record. But, as with *Slang*, it was all second-guessing.

JOE ELLIOTT: We didn't set out to write anthemic songs for *Euphoria*, but we didn't avoid them either. So we had big choruses on tracks like 'Back in Your Face', 'Demolition Man', 'Goodbye' and 'It's Only Love'. Mutt Lange came on board to co-write three of the songs: 'Promises', 'All Night' and 'It's Only Love'.

RICK SAVAGE: After touring the *Slang* album on and off for about two years, we needed to get back to the feel of writing songs.

JOE ELLIOTT: We recorded the album at my studio in Dublin. It was the second time we'd used Joe's Garage as the principal studio for one of our records. By now Pete Woodroffe had taken over from Mike Shipley as our co-producer. Mike had been Mutt's engineer and then when Mike stepped up to co-produce *Adrenalize*, he had Pete as his engineer. When Mike moved away from the scene after *Adrenalize*, Pete became our main guy.

We were running two studios at once when we recorded *Euphoria*. There was the main studio downstairs, where we did all the backing tracks, and upstairs in my office area where we did all the vocals. For this process we built a booth, like a telephone box without a door, then stapled a duvet inside it to soak up the sound.

Pete's assistant, a fantastic engineer called Ger McDonnell, was the guy recording all the lead vocals and backing vocals upstairs. Then, he would take the tapes downstairs to the main studio where they would be added to the backing tracks. Running two studios at once cut out all the waiting around. Once we got one backing track down, it would go upstairs and I would start singing on it while the rest of the band moved on to the next track.

This was working like clockwork until, right in the middle of recording the album, Ger announced that he had to leave to work on another project. So, we needed another 'upstairs engineer', quick. Luckily, through a recommendation from our good friend Ricky Warwick, we found Ronan McHugh, who we still work with to this day. I love working with Ro – he's brilliant at the controls and funny as hell, which makes for a very relaxing environment!

Mutt and the band hadn't worked together for eight years. Joe says: "We were really pleased with ten of the new songs, but we knew there was something missing from these three. We asked Mutt to come over to work on them with us and inject some of his magic."

They had just four days together. "So we blitzed it," Joe says, "with the help of much caffeine intake. That guy has oodles of energy. We'd start at 11 a.m. and he'd still be going strong at four the next morning. Bottled essence of Mutt could replace Lucozade as a re-energizer for the sick and listless. I love 'All Night', it's got a really funky Prince-y feel, a James Brown riff and very tongue-in-cheek lyrics taking the mick out of all the self- styled studs who strut our stages."

Mutt wasn't at all involved with the production of the album. That job was done by the band and Pete Woodroffe, a combination Joe reckons to be "The nearest you can get to Mutt without him being there."

Other standout tracks include Rick Savage's tender "Goodbye." "A good Leppard ballad," Joe says proudly. "With us, ballads come out like wisdom teeth at the dentists." "Goodbye" is very representative of the softer side of Leppard, as is Viv's "To Be Alive."

"Kings of Oblivion" is the polar opposite, a sinewy rocker evocative of "a dark alley and steamy manholes," Joe enthuses. "It's the seamy side of Manhattan at three in the morning. It's also Leppard meets Rush with a large portion of UFO on the side. The title is shamelessly stolen from Bowie's 'The Bewlay Brothers'."

"'Disintegrate' is a Phil Collen instrumental, it's very cool. I love it."

Euphoria, like Adrenalize, was recorded in Joe's studio, downstairs at his Dublin home. It took ten months to make, between May 1998 and March 1999.

"All the lads lived at my house for the duration," says Joe. "Which cuts out the time wasted on travel to and from studios. We worked really hard, normally from Sunday to Friday, we would start work at 12 noon and finish at 1 a.m. unless Mutt was over. All our meals were cooked in-house by our tour manager. And the only days we'd have off were Saturdays."

It's a mighty long way down rock'n'roll from the band's first rehearsal inside a spoon factory in Bramall Lane, Sheffield, UK in November 1977.

Is it a bind having to get out and play 22 years on?

"Never," Joe insists. "It feels better than ever now. You don't think about what's happening to you when you're 21 years old, but as you get more experienced touring and recording gets better and better."

"Def Leppard have never been a five year thing, we've always wanted to keep going like Aerosmith and Stones, improving our sound as we go. They have kept up to date, but never lost their identity. That's what we wanted to do here, make a modern record with the unmistakable Leppard trademark."

And that's Euphoria. Very possibly the best Def Leppard album yet.

RICK SAVAGE: I think we caught the record label by surprise, because when they saw the style of album we were trying to create they were probably expecting another four-year project. But we'd got it down to a finer art by now. The fact we were recording in two studios most of the time meant that we were able to deliver the classic Def Leppard album in a much shorter space of time.

JOE ELLIOTT: Damon Hill lived down the road in Dublin. We used to hang out all the time. One day Damon came to see us recording. I didn't expect him to turn up in a Formula One car but I did think he'd be on four wheels, so it was really funny when he came pedalling along on his bike. Phil handed him a guitar and he could play a bit so we invited him to do the end solo on 'Demolition Man'. He was shitting himself, to be honest. This is a guy who can go round a corner at 180 miles an hour, but playing guitar on a Def Leppard album was really taking him out of his comfort zone.

RICK ALLEN: Damon's a great driver. I'd say to him, 'Don't give up your day job!'

PHIL COLLEN: Euphoria has got some great songs on it. 'Promises' and 'Paper Sun' were both radio hits in America. Whenever we play 'Promises' live, we nail it.
    With 'Promises', I made the riff in the same key as 'Armageddon It' and 'Photograph'. It's basically a rip-off. If another band did that to us we'd sue them. But no one noticed because we were doing it to ourselves.

RICK SAVAGE: 'Promises' is instantly Def Leppard. It has all the ingredients of how people remember us and how I think people want to hear us.

RICK ALLEN: 'Goodbye' is pure entertainment. We always have a certain number of 'serious' songs on every record that we do, but most of them are just about enjoyment and escapism.

PHIL COLLEN: It was only when we got the Diamond Award for *Hysteria*, meaning it had gone ten times platinum, that what we had achieved hit home. We were at the podium and I looked down and saw Elton John, Billy Joel, Dave Gilmour, Jimmy Page – all these amazing musicians – and I finally realised that we'd done something really substantial. We didn't have time to think before that. When we weren't in the studio we were touring.

Diamond Award for Hysteria
Roseland Ballroom
New York
16 March 1999

When Pyromania *went diamond in 2004, Def Leppard became one of only five rock bands that have two or more Diamond Award certifications (the others are the Beatles, Van Halen, Led Zeppelin and Pink Floyd)*

Def Leppard are inducted into the Hollywood RockWalk
5 September 2000

JOE ELLIOTT: The day we got inducted into the Hollywood RockWalk was completely mad. All of a sudden we felt like royalty, being ushered from one room to another to talk to people. Brian May gave a fantastic speech, and then we got to dirty our hands up. It was flattering to see some of the other artists out there who were either side of us, like Jimmy Page.

RICK SAVAGE: It was an honour to have something like that. It's not something that you strive for or think about but it's so nice when it comes along. Selling lots of records is the truest test and then I suppose things like the RockWalk are a spin-off from that.

DEF LEPPARD

Japan Tour 1999

Sep - Oct

DEF LEPPARD

USA/Canada Tour

December, 1999 – February, 2000

DEF LEPPARD

U.S. SUMMER TOUR 2000

JULY 14 – OCTOBER 1, 2000

EUPHORIA

JUN-28-2002 11:18   P.02

FAX IN BRIE[F]
TO: Malvin Mortimer, Def Leppard
FAX: 818 762-5742
FROM:
PAGES (INCLUDING COVER): 3

Monday, June 24, 2002

Received Time Jun.28. 11:06AM

TOTA[L]

New Musical Express Magazine
Album Review
by Andy Capper
July 30, 2002

Def Leppard: "X"-cellent

No-one, not even Bon Jovi, can convey the joy and the pain of the human condition better than Def Leppard. Their tenth album "X" is an emotional minefield. One minute you're feeling wistful and sad because of tearstained ballads like "**Long Long Way To Go**", the next you're plunging headfirst into a world of eroticism and fantasy thanks to hard rock bangers like "**Four Letter Word**" and "**Girl Like You**".

The Dallas Morning News
CD Review
by Teresa Gubbins
July 28, 2002

Def Leppard delivers catchy tunes on "X"

This sounds like faint praise, but it's not: The great thing about older English rock stars like Def Leppard is that they don't muddy up the waters with higher aspirations. Def Leppard has had its creative ups and downs – the last couple of discs, "**EUPHORIA**" and "**SLANG**", haven't been the best – but they just keep on keeping on, happy to do what they do well.

Classic Rock Magazine
Album Review
by Jon Hotten
July 12, 2002

The Joy of "X"

Loaded they may be, but it's not cash that drives Def Leppard. After 20 years, it's their place in music history they're looking to secure.

"If this was about money," Joe Elliott says, "We could have retired in 1988. Clearly we don't need the money. We all believe that we've still got great songs inside us."

The Montreal Gazette
Album Review
by Jordan Zivitz
July 25, 2002

Just this side of Britney –
Def Leppard is comfortable with new album's commercial bent

Many hard-rock acts would slap you upside the head with a double-neck guitar for suggesting they have anything in common with Britney Spears. Def Leppard isn't one of them.

When vocalist Joe Elliott and guitarist Phil Collen previewed the group's 10th album, appropriately titled "**X**", for Montreal media last week, they made no bones about their intentions to "make a very commercial record," as Elliott put it. Of course, the meaning of "commercial" has been revised since the late 1980s, when Def Leppard's behemoth "**HYSTERIA**" album found a home in 16 million households. That's where the group's collaborators on "**X**" came in.

MadBlast.com
Album Review
by Malcolm Michaels
July 29, 2002

Def Leppard are back on top with "X"

"**X**", Def Leppard's brand new album isn't what I expected...and that's a good thing. During the 90s, Def Leppard seemingly tried to please every genre of music fans. It didn't work. Now in 2002, the band has written a pop-rock album (with more emphasis on pop) and it's one of their best albums ever. "**X**" is full of great hooks and brilliant songwriting while still containing that sonic boom that put Def Leppard on top during the 80s.

X

JOE ELLIOTT: *The X cover is the simplest one we've ever done. It was our tenth album (if you include* Retro Active *and* Vault*), so we spent months agonising over all these different ways of representing '10', 'ten' or 'X' on different backgrounds. Then when we were finishing the record off in Dublin, Phil went over to London for the weekend and showed the artwork ideas to his ex-girlfriend Liz. She said, 'Why don't you just put a big fucking cross on it?', and she got a black marker pen and did exactly that. Phil brought it back and showed us, we all agreed on it and there was our cover. Right at the very last minute, as always with us.*

X
Recorded: 2001–2002
Released: 30 July 2002

JOE ELLIOTT: *X*, pronounced 'Ten', was, without a shadow of a doubt, the poppiest record Def Leppard have ever made. We wanted to try something different so we worked with Marti Frederiksen, who was a huge Leppard fan and had worked with Aerosmith, and Andreas Carlsson, Per Aldeheim and Max Martin, who had recorded with the likes of Backstreet Boys and Britney Spears. They wanted to do something with us and we thought, why not?

When I say pop, I'm not talking the Osmonds. It was more like Cheap Trick, who do pop rock. I'm a huge fan of Cheap Trick and I really love the song 'Everyday' on *X* because it reminds me of them.

RICK SAVAGE: Andreas Carlsson, Per Aldeheim and Max Martin used to be in hard rock bands when they were younger and were very much influenced by what Def Leppard were doing in the Eighties. Then they went in a pop direction and made acts like Backstreet Boys very famous. But if you listen to a lot of the Backstreet Boys stuff, it's just like Def Leppard minus the guitars. 'Pour Some Sugar on Me' could have been a Backstreet Boys song. Equally, we could have made their big song 'Larger Than Life' work for us.

JOE ELLIOTT: The album starts off with 'Now', which is definitely a rock song, but then you have 'Unbelievable', 'You're So Beautiful', 'Everyday', 'Long, Long Way to Go', which is all pop music. Then it starts to get heavier again with 'Four Letter Word' and 'Torn to Shreds'. 'Love Don't Lie' is me trying to do Seal, so, again, it's pop with a rock edge. 'Girl Like You' is a good pop song, with Vivian doing most of the singing. 'Let Me Be the One' is the big ballad that I brought to the table. And then 'Kiss the Day' and 'Scar' are big guitar songs, so the rock comes mainly at the beginning and the end of the album.

It's a very varied record and on the odd occasion that I hear one of these songs out of the blue I always think it sounds really good.

VIVIAN CAMPBELL: I'm a pop fan. A lot of people are surprised and maybe disappointed when they ask me what I listen to, thinking that I get up at nine o'clock in the morning and rock out to guitar music. But I actually don't. Crowded House are one of my favourite bands. I love great songs, I love great melodies and I love great singers. That's not to say I don't appreciate guitar or rock music, but my natural inclination is to write pop music.

RICK ALLEN: We all got involved in the songwriting on *X*. We also decided it would be good to collaborate with other songwriters and it paid off. We got a combination of our influence and theirs.

RICK SAVAGE: Andreas Carlsson and Per Aldeheim sent us a tape of the song 'Unbelievable', which they had written with Max Martin. We did not intend to write with them. They just felt that it sounded like a Def Leppard song. We get so many tapes with songs on them that people say 'sound like a Def Leppard song'. Nine times out of ten they sound nothing like us! But this one did have a 'Love Bites' vibe.

Then they invited us to Sweden and they wanted to produce it, which we were happy with. The beauty of this album was that we did not produce every song on it. It was very refreshing to go back to just thinking about being a musician and let someone else have control.

RICK ALLEN: The whole idea was to make a record that sounded like a classic Def Leppard album but with a contemporary edge to it. However, the contemporary sound isn't really in our DNA. That's why we wanted to work with people who knew more about it than we did. We wanted to embrace the new sound, but we didn't switch over completely to machines. We created loops from live percussion, almost like musical collage. It was something I enjoyed doing.

VIVIAN CAMPBELL: The first song that we cut more or less to completion was 'Unbelievable', which was written and produced by Andreas Carlsson and Per Aldeheim. Max Martin was also a writer on the track, but Andreas and Per were the two producers. We recorded it at Polar Studios in Stockholm, which is ABBA's original studio – a great, great room.

Then we went to Los Angeles and cut 'You're So Beautiful', 'Everyday' and 'Now' with Marti Frederiksen at Rumbo Recorders. Those were the sessions that really set the tone for the album. It was liberating because Marti works very, very quickly, whereas Def Leppard was so ingrained in the Mutt Lange school of recording, which was painstakingly slow.

VIVIAN CAMPBELL: Another unusual thing for us was that we recorded live drums and guitar cabinets. Rather than taking direct signals, which is what we normally did, we picked up the ambient sound of the room, using multiple amplifiers and close micing and distant micing.

We carried that earthy, vibrant rock sound and no-nonsense mindset back to Joe's studio in Dublin, where we did the bulk of the album with Pete Woodroffe. As a result, we worked much more efficiently on this record than we had in the past.

RICK ALLEN: I used this beautiful vintage Ludwig kit that sounded wonderful. Marti also brought in some snare drums that were quite interesting, including a free-floating Pearl. The main snare we used was a Ludwig Black Beauty from 1983 or 1984. My tech, Jerry Johnson, brought a 14x22 bass drum, and there was a 14-inch hanging tom, with 16-inch and 18-inch floor toms. The kit just sang. I felt like I was John Bonham.

VIVIAN CAMPBELL: I'd been with Def Leppard for ten years and this was only the third studio album I had made with the band. It was by far the best of the three and the only one that I felt truly happy with at that point.

I think that feeling was universal among the other guys in the band. It was exactly what we wanted and it went very smoothly.

PHIL COLLEN: *X* was quite liberating. We weren't sticking to any rigid boundaries, unlike pretty much all of the other records. I think of this album as a natural successor to *Hysteria*.

VIVIAN CAMPBELL: When you bring the initial idea for a song to Def Leppard's big table, everyone gets the knives out. It's a sort of Ginsu method of production – we chop and change. We all get involved in everyone's material, and we don't just settle for the first version. Sometimes we go round the houses and end up back where we started, but the fact that we're prepared to go down all these different avenues hopefully results in a better song.

'Girl Like You' is typical of how Leppard works. It started with a little rock riff that I was playing with on the Euphoria tour. Then I got home and made a demo in my spare bedroom using Pro Tools for the first time. That demo became the master, but when I brought it to the band we changed the verse a lot, cut out parts here and there and altered the tempo significantly.

PHIL COLLEN: I had to move out of my house for six months when it flooded and my entire ceiling collapsed. While it was being fixed I rented a house in Laguna Beach, which had a piano at the top of the stairs. I remember running up the stairs and my hands falling on the piano with the first chord of 'Now'. It was one of those songs where a single word kicked things off. I worked out how the song would go and then Marti and I started writing it and getting the acoustics worked out. It was different from anything we'd done before. The chorus came even before any lyrics were written. Then Joe got involved and wrote the lyrics. I really like the way he left the meaning open to interpretation.

JOE ELLIOTT: We played 'Now' every night during our 2019 residency in Vegas and it went down an absolute storm because people weren't expecting it. We really love that song. Phil came up with most of it and then everybody threw in their little bits.

VIVIAN CAMPBELL: 'Now' was a bit of a sleeper. I remember that when my wife first heard it she said, 'That's the single?' But then after hearing it a couple more times she really liked it. The first single is always a tough choice, especially for a rock band. You don't want to lead with a ballad or anything that's too pop. We decided that 'Now' was the right choice for the first cut because it had the rock element, it sounded fresh and it grew on people.

JOE ELLIOTT: In Leeds, as part of the Queen's Golden Jubilee tour, we played a three-song set, and then we met the Queen and Prince Philip. I have a photograph from the front page of the *Sheffield Star*. Then, two days later, we did Stoke-on-Trent and Sheffield on the same day. We were doing promo for *X*, which was released later that month. They weren't full gigs, just four-song sets on the same bill as various pop acts. We played 'Now', 'Let's Get Rocked', 'Animal' and 'Sugar', then legged it to the next gig.

Because we weren't really sure where we stood in the business at that time, we made the sensible decision to book smaller venues for the UK leg of the X tour proper. We played Ipswich Regent Theatre, where (when it was called the Gaumont) UFO had blown our minds in 1978. Back then, it would have been a dream to have played there but by 2003 it was a bit underwhelming.

PHIL COLLEN: Our bus broke down outside the K West Hotel in London. It started rolling back, so we all had to get out, including my dad who was around 80 at the time, and push against the bus so that it wouldn't hit the wall of the hotel. Then we had to walk all the way from Shepherd's Bush to Hammersmith Odeon, where we were playing, and just walk into the venue off the street.

Another memorable thing about that show was Brian May coming on at the end. We played 'Tie Your Mother Down' with him.

X

DEF LEPPARD

X

DECEMBER 2002 - US TOUR

EDR
MEAL PASS

MANDALAY BAY
Resort & Casino · Las Vegas

DEF LEPPARD

12/8/02
EVENTS
CENTER

McGATHY PROMOTIONS
& THE CONCLAVE 2002

DEF LEPPARD

EARSHOT
THEORY OF A DEADMAN
SPARTA   DRAGPIPE

Friday, July 26, 2002
@ The Quest Club
110 North Fifth St. Minneapolis, MN

98 ROCK
LIVERROCK
13
APRIL 25-27
ALL
ACCESS
417

DEF LEPPARD
all access

DEF LEPPARD
all access

394

The Quest Club
110 North Fifth St. Minneapolis, MN

Backstage pass
Artist

Joe Elliott
Vocals

Novamedia © 2002 BingoLotto Sweden

DEF LEPPARD

Japan Tour 2002

ジョー
Joe Elliott

DEF LEPPARD
all access

DEF LEPPARD

All Area Access
2003
promoter

10th Annual
music midtown
FRIDAY, SATURDAY & SUNDAY · MAY 2, 3 & 4
2003

YEARS OF MUSIC, FOOD & FUN

ARTIST

DODGE
96 ROCK
UPN ATLANTA
STAGE

BEST BUY   nashville
river stages
BEST BUY
2003
SATURDAY
ARTIST

Working DEF LEPPARD

guest
DEF LEPPARD

33 33 33 33
33 33 33 33
33 33 33 33
33 33 33 33
33 33 33 33
33 33 33 33
AR   0092
RICK SAVAGE
33 33 33 33

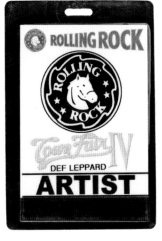

ROLLING ROCK
ROLLING
ROCK
Tom Petty IV
DEF LEPPARD
ARTIST

Working DEF LEPPARD

after show
DEF LEPPARD

PHIL COLLEN: The *Best Of* album was the label's idea. *Vault* always sold so well – it's gone five times platinum in the US – and every Christmas it sells like crazy. But it was missing some of the classic songs, so I think that's why they wanted to release another compilation.

CURRENT VAULT:

1. Pour Some Sugar On Me
2. Photograph
3. Love Bites
4. Let's Get Rocked
5. Two Steps Behind
6. Animal
7. Foolin'
8. Rocket
9. When Love & Hate Collide
10. Armageddon It
11. Have You Ever Needed Someone So Bad?
12. Rock Of Ages
13. Hysteria
14. Miss You In A Heartbeat
15. Bringin' On The Heartbreak

POTENTIAL ADDITIONAL GEMS FOR "VAULT x 2":

1. Long Long Way To Go
2. Rock Rock ('Till You Drop)
3. Let It Go
4. Women
5. Tear It Down
6. Another Hit & Run   *- love it, but is it greatest hits material?*
7. High 'N Dry (Saturday Night)
8. Wasted
9. Rock Brigade
10. Action
11. Run Riot
12. I Wanna Touch U
13. White Lightning
14. Switch 625   *- should have been on 1st one, would be strange w/o as #14. Bringing on heartbreak*
15. Promises
16. Slang
17. All I Want Is Everything
18. Paper Sun
19. Stand Up (Kick Love Into Motion)
20. Tonight
21. Heaven Is
22. Long Long Way To Go (Acoustic)
23. Two Steps Behind (Electric Version)
24. Miss You In A Heartbeat (Electric Version)

12-15

now?

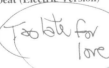 *Too late for love*

＊ how about something really hard to find like Ride Into the Sun? or something from that EP they put out themselves?

Best of Def Leppard
Recorded: 1979-2004
Released: 25 October 2004

Rock of Ages: The Definitive Collection
Recorded: 1979-2005
Released: 17 May 2005

PHIL COLLEN: On *Rock of Ages*, the US version of *Best Of*, disc one is the greatest hits but disc two is really what people wanted to hear – stuff like 'Wasted', 'Mirror, Mirror' and 'Paper Sun'. I think more than anything else the record label wanted to introduce Def Leppard to a younger generation. It's the teenagers that really make something special. You need them on your side for it to work on a bigger scale.

JOE ELLIOTT: It was a great way of letting people know that we were still around.

We were keen not to exclude any part of our career. It would have been so easy to focus on *Hysteria*, *Pyromania* and *Adrenalize*, but I think that would have been a little unfair on us as artists and on our hardcore fans.

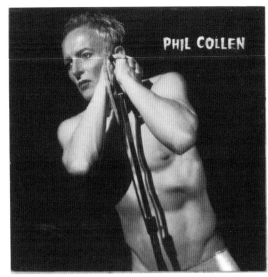

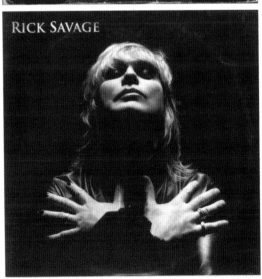

Yeah!
Recorded: 2003–2006
Released: 23 May 2006

YEΔH!

JOE ELLIOTT: *For the inner sleeve artwork of* Yeah! *we wanted to recreate some of the iconic images of Seventies rock music. So, we had Vivian as Marc Bolan's* Electric Warrior, *me in the phone box doing David Bowie, Phil as Iggy Pop on the Stooges'* Raw Power *cover, Rick doing Lou Reed's* Transformer *cover and Sav as Freddie Mercury, with black fingernails and the whole bit.*

We were paying homage to our Seventies heroes and what better way to do that than to ask Mick Rock, the man who shot the Seventies, to photograph us? This was the guy whose pictures we saw every week in Sounds, Melody Maker, Record Mirror, Disc ... everywhere, basically. In fact, it was Mick who had shot the original Freddie Mercury, Iggy Pop and Lou Reed photographs that we were restaging.

Mick did a brilliant job of replicating those five images. If you look at the picture of Vivian and compare it to the front cover of Electric Warrior, *it's scary how similar it is.*

JOE ELLIOTT: In 2004 we didn't do any gigs the whole year, which was unusual for us. It was just a different time in our lives. I was getting married in September that year so I was glad not to be working. We'd never had any proper time off, ever. When we've got three years between albums, it's because for the first year or two we're touring the previous album, then we get a couple of weeks off, and then we're making the next album. In 2004 we didn't have anything planned – no tour, no new album.

RICK SAVAGE: The fans throughout the years have been absolutely fantastic. It's not always easy being a Def Leppard fan, because we take so long to make records that they must be wondering whether we've split up. So, it's great that they're always there for us whenever we do finally release something.

JOE ELLIOTT: After a while we got a bit itchy and decided to make a covers record, which became *Yeah!* We'd actually chosen the tracks during the 2003 tour – well, they kind of chose themselves. They were all songs that had had a big impact on us growing up – mainly the stuff we saw on *Top of the Pops* like Slade, Sweet, Bowie, Bolan, Blondie and Queen. And then there was the odd song we loved by artists whose albums we wouldn't necessarily buy. We all thought 'Rock On' by David Essex was brilliant and we loved the John Kongos song 'He's Gonna Step on You Again' – the drum technique was one of the things that fed into 'Rocket'.

RICK ALLEN: Every five years or so Joe would say, 'We need to do a covers album!' Finally, we just recorded it and told everybody after the fact.

The idea was to choose songs that had inspired us prior to our signing a record deal but we didn't want to pick anything that was too obvious, such as Stones or Beatles songs. Interestingly enough, we all came up with similar lists!

VIVIAN CAMPBELL: We decided to make a record that reflected where we had come from. The songs, for the most part, represent our formative musical years. People are always pegging us as a heavy metal band, which we're really not. Our primary influence is pop music. Ultimately, we're a sheep in wolf's clothing. If you strip away the bombast of Def Leppard, you'll find pop songs with choruses underneath.

RICK SAVAGE: When deciding to record some of the songs that were so influential in our youth, I thought we would be facing a nightmare task just to narrow the number down to 50 or so. How wrong could I be? It soon became apparent that many of the songs appealed to all five of us, stirring up our own individual memories and feelings of a period in time that was to shape just about everything we've tried to achieve as Def Leppard.

We had a lot of fun making that album – and we still have a lot of fun listening to it.

PHIL COLLEN: We have a briefing for every album and the briefing for *Yeah!* was that we didn't want to choose the songs that everyone knew. So, instead of doing 'The Jean Genie' or 'Ziggy Stardust', we did 'Drive-In Saturday'. That was a Bowie song I'd never heard anyone cover before. Avoiding the obvious moved the album into a different sphere.

We did do 'Waterloo Sunset' by the Kinks, but that was great because we made it sound like us. We didn't force any of the songs. 'No Matter What' by Badfinger sounds like what we'd been trying to do ever since we started.

VIVIAN CAMPBELL: There was a lot of politicking. Some people were fonder of certain acts than others. We covered an ELO song. I wouldn't say I was a big ELO fan but Sav was, so he lobbied for that. And Joe was a huge Bowie fan. We put our version of 'Dear Friends' by Queen on the bonus EP, but we should have done a Queen song for the main album. They were a massive influence.

JOE ELLIOTT: Every single one of us blurted out 'No Matter What' by Badfinger, so that was a no-brainer. Roxy Music was another must-have for Phil and me, and also '20th Century Boy', which I felt was the most representative T. Rex song for us to do. The ELO song '10538 Overture' was a way to get to a Jeff Lynne/Roy Wood sound, as Roy Wood was only in ELO for that one record. Plus, that guitar lick at the beginning is fantastic.

The only real rock songs on the album are 'Don't Believe a Word' by Thin Lizzy, 'Little Bit of Love' by Free, which is really a pop rock song, and 'Stay with Me' by the Faces, which is the one that Phil sang. Then you have Sweet's 'Hell Raiser', Mott the Hoople's 'The Golden Age of Rock 'n' Roll' and Bowie's 'Drive-In Saturday'. These were the singles that as kids we all went out and bought.

The guys came to Dublin for a couple of weeks, banging the backing tracks down in my studio. We had a new co-producer to work with. Pete Woodroffe decided he wanted to spend more time songwriting and demoing in his home studio, so Ronan McHugh made the step from engineer to producer that Pete and Mike Shipley had done before him.

After everyone else had gone away again, I spent the summer of 2004 dipping in and out of the studio between wedding preparations. I remember one day when I did the vocals for four of the tracks. I went from Bryan Ferry to Debbie Harry before lunch and then from David Essex to Ian Hunter after lunch. It was really weird – I felt like I was schizophrenic.

JOE ELLIOTT: In 2005 we changed management from Peter Mensch and Cliff Burnstein at Q Prime to Howard Kaufman. Howard's forte was re-breaking famous bands. He did it with Fleetwood Mac, the Eagles, Aerosmith – bands that had sold millions of records but had gone under the radar for a while. He would bring them back up by getting them out live in front of as many people as possible and rebuilding their fan base.

He didn't really care whether these bands made new music ever again; he was all about the touring. When we got to know him and discussed how we wanted to go forward, we were adamant that we would still want to be making new music. We saw *Yeah!* as an important stepping stone in that process as it would give us something to take on tour, but the label had been reluctant to release it. Howard seemed to have more clout with the label than our previous management – possibly his personal relationship with the CEO in America had something to do with that – and so all of a sudden they were happy to put the record out and get behind it and it did really well.

PHIL COLLEN: I went to a gig and met someone called Trudy Green, who said, 'You shouldn't be split headlining. You should be out there headlining yourself. You guys are Def Leppard.' She offered to introduce us to her business associate Howard Kaufman, who managed acts like Aerosmith, Lenny Kravitz and Stevie Nicks.

I met him the following week. He laid out this plan to get us back to filling bigger places that he said would triple our income within a year. I was sold. I loved everything he was saying. We had been loyal to Q Prime for a long time and they'd done amazing things for us but they'd taken us as far as they could. They had other bands and they didn't see the value in us touring.

So, Howard became our manager and literally everything he promised – from the size of the venues, to the number of people that would be coming in, to the increase in revenue – he nailed.

He told us we should go out and tour with Journey. The first gig we did was in Camden, New Jersey: 23,000 people, sold out; 3,000 people couldn't get in.

From that point, everything started to change. It gave us a new lease of life and we all started getting excited about the band again. We always believed in ourselves, but part of you does start to question your relevance and validity when nothing much is happening for years. But suddenly we went from that to thinking, 'Wow, shit. We should be in the Rock and Roll Hall of Fame.'

Opposite:
Rehearsal and show
Live 8
Philadelphia Museum of Art
2 July 2005

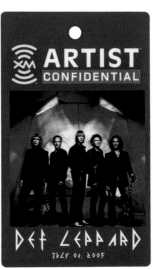

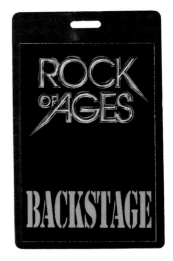

LIVE

ARTIST GUEST

Philadelphia
July 2, 2005

ACTION
LET'S GET ROCKED
WOMEN
FOOLIN'
HYSTERIA
PROMISES
NO MATTER
LOVE BITES
ARMAGGEDDON
ROCKET
HAVE U EVER
PHOTOGRAPH
ANIMAL
ROCK OF AGES
HEARTBREAK
SUGAR

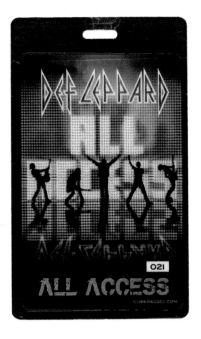

JOE ELLIOTT: *Yeah!* came out on 23 May 2006 and then two days later our old friend Brian May joined us on stage to play '20th Century Boy' at the VH1 Rock Honors show in Las Vegas. Soon after that, we kicked off the 2006 tour where we co-headlined with Journey. 'No Matter What' and 'Rock On' had some enormous airplay in the States on FM rock radio, which really bolstered the ticket sales. That tour was our biggest selling in America since 1988, even bigger than 1992.

Things were quieter in the UK. We only did a couple of gigs in England – Sheffield Arena and Hammersmith Apollo – but we always said we'd never not play our home country. We had Cheap Trick and the Sensational Alex Harvey Band opening for us, obviously without Alex, but it was fun for me watching them play those two nights.

We treated *Yeah!* like any new record and played two or three songs from it in our set, mixing them in with the crown jewels like 'Let's Get Rocked', 'Sugar' and 'Photograph'.

RICK ALLEN: These days, a lot of people work out songs using drum machines, but back when the songs on *Yeah!* were written there was no such thing as a drum machine. Playing the drum parts on those songs live gave me the chance to rediscover aspects of drumming that had become something of a lost art. It's only when you play a song live that you figure out what the song really means and wants to be.

JOE ELLIOTT: The relationship between recording and touring was being turned on its head. Albums were no longer being promoted by tours; tours were being promoted by albums. Suddenly ticket sales were more important than record sales. We were doing great with ticket sales, so we were comfortable with that. We knew the record wasn't going to sell like hotcakes but the tickets did, so it was a good payoff. We had a great tour, we finally got the record out and we were happy little piglets because we had new management and the enthusiasm was back.

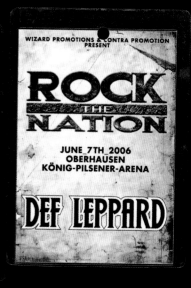

PHIL COLLEN: Our tour with Journey was billed as a double headliner, but we went on last every night. That was an amazing tour. You had all of the Journey songs and all of our songs, but there was no sense of competition between the two bands. It was just presented as a great night of music and it really was.

Songs from the Sparkle Lounge
Recorded: 2006–2008
Released: 25 April 2008

SONGS FROM THE SPARKLE LOUNGE

JOE ELLIOTT: Songs from the Sparkle Lounge *was written during the Yeah! tour in 2006, recorded in 2007 and released in 2008. The title of the album comes from our name for the backstage area where we wrote the songs. We would ask the crew to find a room in each venue for us to work in. We used this miniature drum that literally came out of a suitcase and folded out, and a tiny amp the size of a loaf of bread for the guitars and bass. After a few weeks, the crew started messing about by stringing fairy lights over the gear so it got christened the 'Sparkle Lounge'. And then 'sparkle' became our codeword for songwriting on the road: 'Let's get in there and sparkle. Let's see what we can come up with.'*

RICK ALLEN: The 'Sparkle Lounge' gave us the opportunity to present song ideas to each other and do some rough recordings while we were on tour. Some of those ideas made their way to the studio when we were ready to record the next album. The last thing we wanted was to get off the road and think, 'Oh shit, now we've got to come up with a new record!'

VIVIAN CAMPBELL: I don't normally write on the road, but occasionally I have. You never know when you're going to be inspired by something. If I come up with an idea while I'm on tour all I'll do is make a note of it. I don't demo it on the road, as I prefer to use my full Pro Tools rig at home.

To be honest, I find writing for Def Leppard a bit of a struggle anyway. It's not really my natural inclination to write Leppard-like songs. I always find that I have to step outside of myself and try to think whether what I'm writing is going to work for Joe. On my demos I tend to be more of a soul-type singer, but I've come to realise that Joe has a different approach to melody.

JOE ELLIOTT: By the end of the tour we had the guts of a lot of songs that we could take into the studio and finish. Some of them came from ideas that we'd had before 2006 and then put to one side. For example, I'd written the music for 'Bad Actress' at some point in the Nineties, but we'd sat on it and sat on it and sat on it.

The songs on *Sparkle Lounge* are a little different. To me the album is like a hybrid of typical Def Leppard and the harder-edged *Slang* sound.

Songs like 'Go' and 'Nine Lives' were pretty AC/DC-ish. Sav wrote 'C'mon, C'mon', which is classic glam and very Leppard but, again, a bit rawer in its execution. He also came up with 'Love', which was the first time that we'd worn our Queen heart on our sleeves so blatantly. I wrote 'Come Undone', which was like a shortened version of an eight-minute Led Zeppelin epic. Vivian came up with 'Cruise Control', 'Only the Good Die Young' and 'Gotta Let It Go'.

It was a weird time because we knew we were coming to the end of our recording contract and that it wasn't going to get renewed. It was clear that the label were happy for us to go off and do our own thing somewhere else – which is exactly what we did. The guy in charge wasn't a big fan and there's not much we could do about that. So, *Sparkle Lounge* was our last album for Universal.

PHIL COLLEN: The first song we recorded for *Sparkle Lounge* was 'Nine Lives', which we did with Tim McGraw. Rick's brother, Robert, who used to be our tour manager, was now working with Tim McGraw and Faith Hill. Robert had told Rick that Tim would love to do a song with Def Leppard, so I had this idea for a song percolating in my head if I ever met him.

Then we played the Hollywood Bowl, and Tim was backstage with a million other people and someone introduced us. I said, 'Hey, Tim, I've got an idea for a song. It goes like this.' I'd literally just met him and shaken his hand. And then I started singing my idea to him. Then he said, 'Well, what if the vocals did this?' And he started singing back to me. Then he said, 'And then it stops. And Joe comes in and the band kicks in.' We wrote most of the song literally within a minute and a half of meeting each other. It was amazing.

We started recording it while we were on the tour with Journey. I did the backing vocals in a shower area backstage. They didn't sound great and I assumed we'd re-record them later. We never did.

JOE ELLIOTT: When *Sparkle Lounge* was released in April 2008 it got good coverage across the mainstream British press not just the rock magazines, which set us up for a pretty successful British tour that year. Then we came back to headline the Download festival at Donington a year later as a kind of lick-the-envelope seal on the tour. We felt vindicated because, without much label assistance, we had managed to get our name back out there by talking to anybody who wanted to talk to us. We didn't refuse anyone and our willingness was rewarded.

This was a good time for us because we were establishing a great relationship with our new manager, Howard Kaufman. I think he was impressed with the fact that we knew what we wanted. We weren't just sitting around, waiting for him to tell us what to do.

As part of the 2008 tour we went back on the festival circuit in Europe for the first time since 1996. We toured all over with Whitesnake, taking turns to headline depending on where we were.

We went out in 2008 with a new album and then we basically toured that album for three out of the next four years. We just tweaked the set list and brought in different opening acts, including Heart, Poison, Journey, Mötley Crüe, Joan Jett and Cheap Trick – all big ticket sellers in their own right. We always loved a good package.

PHIL COLLEN: We started *Sparkle Lounge* while we were on tour, so we didn't have the usual thing of taking six months off then having to re-establish some momentum in the studio. When you're on tour you're performing almost every day and there's more aggression to your playing and singing. But when you're off tour you become more comfortable. I think that's the main reason why there was a bit more spark to this album than the other studio stuff we'd done previously.

VIVIAN CAMPBELL: We always try to capture the energy of our stage shows on our albums, but bottling lightning is hard to do. Def Leppard are notoriously slow at making records, but *Songs from the Sparkle Lounge* seemed more fluid in style and a lot less mechanical. But then, you can never really replace a live audience for motivation.

PHIL COLLEN: When you play songs live, you make a collage of what is prominent on the recording and focus on those elements. There's no way you can play live all the vocals and counter vocals that you did in the studio, and there may be a high harmony that's impossible for any of us because Mutt Lange had originally sung it. So, we do a version of it that sounds there or thereabouts.

It's the same with the guitar parts. Say you had four guitar parts going off – you would listen for the most prominent parts on the record and create a two-guitar version of that. Really what you're doing is orchestration.

RICK SAVAGE: A lot of bands go in the studio and try to make it sound as live as possible, whereas we try to make the best recording possible. If that means spending loads of time doing different backing tracks, then that's how we'd rather do it. We want people to listen to our albums in ten years' time and think, 'Well that still sounds pretty good.' When you're playing live you can't replicate everything you can do in the studio, but there's an energy on stage that makes up for it. On the other hand, when you're in the studio it's very hard to recreate the energy that you get from playing live. The two are totally different things.

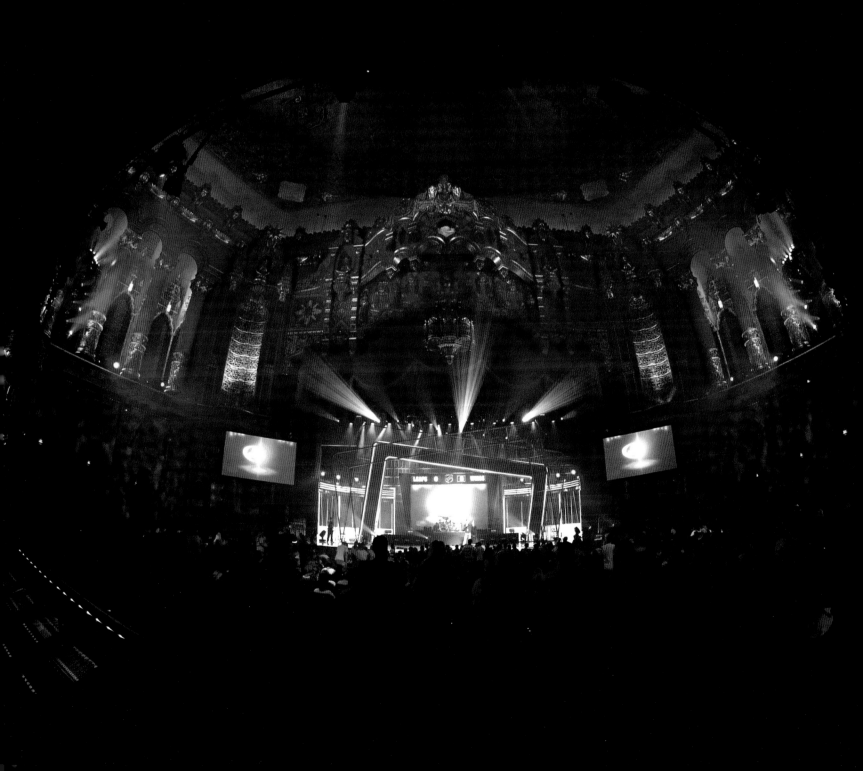

JOE ELLIOTT: While we were on the road in 2008 our tour accountant walked on the bus with his laptop open. He said, 'Have you seen this?' It was an interview Taylor Swift had done, where somebody asked her whether she planned to go on the CMT show *Crossroads*, which pairs country performers with artists from other genres. Her reply was that the only act she'd ever do it with was Def Leppard.

Taylor's parents were huge Leppard fans. She was born in 1989 so she would probably have heard *Hysteria* in the womb.

We immediately got in touch because we thought it would be amazing to do something like that. This girl was the new generation and was selling billions of records. She was a fan of our music. What could go wrong with this picture? Not a lot. So, we were blown away when she agreed to do it. We learned five of her songs and Taylor learned six of ours. She insisted on 'Two Steps Behind', and 'Love' off *Sparkle Lounge*. I enjoyed the challenge of singing songs like 'Love Story' from a man's perspective.

There was one funny moment: Taylor said there were a couple of lines in 'Sugar' she just couldn't sing. 'You got the peaches, I got the cream' was never going to be right for her, but she was OK with everything else.

We rehearsed individually to tapes and then we got together in Nashville and did a two-day rehearsal with Taylor and her band. We shot it on a Friday or a Saturday and then she invited us all around to her house on the Sunday for a barbecue. It was a fun week and then we all went back to our daily lives as Def Leppard and Taylor Swift.

Since then, I've followed her career with interest. We did get together one more time when we were jointly nominated for performance of the year at the CMT awards in 2009. We didn't win it, but we got to close out the show with Taylor doing 'Pour Some Sugar on Me' again, which went down an absolute storm.

PHIL COLLEN: Taylor Swift's mum and dad were huge Def Leppard fans and that filtered down to their daughter. She also really loved Shania Twain and obviously there's a huge connection between Shania and us because Mutt Lange wrote and recorded all of those songs with her.

The idea behind the *Crossroads* TV show is to bring two acts together to play each other's songs. It was really fun. Taylor was only 19 at the time and still trying to define her sound. You could hear the country in Shania's stuff but with Taylor, if it wasn't for Caitlin, her fiddle player, you wouldn't really have said that her songs were country at all. She didn't have the twang in her voice. She had a pure pop voice, which was so appealing. She was having that hybrid moment. It wasn't country. It wasn't pop. It was just great songs.

RICK ALLEN: Doing *Crossroads* with Taylor was a pivotal moment for Def Leppard. Collaborative work like this was a new thing for us. I knew from my brother Robert, who is still an integral part of her management team, what a true talent she was. Her staying power is further proof that her songs, like ours, stand the test of time.

Top: Crossroads *recording*
Roy Acuff Theater
Nashville, Tennessee
6 November 2008 (broadcast 7 November)

Centre and bottom: 2009 CMT Music Awards
Sommet Center
Nashville, Tennessee
16 June 2009

Joe Elliott
Performer
Def Leppard

JOE ELLIOTT: The *Mirror Ball* live album was mainly recorded on the Sparkle Lounge tour in 2008 and 2009 and came out in 2011.

Technology had moved on. We no longer needed to hire in the Rolling Stones Mobile for two nights and hope we didn't make a mistake. Ronan would record every night onto a hard drive. Because you're recording every night you don't get red light fever; you don't even think about it anymore. He sifted through and picked the best performance of each song and then glued it all together. There's not an overdub to be seen – or heard.

We wrote three new songs, which went on the end of *Mirror Ball*. It's a trick that a few bands did in the Seventies and Eighties. KISS did it on *Alive II*. Ian Hunter did it on *Welcome to the Club*. I wrote 'Undefeated', Sav wrote 'Kings of the World' and Phil and his mate C.J. Vanston wrote 'It's All About Believin''. And I swear to God, those are three of the greatest songs we've ever done. We thought we would put them on the live album as a teaser and then remix them for our next studio album. But when the next album came out four years later, it turned out we didn't need them.

VIVIAN CAMPBELL: It was the band's first ever live album. The three new tracks on the record were very different from each other. Joe's song 'Undefeated' is a classic Def Leppard tune and it worked very, very well for us live.

Mirror Ball – Live & More
Recorded: 2008–2011
Released: 3 June 2011

JOE ELLIOTT: In 2011 we hit a disagreement with Universal over digital rights for our back catalogue. Howard Kaufman had negotiated a smoking deal for the band in 2010. They shook hands on it but over Christmas someone else at the label read through the contract, had second thoughts and pulled the deal.

We had our lawyer draft a two-pager to Universal saying, 'Dear Sirs, from now on this is how it is. Contractually, you are not allowed to delete our back catalogue. We are going to keep an eye on that. We also aren't going to ever let you put our records in mid-price. And you can't put our songs on any compilation record without our permission.' Basically, what we were saying was, 'If you ask the question the answer's going to be no.'

We also decided to sell new recordings of some of our hits online so that the label wouldn't make a penny out of them. We'd already released re-recorded versions of 'Sugar' and 'Rock of Ages', which we'd done for the *Rock of Ages* movie back in 2012, so that gave us some momentum. Then, we re-recorded the song 'Hysteria' in 2013. So, for the best part of six years we only had *Mirror Ball* and three of the re-records up online and that was all you could buy digitally. No studio albums, just the live album and the re-records.

We didn't feel we needed a record company. As a band we'd always had our own record label in Bludgeon Riffola, which is the name we put on the label of our self-released EP before we had a record deal. Now we were going back to Bludgeon Riffola as a label name for our new releases, but licensing them through Jimmy Buffett's label, Mailboat, which was part-owned by Howard Kaufman.

The stand-off with Universal continued until 2017 when Bruce Resnikoff and David Rowe got involved and made a determined effort to build bridges. All of a sudden, the digital deal was done. Sadly, Howard passed away before the deal was finalised but he and his associate Mike Kobayashi had already set everything up so it all went through smoothly. We put the digital up in January 2018 and as of August 2022 our songs had been streamed six billion times.

JOE ELLIOTT: The Mirror Ball tour was a tour to promote a recording of a band on tour. That sounds crazy, but we weren't the first band to do it and we certainly won't be the last.

As you get older it gets increasingly difficult to keep spewing an album out every year or two years, because life gets in the way. Dropping everything to go and work in a studio for four months is what you do when you're 18 to 25. As you move into the middle part of your career you're surviving on the adrenaline, but then you have to start thinking about how you're going to keep going without burning out.

Touring was taking its toll as well. Eventually, I put my foot down with the new management. I told them we weren't going to play three nights in a row anymore. It was killing my voice. After a while everybody else in the band who sang realised they were singing better by not having to do the third night.

VIVIAN CAMPBELL: While it is a very gruelling schedule, we make it as comfortable as we possibly can for a bunch of old guys who are still out there on the road. When I joined the band we played a lot more shows per week but in recent years we have definitely slowed down. We have to make sure that we're physically able to do the show justice – and, take it from me, it really is a physical show.

JOE ELLIOTT: The Mirror Ball tour took up basically the second half of 2011. Then we went at it again in the summer of 2012 with 40 or so North American shows, which followed on from a set we played at the premiere of the Tom Cruise movie *Rock of Ages*.

JOE ELLIOTT: Download is a great festival. When we headlined in 2009, it was the first time we'd been back to Donington since that memorable gig in 1986 where Rick made his comeback after losing his arm. So, the 2009 Download had felt like a homecoming for all of us, but especially for Rick.

All of a sudden, we were headlining again in 2011. That made us the first band to play the festival three times. And we're the only band, to this day as far as I'm aware, to headline it twice in three years.

JOE ELLIOTT: In 2013 we did a Las Vegas residency called 'Viva! Hysteria'.

Vegas was always thought of as the elephants' graveyard, where artists went to die, but all of a sudden it had become a very rock and roll town. You had people like Prince, KISS, Mötley Crüe and Aerosmith all doing residencies there. So, the timing couldn't have been better. They asked us to play *Hysteria* in its entirety and in its correct order. We thought, 'Wow, that sounds tough. Let's do it!'

PHIL COLLEN: Plenty of bands play a full album on tour, but there aren't many records that have the status of a diamond album like *Hysteria*. It was going to be a real challenge. A lot of the songs on there are hard to sing and play at the same time.

RICK SAVAGE: The seven or so songs on *Hysteria* that we played regularly on tour weren't a problem. It was the other four or five, like 'Don't Shoot Shotgun', 'Excitable' and 'Love and Affection', that needed the work. We spent 80 percent of our time in rehearsals getting them up to standard.

JOE ELLIOTT: I have mixed memories of that time because on the morning of the first rehearsal Vivian told us that he had cancer and not just a bad cough. We had to circle the wagons, because he didn't want to go public with it yet. It was hard to be a hundred percent excited when one of you has just been diagnosed with the big C, but we never let it interfere with our performance.

VIVIAN CAMPBELL: I'd been feeling run down, on and off, since late 2011. It wasn't full-on, knock-you-down sickness, it was a head cold thing. I'd go and see the 'rock doc' and he'd give me antibiotics but then as soon as I'd finished taking them it would come back again. So, he'd give me some more antibiotics. Next, he sent me to a respiratory doctor, who gave me a nasal spray and an inhaler. I was sure there was something else going on and so I asked for a chest X-ray, but he said I'd be fine, gave me a stronger inhaler and told me to come back in a month. This went on and on until finally they gave me the X-ray.

Having done the X-ray, the doctor sent me for a PET scan that afternoon and having done the scan he sent me to the oncologist the next morning. Then I had a biopsy the following week and I was told that I had Hodgkin lymphoma. It was at a pretty early stage, but I could have caught it even earlier if I had been more insistent instead of deferring to the doctors. Nobody knows your body better than you do.

I've done various different treatments and therapies and there's new stuff coming down the line all the time. I'm fortunate enough to be able to afford great healthcare. So, I'm not worried about it, but it's been quite a journey.

I've learned how to roll with it. I'm stubborn and I'm Irish, so I've always had the mindset of 'Fuck you, cancer, you're not going to get me.' I'm very thankful to my bandmates in Leppard for allowing me to keep working as much as possible, even when I've really been on the ropes. There have been a couple of times when we weren't sure if I was going to be able to make a show. But we got away with it. Having the band as a focus has stopped me from obsessing about the disease and capitulating to it. That's really helped me a lot.

PHIL COLLEN: As a band we've spent more time together than we have with our blood relatives. Terrible things happen in regular families, so the odds are they're going to happen in this other family sooner or later. You know you're just going to have to deal with it and make things as easy as possible for whoever's going through it.

VIVIAN CAMPBELL: I take immense pride in my work, so the thought of bringing in a sub doesn't sit well with me. I always feel like they'll never be able to do as good a job as I will, because I have this work ethic and I want to be perfect. I know that I'm never going to be perfect, but that's what I'm aiming for.

PHIL COLLEN: We had Steve Brown stand in for Vivian when he was receiving stem cell treatment. Steve stood in for me as well when my son Jaxson was born in 2018 because my wife died in childbirth twice. They got her back to life and Jaxson's a miracle baby. The show goes on – we just have to navigate around whatever life throws at us.

Viva! Hysteria
Recorded: 29–30 March 2013
Released: 22 October 2013

10,210

DED FLATBIRD
WORLDS BEST
DEF LEPPARD COVER BAND
WORLD TOUR 2013
LAS VEGAS

JOE ELLIOTT: We decided we would open for ourselves with our own alter ego band, Ded Flatbird.

PHIL COLLEN: When my eldest son's mum was pregnant with him and having ante-natal classes, one of the other women there said, 'Oh, your husband's a musician, isn't he? What's the name of his band?' She replied, 'Def Leppard.' And the woman said, 'Dead flat bird?' So, that became a thing. Peter Mensch made up a T-shirt with the logo and everything.

JOE ELLIOTT: We thought we might go mad, playing the same main set of 12 songs on the same stage for a month, so I suggested we never play the same opening set twice as Ded Flatbird. On one of the two nights that were recorded for the *Viva! Hysteria* live album and DVD, we played seven of the ten songs from *High 'n' Dry*, the closest we've ever come to doing that album from start to finish. We played side one and then 'On Through the Night' and 'Mirror, Mirror' off the other side.

PHIL COLLEN: We used aliases in Ded Flatbird. They were in the tradition of the ridiculous names we came up with when checking in to hotels on tour so that people wouldn't phone our rooms in the middle of the night and stuff. We were all sitting in the dressing room and on the walls they had old covers of *Rolling Stone* magazine. The idea was to take a name or title from one cover and combine it with a name from a different cover based on your month and day of birth. My two names were a rapper called Chingy and Tracy Chapman, so we put them together to make Chingy Chapman. Joe's name was Booty Ruben, from a Destiny's Child cover promoting their song 'Bootylicious' and *American Idol* winner Ruben Studdard.

JOE ELLIOTT: We even used different gear as Ded Flatbird so that we looked like a crappy support band. Rick played on this tiny little kit. We roped off the ego ramp so that Booty Ruben couldn't go down it. And Booty would slag off the headline band: 'That fucking Joe Elliott won't give me any room.' A famous singer came to see us and one of his entourage said to me, 'Dude, you should have a word with the singer in that opening band because he was having a real go at you.' I didn't have the heart to tell him it was me.

PHIL COLLEN: We'd go on stage wearing hats and all this stupid gear. Most of the audience realised it was us but some of them didn't get it. They were upset that this band was ripping Def Leppard off. And so we'd have a bit of fun with that, saying things like, 'Wow, really? A guy cuts his arm off just to look like the drummer. A bit extreme?'

JOE ELLIOTT: It was weird to be having such a great time messing about as Ded Flatbird when we'd only just heard that Vivian had cancer, but he was convinced he was going to get through it fine and his positivity meant that there wasn't any kind of horrible, morbid atmosphere.

PHIL COLLEN: We wrote out a list of all the songs that we wanted to do. One of the songs on the list was a track called 'Good Morning Freedom', which was the B side of the first single from *On Through the Night*. When we first played it in rehearsals Rick just suddenly stopped. He said, 'Last time I played this I had two arms.' He figured it out but it was his muscle memory telling him to play a certain way. It was quite a moment.

RICK ALLEN: Some of the older songs – the two-arm songs – can get a bit challenging. 'Rocket' is always a little tricky, but very satisfying to get right.

That whole *Hysteria* album conjures up the ups and downs we all go through in life before ultimately succeeding with gratitude in our heart. That record leaves me in a really good place. It's saying to me, 'Don't move anything, because everything is OK exactly where it is.'

PHIL COLLEN: I would have a shower in between our Ded Flatbird set and our Def Leppard set, which is kind of my ritual to wake me up and get me into whatever I'm doing. Then we'd come on and play *Hysteria* in its entirety. It was pure theatre and we loved it.

JOE ELLIOTT: There was no need to soundcheck once we'd got it all down, and no travelling, of course, so we had lots of time to write some new songs. What a luxury! I was even able to come up with some stuff for my other band, Down 'n' Outz, which has been going since 2009.

RICK SAVAGE: We played 11 shows spread over three weeks or so. It was one of the best things we've ever done. It was great to just play your gig and then not have to get on a bus and travel 300 miles to the next show. You just got in a service elevator and there was your bed, if that's what you wanted. It was all the positive things about playing live without any of the negative things.

PHIL COLLEN: I was getting in a boxing ring with boxing gloves on and, as I went under the rope, I touched the floor really lightly just to get my balance and my hand went all squishy and numb. I took off the boxing glove and the tendon had torn off at the knuckle. It had been going like that for ages from doing left hooks during my kickboxing training. I think I had the wraps on too tight and for too long, and I was hitting too hard. Eventually it just went.

I thought I'd be OK in a week, but then Rick and I were rehearsing in Paris and suddenly I couldn't play. My friend got in touch with a local surgeon he knew, Dr Jean-Noël Goubier, who sews people's fingers and hands back together if they've been blown up or in a chainsaw accident. He said he could fix it no problem, but that I'd be out of action for two months after the operation.

So, I struggled through the European tour that summer. We did Hellfest in France and some other dates with Europe and Whitesnake. The body's so amazing. The first night I was making all these terrible mistakes, but after a few more shows I'd figured out how to play around the injury. It really hurt, though. I'd hit a note with one finger and then it would pop and I'd swear like mad. After the tour I went back to Paris and had the operation and then I was in a cast for six weeks.

Then I had to learn how to play again, which was really weird. After playing for so long, all of a sudden you can't. Your dexterity disappears so quickly. Rick had the same thing when he lost his arm. Whenever he stood up, he'd lean over to the right because he was used to being balanced with two arms. You take things for granted until they're not there anymore.

JOE ELLIOTT: The first time I came into KISS's orbit was the summer of 1976. I headed to Bradley's Records with my pocket money like I always did on a Saturday morning. There was a six-foot poster of the *Destroyer* cover in the window with these guys standing like cartoon superheroes on top of a burning hill. I'd heard of KISS but I'd never actually heard any of their music. I remember thinking that if they sounded like they looked, they were going to be amazing. Abandoning whatever record I'd planned to buy that week, I took *Destroyer* home and it did not disappoint at all.

From that moment on, I was a total fan. The first time I saw them live was at the Bingley Hall in Stafford in 1980 when Phil was opening for them in his band Girl. It was a horrible echoey place so I couldn't judge how they sounded. But they were such a brilliant spectacle that it didn't really matter.

The next time I saw them was 1996 when we were playing Wembley Arena the night after they did. So, I'd only actually seen them live twice in all the time that I'd been a fan. But that's not because I didn't want to, I just never got the chance.

PHIL COLLEN: KISS achieved success by being the first rock band to approach their career from an extreme theatrical angle. They act out these parts as younger men on stage. Being larger than life means they don't have to deal with the bullshit that other bands face. They can take the makeup and costumes off and go back to being kind of normal. I think they maintain probably about 50 percent of their onstage character off stage.

So, touring with KISS was wonderful, as it made us realise how important the show is as a piece of theatre. Just being a part of that with everyone in the crew and both bands pulling together was really cool. It lifted us to a different level, kept us going on an upward trajectory.

I went on stage with them in Atlantic City for one of their songs and I had to borrow Paul Stanley's spare boots. Otherwise, I'd have looked ridiculous standing next to these seven-foot giants. That was hysterical. They walk around in those boots all day, but I could barely manage the four minutes on stage without toppling over.

JOE ELLIOTT: The tour with KISS was all very relaxed. I think that came across in the joint press conference we held in the House of Blues in Los Angeles. The two bands sat down on stools and you could tell instantly that there was a mutual respect. I knew Paul Stanley and Gene Simmons quite well and I'd met Eric Singer and Tommy Thayer over the years. In fact, when I'd played Sheffield City Hall with the Down 'n' Outz back in 2010, Gene and Eric were actually stood at the side of the stage.

House of Blues
Los Angeles
17 March 2014

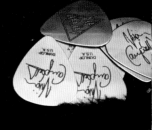

Def Leppard
Recorded: 2014–2015
Released: 30 October 2015

Def Leppard *originally came out in the UK as a free CD with copies of* Classic Rock *magazine. The album was then released conventionally two months later on Bludgeon Riffola/Mailboat. It debuted at number 11 in the UK and number 10 in the US.*

DEF LEPPARD

JOE ELLIOTT: *In February 2014, the guys came over to my house in Dublin for a month to record some of the new tracks we'd written during the Vegas residency. We thought we were going to do what we had done for Mirror Ball – just three new songs. But by the end of the session we had the basics of 12 songs done. We couldn't believe it. Songs were flying in from all directions.*

When everyone came back in May, not only did we finish the 12 off but we wrote two more. So, suddenly we had a 14-track album that we didn't set out to make.

We called it Def Leppard, *because it had the many different aspects of the Leppard sound all in one place.*

PHIL COLLEN: *Everything about the* Def Leppard *album was really good. For once, we didn't give ourselves a briefing. So, then a lot of the pressure that you put on yourself to make a certain kind of record disappears and things just naturally flow.*

From the end of Adrenalize *to the* Slang *and* Euphoria *period, we were playing a lot of state fairs. We would have ended up as a casino band if we had carried on like that. But we knew there was still value in playing all these massive songs that people wanted to hear.*

Things happen in cycles in music. In sport, you only get one chance; if you have a bad injury it's all over, and you're old at 30. But in music, if you keep going and you represent your art the right way, you can have multiple windows opening up. You just have to be prepared to ride out the downturn.

The Def Leppard *album led us into a few other tours that then headed us towards the Rock and Roll Hall of Fame. Before we knew it, we had been inducted and that made a huge difference to people's perception of us. And another little window opened up …*

DEF LEPPARD

JOE ELLIOTT: For every tour we need to get fit and that gets harder each time. For me it's a lot of vocal gymnastics, but at the same time I still work out as best I can. You owe it to yourself, your bandmates and your audience to be in the best shape you can be.

PHIL COLLEN: When I'm preparing for a tour, I can't hit a note to begin with and then within about a week I can get there. You start with the new stuff and I also focus on songs where I have to play a prominent guitar part and sing at the same time. It's a bit like rubbing your tummy while patting your head.

JOE ELLIOTT: Band rehearsals are a bit like getting back on a bike. After about two days, we're bored shitless of doing songs like 'Photograph' and 'Rock of Ages' because they're burned into our DNA, so we spend all our time focusing on the new stuff. A song you've never played live has to stand up next to a song that you might have played 1,500 times.

PHIL COLLEN: People think we're using tape samples for our harmonies, but we're not. We work hard at it. And we're actually just really good at it. When we're all singing during rehearsals it's like I can hear monitors. I have Vivian panned to my far right, Joe in the centre, and me on the left, because that's where we all are on stage. We've been playing and singing together for so long that it sounds like a record.

I was fortunate enough to know Phil Everly for a while before he died, and I asked him how they did those harmonies in the Everly Brothers. He said, 'Well, me and my brother grew up singing since we were babies. After a while, it became almost like a single spirit.' We have a similar thing going.

I always listen to Vivian when we're doing vocals because he has perfect pitch. Sav has perfect timing as a singer and Rick is like a metronome. He doesn't stray. Sometimes we'll use a click machine to keep us in time, but with Rick we don't really need one. So, everyone has their roles within the live musical structure.

JOE ELLIOTT: Before a show we're normally in one big dressing room. We tend to just potter around shaving and trying on clothes. The vocal warm-up is the major ritual.

Everybody has their own way of preparing. Some people sit quietly, just getting their head together. Phil does a full-on physical workout. He'll lift weights or punch a bag. Vivian, Sav and I always used to do a little shot of Irish whiskey before we went on but when Vivian stopped drinking alcohol because of his medical situation Sav also stopped doing it.

Humour plays a huge part backstage. We're there to entertain people so it's best that we're in a good mood when we go on stage. We don't half fuck about. Somebody will say something silly that will trigger a look between Phil and me, and then we'll both puke out the same Blackadder or Basil Fawlty response at the same time. We can't help ourselves.

RICK ALLEN: My relationship with Sav is all about intuition. We anticipate what the other will do without needing to say a word or make a sign. It's nice because I can relax and I rely on his timing sometimes, where if something is a little challenging he'll be right there with me.

PHIL COLLEN: As a band, we're looking to the singer to narrate the whole thing. The rest of us are just backing him up. The song is king, and then you have a narrator leading it and each band member is part of the orchestra. You have to make it look cool as well. You've rehearsed it enough, then the rest is pure performance. It's putting all these integral parts together.

RICK SAVAGE: You can't have everybody fighting for the spotlight. As a bassist, your job is to be the perfect bridge between the rhythm and the colour. I'm probably the least important member from an individual point of view – I've always felt that if I can make the guitars sound as good as possible, I'm happy. People want to hear the harmonies and the lead singer.

Sometimes I see someone digging in on the bass too much. It's like they're at the wrong gig. As a guitar player myself, I sometimes think, 'How would my guitarists want me to play this?' If that means staying on a groove and not moving much melodically, then that's what I do ... because two guitar players can sound amazing.

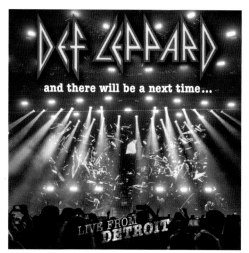

JOE ELLIOTT: I had this idea that we should film one of the shows from the 2016 tour because, apart from the 'Viva! Hysteria' shows, we hadn't actually had a live performance filmed since 1988. With a new album out that was being so well received, it was just a case of where to do it. We ended up choosing an outdoor venue just outside Detroit. The moment the house lights went down we could see the sun setting from the stage and the energy from the crowd seemed to intensify.

And There Will Be a Next Time ... Live from Detroit
Recorded: 15 July 2016
DTE Energy Music Theatre, Clarkston, Michigan
Released: 10 February 2017

The Story So Far – The Best Of
Recorded: 1981–2018
Released: 30 November 2018

VIVIAN CAMPBELL: There was a strong resurgence for Def Leppard in 2018. We had completed a massive North American tour where we mainly sold out these huge, iconic ballparks with Journey opening for us. The surprising thing was that 30 to 40 percent of our audience were young enough to be our children.

Not only that but we were also nominated for the Rock and Roll Hall of Fame. It seemed quite fitting, then, to call our latest 'best of' *The Story So Far* because it really did feel like an ongoing journey.

PHIL COLLEN: I never get stage fright because that's not me on stage; I have an avatar. I'm playing a role. As long as I can sing and play guitar to a certain level, and my body's in shape, then my avatar stays nourished. When we played Rock in Rio in front of 95,000 people and they announced, 'Def Leppard', I thought, 'OK, we've got about 30 seconds. I'll check my pulse just as a little experiment.' Nothing. It didn't move at all.

VIVIAN CAMPBELL: I thoroughly enjoy playing live. That's the main reason why you pick up your instrument in the first place. You get that instant gratification in front of an audience. I don't really get nervous before a gig. There's an excitement and a flow of adrenaline. But nothing lasts forever, so you have to enjoy it while you can.

JOE ELLIOTT: In almost every gig I'll forget some lyrics. The others mess up as well. But we've never berated each other for making a mistake; we just point and laugh. We'll come off stage and Phil will say, 'Fucking hell, I was playing like I had boxing gloves on tonight.' And I'll say, 'Yeah, well, you should have heard what I was singing in the encore.'

One time I was at the end of the ego ramp with Phil and Viv, doing the acoustic version of 'Bringin' On the Heartbreak'. I walked up to the mic and I couldn't for the life of me remember the beginning of the second verse. I stood there smiling at the crowd, pretending I was messing with them, and then I leaned over to Phil, the way that you see Jagger and Richards leaning into each other. I whispered, 'What's the next line?', through my teeth. He leaned back into me and said, 'You're such a secret.' I said, 'Thank you', turned to the mic and switched back into full rock god mode. It was a difficult 15 seconds or so, but I don't panic in those situations. I'm not Pavarotti; I'm just a guy in a band. I get it right most of the time.

PHIL COLLEN: In all the time I've known Joe, which is almost 40 years, I can probably count on one hand the times he's completely forgotten the lyrics, and that was one of them. It's a real shock when he does it because he's normally so good. I forget words all the time, so it doesn't shock me – it just irritates me. But Joe hardly ever does. He's like an elephant.

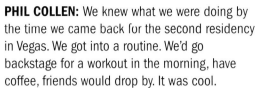

PHIL COLLEN: We knew what we were doing by the time we came back for the second residency in Vegas. We got into a routine. We'd go backstage for a workout in the morning, have coffee, friends would drop by. It was cool.

The first residency back in 2013 was at the Hard Rock Casino, which is a bit out of the way. It made a huge difference to be on the Strip this time because you could just walk out of the hotel and be in another casino or mall. There was so much going on. It was just more fun the second time round.

I had a great time but being in Vegas is more exhausting than being on tour because you're on all the time. You get recognised a lot and it's a very unhealthy existence. I made a point of going out for a walk as often as I could, but it was hot – 110 degrees – the whole time we were there.

RICK ALLEN: When I was at school I was a marathon runner and when we were doing the long Vegas shows I tapped into that. It was good for my technique.

VIVIAN CAMPBELL: The joy of playing a Vegas residency is that you get to write the rules. It's not like a conventional show, where you're beholden to the hits; with a residency, you know that people are going to fly in from around the globe and if they're willing to do that they must be diehard fans. So, you want to give them something different. That means we get to blow the cobwebs off obscure cuts and throwbacks like 'Rock Brigade' and 'Billy's Got a Gun'.

ROCKET
ANIMAL
LET IT GO
FOOLIN
LOVE & HATE COLLIDE
LET'S GET ROCKED
ARMAGEDDON IT
ROCK ON
2 STEPS BEHIND
MAN ENOUGH
LOVE BITES
HEARTBREAK
SWITCH 625
HYSTERIA
SUGAR

ROCK OF AGES
PHOTOGRAPH

PHIL COLLEN: People have taken us a lot more seriously since we were inducted into the Rock and Roll Hall of Fame. It shouldn't mean anything, but it does actually open doors.

I wasn't at all surprised that it took so long. If you ever meet the people who are on the voting panel, it's a bunch of old white businessmen and they're all about the ratings. They just choose who they feel are the hippest bands. We've never really been that trendy. It was annoying to see these other bands being inducted that we didn't feel had made as big a contribution to music as we had. But we obviously accepted it when we got the call.

Personally, I hate awards events. It was wonderful what Brian May said about us in his induction speech, and it was wonderful that it finally happened, but I'd rather have been at home.

RICK ALLEN: To be honest, when I heard that we'd been inducted it was a bit of an inconvenience. I'd just finished touring and was looking forward to being at home with the family. But I soon realised that this was a massive deal. Everything surrounding the event, from going on Howard Stern's show to Brian May and Ian Hunter getting involved, was incredible.

Most important was that we topped the fan vote that year. Our fans loved us, but we always felt we didn't get enough love from the industry. Standing on that stage and looking out at rock royalty giving us a standing ovation was when I finally felt the love. The emotions came flooding over me as I remembered everything I'd gone through to achieve this. It was nothing short of a miracle.

Rock and Roll Hall of Fame induction ceremony Barclays Center, New York 29 March 2019 (broadcast 27 April)

JOE ELLIOTT: Recording *Diamond Star Halos* was a different kind of challenge. Because of the pandemic, we had to do everything remotely; we never saw each other during the whole process.

We all wrote stuff and shared it with each other as MP3s. Phil would send me something while I was asleep in Dublin. Then I'd work on it while he was asleep in California and Dropbox it back to him. He would listen to it when he woke up in the morning and call me to say what he was going to do next. And so it went on until between the five of us we had all the parts of a song. Then we'd send the files to Ronan and he'd piece it all together, like he was building a model aeroplane.

RICK ALLEN: One of the nice things about modern technology is that we can be all over the planet and still sharing ideas for new songs.

RICK SAVAGE: I had to become a roadie, engineer and producer as well as a musician. I even had to change my strings myself, which I hadn't done for years! The experience served us well, though, because it allowed us to record alternative takes. Nobody was there to say, 'No, no, you have to leave room for me to record my guitar solo!' It was really free.

PHIL COLLEN: Every part of making *Diamond Star Halos* was brilliant. Because of the lockdown there was no time pressure. I got to spend two and a half years seeing my young son learn to walk and talk, which was awesome.

VIVIAN CAMPBELL: Phil came up with the *Diamond Star Halos* title, which, of course, is from the T. Rex song 'Get It On'. We didn't set out to make a record that reminded us of our youth, but the further we got with it the more we were thinking, 'Hang on. This has got some juicy Seventies parts to it.'

Diamond Star Halos
Recorded: 2020–2021
Released: 27 May 2022

DIAMOND STAR HALOS

PHIL COLLEN: *The album cover was like a Seventies vinyl masterpiece. It had so many cool artistic elements. There were little references to our past – like the diver from* High 'n' Dry *and the cross hairs from* Pyromania. *I think that the cover design complemented the sound of the record really well.*

JOE ELLIOTT: *We wanted the cover to be like one of those classics from the Seventies – like Elton's* Captain Fantastic *or* Goodbye Yellow Brick Road, *or any Bowie album – where you'd be so struck by the sleeve that you'd buy the record without knowing what the music was like inside. I bought plenty of music like that as a kid.*

The Munden Brothers did the design. We had the basic idea of tattoo art and it went from there. We wanted the artwork to have a mystique and things look more mysterious in black and white. The contrast between the black and white and our red and yellow logo looks great. A lot of the imagery on the inner sleeve is late Victorian fairground in style – a little eerie but not scary.

There are a lot of 'Easter eggs' hiding on the front cover. The vase at the bottom right represents the song 'Liquid Dust'. The girl with her hair covering one eye and a boat on her head represents the lyric 'I feel like a shipwreck washed up on your shore' from 'Lifeless'. The flames coming up from the bottom illustrate 'Fire It Up'. It's like a multitude of interlinking micro-stories.

Diamond Star Halos *is not strictly a concept album like* Tommy *or* Quadrophenia, *but the way we recorded it during lockdown gave the music a thread. Once we started putting the running order together, we found that certain songs overlapped each other. We wanted the sleeve to be like its own concept within the idea of what we were doing, although it wasn't our concept. The music and the lyrics were ours. The sleeve was not dictated by us, but evolved through a process of suggesting, listening and then accepting.*

VIVIAN CAMPBELL: The first songs that came in were piano ballads that Joe had written on the road. I was thinking, 'God, this is gonna be a very grown-up record!' But then Phil weighed in with some classic Def Leppard rock songs, and Sav wrote a couple of great songs – 'Take What You Want' and 'From Here to Eternity' – that we used as the first and last tracks on the album.

RICK SAVAGE: The inspiration for 'From Here to Eternity' came from Led Zeppelin, as well as from the Beatles and Queen. I also had a Forties black-and-white gangster film in my head while I was writing that song.

PHIL COLLEN: I was working with some outside writers for non-Def Leppard projects, and trying to write a glam rock kind of song. In doing that, we came up with this song called 'Kick'. I played it to Joe and told him I was planning to hand it over to someone else. He said, 'No you're fucking not!'

VIVIAN CAMPBELL: Alison Krauss's singing on 'This Guitar' and 'Lifeless' elevated those two songs from good to brilliant. She's such an incredible musician – she sings like an angel.

PHIL COLLEN: I wrote 'This Guitar' with my friend C.J. Vanston in 2003. Joe's always been a champion of the song. It sounds a little bit country, so we never really attempted it. The song is about the feeling of artistic release. You undo the creative valve, let the inspiration flow and that stops you from going bonkers. I'm really proud of that one.

RICK ALLEN: We have survived as a band because we're constantly writing new music. That keeps us vibrant and fresh and moving forward.

'Kick' video shoot
Ken Fox Wall of Death
Cambridgeshire
February 2022

JOE ELLIOTT: The Victorian fairground imagery of the cover tied in nicely with the video for 'Kick'. We spent two days with a circus troupe in a wall of death in rural Cambridgeshire. It was like *American Horror Story* meets *The League of Gentlemen*.

And it was freezing – eight degrees below zero in the middle of a field. The 'freaks' that you see in the video were dressed in their full regalia all day. There was a long-legged girl doing all the high kicks and the poor thing had hardly any clothes on. They had to keep wrapping her in a blanket when the cameras weren't running. We would keep stepping in and out and going back to our nice warm trailers with food and coffee machines and teabags. We started at noon and finished at about 8.30 at night and we got a four-minute video. It's all for the cause.

JOE ELLIOTT: The pandemic was like a reset button for the band. It led to a complete overhaul of our image and the way we work.

The new look came from having Maryam Malakpour as our stylist for the photoshoot with Anton Corbijn. She works with Steven Tyler and has worked with The Rolling Stones for decades, and she has a good relationship with Anton. To be able to collaborate with Anton was incredible. He's shot Depeche Mode, U2, Bowie, Miles Davis, Nelson Mandela ... and now this guy wanted to shoot us! I feel a bit taller today because Anton Corbijn wanted to do this photo session.

By the time we did the shoot, in February 2022, after various lockdown delays, things had to be turned around quickly. We were approving photographs for the album artwork the day after Anton took them. That's how tight it was. It wasn't a problem because we're good under pressure and Anton doesn't take a bad photo. Having worked with the band for the two days, he fell in love with us because we had a similar sense of humour. He's Dutch and we had spent two years living in Holland recording *Hysteria*, so we knew how to swear at him in his mother tongue. He was very, very relaxed. We were really impressed: he was quick and he was productive and he was great fun to work with.

PHIL COLLEN: I hadn't seen Vivian, Joe or Rick for more than two years, so when we finally got together it was quite emotional. We'd obviously seen each other on Zoom, comparing our beards and all that stuff, but when we shaved them off and got back into the groove it felt amazing.

A lot of bands don't have what we have. We've spent so much time together over the years and we know each other intimately well. We've been around each other's pain and suffering, as well as the wonderful stuff like kids and marriage. So, we can relate to each other on so many levels. And then when we make music together it's amazing. I'm sure we all feel very grateful for what we have as a band. I know I do.

JOE ELLIOTT: We rehearsed in Mates in California in May. It was very intense, yet relaxed. We worked a lot on the four new songs we had decided to put into the pile: 'Take What You Want', 'Fire It Up', 'Kick' and 'This Guitar'. The toughest one was 'This Guitar' because we were doing it on acoustic guitars without Alison Krauss, so it was very different from the album version.

We hadn't seen each other for a long time, but we fell straight into the old routines. It didn't feel like two years had passed – but, when you've been a band for 45 years, a couple of years is just like a long weekend.

PHIL COLLEN: You don't want to bore people with all the new stuff. You have to be creative about where you put the new songs. The Stones are really good at that.

The first two songs on *Diamond Star Halos* were genuine rock anthems, which we hadn't really had since 'Pour Some Sugar on Me'. Those are the hardest songs to write and we've constantly been trying to come up with them throughout our career. They've got to have a credible element so they don't sound silly, while also making you feel good. I think we actually nailed it this time. You can't force something like that because otherwise it sounds forced. These ones came naturally.

JOE ELLIOTT: At the end of rehearsals we did a one-off show at the Whisky a Go Go for Sirius XM, a network of hundreds of internet radio channels. It was our first gig in two and a half years and we were broadcasting it live, so there was no room for error. Not only that, but it was also being filmed.

It was an invited audience. Right at the front were the hardcore fans, then eight feet back you had a lot of industry people. They tend not to leap up and down as much, but they were clapping at the end of each song and it was a great night. I didn't really have the headspace to mind how everybody reacted. It was more about how we reacted to being back in front of a crowd.

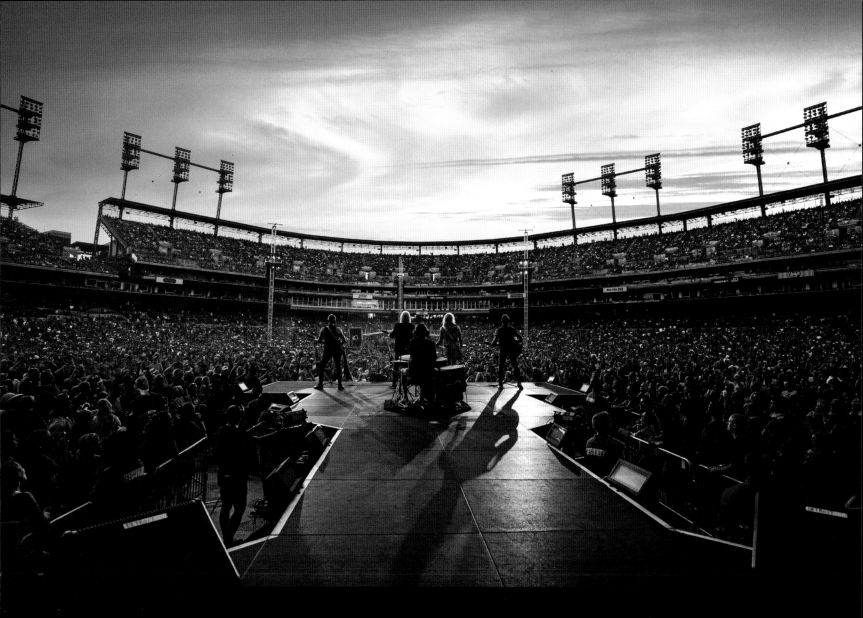

JOE ELLIOTT: The Stadium tour was essentially a festival show featuring five bands: us, Mötley Crüe, Poison, Joan Jett and the Blackhearts and Classless Act, a band of young kids who opened every night. We took turns with Mötley Crüe to close the show. That daylight spot was great if you had a really long drive, because it meant you could leave early and miss the show traffic.

With the festival format there was no soundcheck, so we played every show blind. You're performing to some of the biggest crowds of your career, so you've got to have a big pair to be able to just go out there and play. But we had a fantastic crew and the sound was never an issue. Every show we were able to play a little more confidently than the one before.

Going on the biggest tour of our career to date with a new record to promote was the most beautiful, heart-warming situation that I could have imagined at this stage of my life. The band was on fire and everything about what we were doing was just brilliant. We were having fun. We were making progress. We were selling well. We were getting good reviews. What more could you ask for?

The audiences were some of the best we'd ever had. There were probably as many people in the crowd who weren't even born when we toured *Hysteria* as there were people who had been at those gigs. As a music fan myself, I've been that kid. I used to go and see bands that were having hits before I was born, and loved it. Age has got nothing to do with it. Music is music.

The show was a celebration of our history and the new record all rolled into one, and our enthusiasm spread into the audience. We couldn't wait to get out there each night – we were frothing at the mouth at the thought of playing to 43,000 people in Denver. So what if we were singing a mile above sea level? If I got out of breath and started seeing sparkles, I didn't care.

Millions of people would swap places with me right now. But they can't have my space. I'm staying right where I am.

VIVIAN CAMPBELL: We all really do love our work. We genuinely feel humble about what we do and there is a very deep sense of gratitude among the members of the band. We don't take any of it for granted. There's also a very high work ethic in Def Leppard – I've always noticed that from right back when I joined the band. You have to remember that I'm still the new guy!

RICK ALLEN: I joined the group on my fifteenth birthday and we've grown up together. We've all been through a lot and had enough setbacks to realise that we're really strong as a team. That's what keeps us together.

RICK SAVAGE: We've never gone out of style or dropped off the cool list because we were never there in the first place! Even now, we're not sure what kind of image to project or what we should be wearing. But give us an acoustic guitar and a piano and we're completely at home … we'll write you a couple of songs in an hour!

JOE ELLIOTT: Def Leppard exists as a microcosm within the music world. Always there, doing our own thing, writing our own rules. We're willing to listen to good advice but we won't do things just because people tell us to. It was hard work getting up that hill, but we did it and now we're skiing down and having a good time.

PHIL COLLEN: There's no plan B. We haven't achieved what we set out to do yet. We've got this wealth of music to share with everyone.

When a painter creates art, whether they're Picasso or someone completely unknown, they want people to see it. There's an ego involved. And that's the thing … people haven't seen all our paintings yet.

ACKNOWLEDGEMENTS

Def Leppard would like to thank all of their families, friends, and fans past and present.

The publishers would like to thank:

Joe Elliott, Phil Collen, Rick Allen, Rick Savage and Vivian Campbell for their commitment, time and great enthusiasm for this project

Pete Willis and the Estate of Steve Clark

Mike Kobayashi, Emilie Fabiani and Kaylie Norris at CSM Management for all their support and encouragement

All Def Leppard fans around the world

A special thanks to Brian May and David Fricke for their Forewords

Additional thanks to:

All the photographers, with a special mention for Anton Corbijn, Ross Halfin, Kazuyo Horie and Ryan Sebastyan

Brad Mindich and Jason Kendall and the Inveniem team

Jessica Squire

Universal Music

Dave Bates

David Church

All of the generous contributors who helped make this book happen

The Genesis Team, especially Sally Millard and Nicky Page

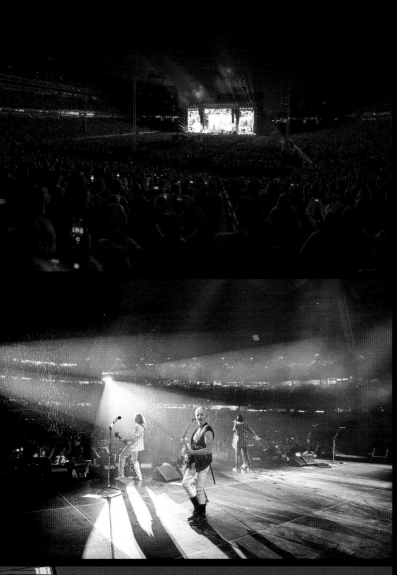

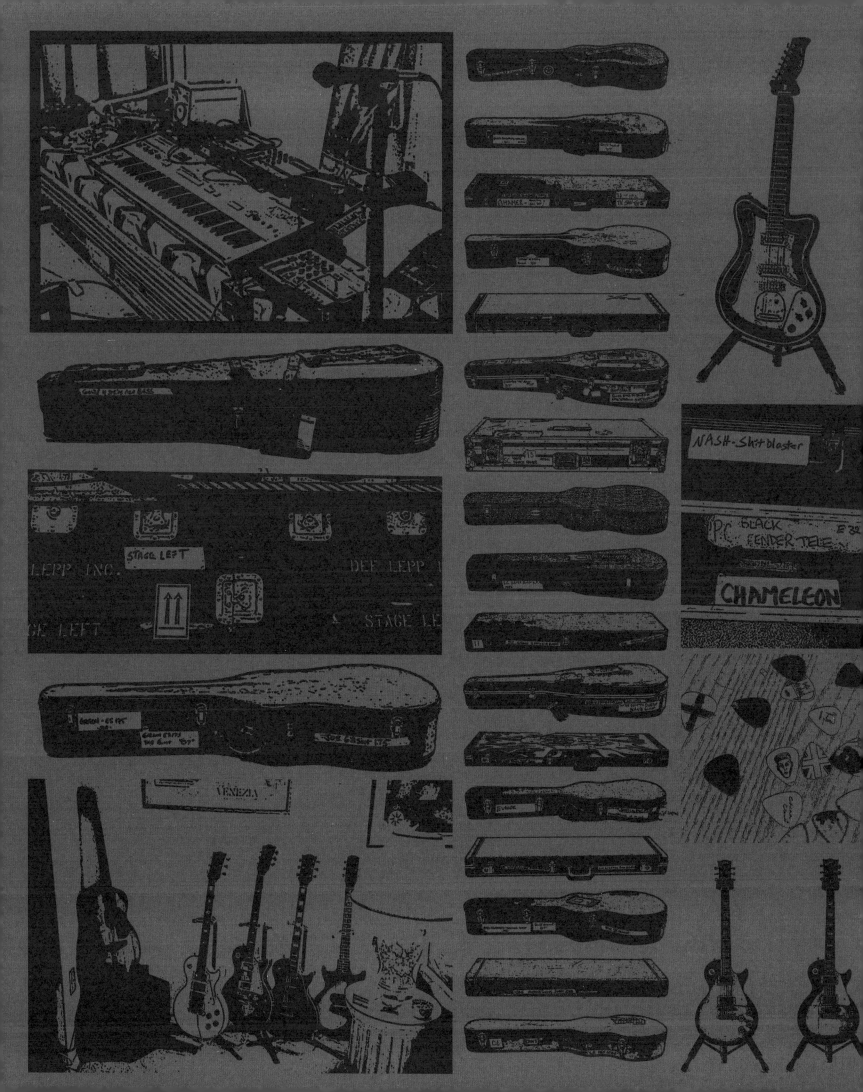

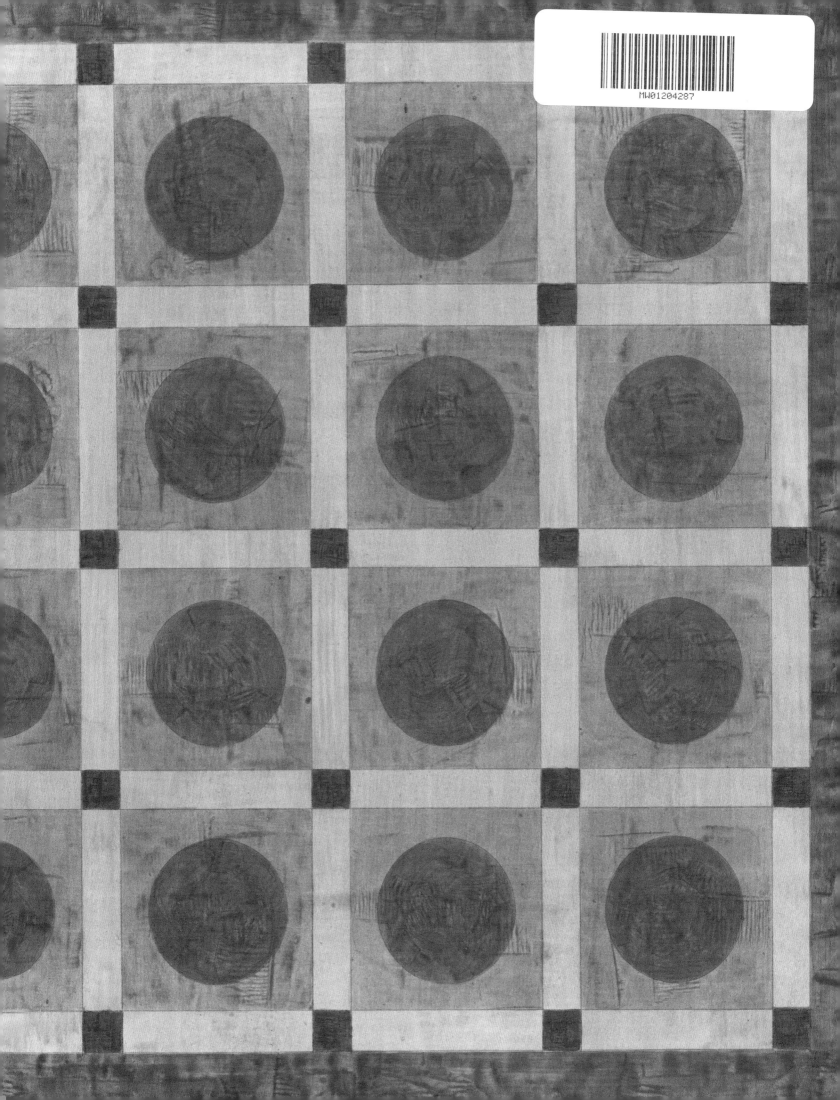

THE
ELEGANT
LIFE

EAT A
PEACH

THE ELEGANT LIFE

ROOMS THAT WELCOME AND INSPIRE

ALEX PAPACHRISTIDIS

Written with Mitchell Owens

Foreword by Harry Slatkin

CONTENTS

FOREWORD

Alex Papachristidis's sense of style is all-encompassing, from the grand yet cozy atmosphere of the living rooms he decorates to the luncheons and dinners he hosts, where the accoutrements of the tables complement wonderfully delicious foods. Nothing—and I mean nothing—is ever missed or overlooked. Everything Alex does bears witness to his dedication to getting things right for his family, his friends, and his clients. He really cares about every aspect of the world around you and the pleasures that even the smallest gesture can bring.

Twenty-nine years ago, the eve before Christmas, Alex walked into our lives, opening the door to Slatkin & Co., which would eventually become known for our home fragrances. The shop was small, and you needed to be buzzed in, whereupon you turned a beautiful, gilded handle modeled after a Jean Schlumberger cuff link. On any given day it was not unusual to find Jacqueline Kennedy Onassis or Oprah Winfrey, Elton John or Valentino mulling about the store. My wife, Laura, waited on Alex, and he admired the Christmas tree and its ornaments and said—with what I would soon learn is a typical Alexism—"I'll take it! The entire tree and its ornaments!" And, then to everyone's surprise and delight, he helped wrap every ornament on the tree—an early insight to his kindness.

Alex, Laura, and I quickly became best friends, and as we got to know his entire family, we learned that he shared the same joie de vivre and boundless curiosity as his mother, Mariya, and his amazing sister, Ophelia. For them, everything is always bigger than life, very *Auntie Mame*, but done with great care and deep affection. If Alex had a motto, it would be "Live, live, live!" His infectious attitude and generosity of spirit ensure that his clients become his friends and that his friends become friends of his clients. That talent, kindness, and style has led to a world of admirers, and Laura and I are at the front of that line.

—*Harry Slatkin*

INTRODUCTION

It is a luxury to decorate your home with an interior designer, and the process should be joyful. Selecting fabrics, creating a color palette, choosing the most inviting chair, designing the most comfortable and stylish sofa, shopping for antiques—these are pleasurable activities. You and your family will love your home even more when you are active participants in its creation. It will be a wonderful backdrop for you to live in, entertain in, and enjoy.

I have been decorating for years now—OK, decades, starting right after college—and working with clients never gets tiring. We get to joke and laugh and shop. I want them to be so happy that each meeting is something they look forward to and when we finish the job, they can't wait to do their next project. The point is that our shared journey should be a delightful one. The spaces that you occupy should make you smile and bring you satisfaction, reflecting your life, your loves, your values, and your interests, from the entrance hall to the kitchen. To my mind, there is no such thing as an unimportant space; each one deserves respect and attention—after all, a living room is called a living room because you are supposed to live in it, not just look at it. The only way you can write that story is to understand how you want to live, in as much detail as possible.

Helping clients identify their needs and their desires is one of the pleasures of my job. Often people need guidance and part of the process is sharing ideas and refining concepts. We sometimes travel the world in search of a singular mix of art, objects, and furniture, all the ingredients that make a beautiful home. From London antiques shops to the Paris flea markets to auction houses and shops around the world, the resources are endless and exciting, and my clients and I get to explore them not only as a team but as friends.

That relationship is always a learning process. My taste is broad—I love everything from a 1970s metal console table to an incredible eighteenth-century giltwood chair—but I learn from my clients as they do from me. That being said, no matter how elaborate or simple the rooms, the goal is that your home should be your personal wonderland.

LIVING WITH WHIMSY

My nephew Michael and his wife, Sabrina, wanted their children to live in an apartment that felt like a house, so they found a duplex where she could grow vegetables and flowers on the roof and they could entertain outdoors in sunny weather. They are a family that really love nature, everything from beaches to mountains. We collaborated with architect Alan Orenbuch to establish a plein-air feeling indoors, too, right from the moment that the front door opens. The entrance hall of the apartment may be small in proportion, but its impact is vast, thanks to a fairy-tale de Gournay wallpaper adapted from a photograph of a forest. It is a soothing antidote to a streetscape of skyscrapers and traffic. The floor is paved with pretty glazed tiles in a grass-green color, so the space feels like a glade, and the furnishings and front door are made of unpainted wood, which makes a visual connection to the tree trunks. When you step inside the apartment, the entrance

OPPOSITE: A de Gournay custom mural—adapted from a photograph—wraps the foyer. The ceiling fixture is by Apparatus. A vintage T. H. Robsjohn-Gibbings side chair stands next to a Swedish Modern table from Hostler Burrows. The Moroccan floor tiles are from Mosaic House. RIGHT: A Venetian chandelier from Gerald Bland is suspended above the staircase; the painting is by Brian Alfred.

hall makes it clear that you are entering a cheery, bright, and contemporary space designed to reflect one young family's love of color, activity, and casual living.

The scheme for the living room began with the carpet, always a foolproof place to start when you are decorating. We chose an overdyed Oriental carpet, with lots of pink and turquoise motifs, that resembles an abstracted garden. From that, we pulled out the colors for the space: a family-friendly L-shaped sofa in blue, iridescent blue-green tiles for the fireplace, a raspberry-pink armchair and patterned pink cushions, as well as a colorful, classic, mid-century modern Arredoluce Italian floor lamp. Since I love furniture with a sculptural shape that adds another dimension, I settled on a pair of vintage Brazilian mahogany armchairs and bleached them to a lighter shade so they did not have such a heavy presence. As for the yellow curtains, they feel like eternal sunlight.

That same cheerful attitude is felt almost everywhere in the apartment, from the invigorating pink breakfast room to the playful family room. The dining room is clad in a dynamic Indian scenic wallpaper (a country beloved by my niece), inspired by Mughal-era watercolors of an Indian prince's

LEFT: Flanked by Remains Lighting sconces, a Michael S. Smith mirror joins a custom vanity in the powder room. The custom wallpaper is by Studio Four, the ceiling fixture is by Kelly Wearstler, and the flooring is from Mosaic House. OPPOSITE: In the foyer, a hidden door opens to the powder room.

RIGHT: A Sophie Cooper painting surveys the living room, where a Manuel Canovas silk velvet covers the custom-made sofa, flanked by Vaughan tables and Christopher Spitzmiller lamps. The curtains are made of a Cowtan & Tout chintz, a Studio Four linen fabric covers the slipper chairs, and a Larsen fabric dresses the teak armchair from Glen Dooley. A Vaughan coffee table stands on a carpet from ABC Carpet & Home.

wedding. The room is filled with T. H. Robsjohn-Gibbings dining chairs surrounding a custom table and a Charles of Paris bubble chandelier.

In the primary bedroom, though, the palette is much lighter and more soothing; bedrooms are private spaces where you should be able to relax at the end of a busy day and take stock. The decor has modern elements—the bucket chair is very 1960s—but also classical ones; the desk is eighteenth-century Swedish, and the bed is upholstered in vintage-inspired fabrics. The only trouble with the space was a structural column that could not be removed. I camouflaged it with plaster and fluted the surface, so it has the effect of a Greek column. That's one of the most valuable lessons in decorating and architecture: if you can't get rid of something unattractive or awkward, transform it into something alluring. These whimsical rooms are filled with a welcoming spirit, hospitality and home-cooked meals.

RIGHT: In the living room, an Eve Kaplan mirror hangs beside the custom mantel, which incorporates Ann Sacks tiles, and is surmounted by a John Smith painting. Manuel Canovas fabrics cover the vintage T. H. Robsjohn-Gibbings club chair, from Arenskjold Antiques, and the custom sofa, made by J. Quintana Upholstery. The Triennale floor lamp is by Arredoluce.

RIGHT: The dining room features a Canovas wallpaper, a custom dining table by Jonathan Burden, and vintage T. H. Robsjohn-Gibbings chairs, cushioned in a Canovas fabric. An Anish Kapoor digital print hangs above a Swedish Modern cabinet by Paul László; alongside it stands an Ugo Rondinone sculpture.

ABOVE AND OPPOSITE: In the breakfast room, Jonathan Adler chairs, with Canovas fabric seats, surround a Saarinen table by Knoll. Phillip Jeffries grass paper brightens the walls, and the chandelier is from Objets Plus. Waterworks pendants light the kitchen beyond. Nina Boesch created the collage.

RIGHT: Lively Canovas fabrics are deployed in the playroom. A painting by Petra Cortright is displayed above a sofa from John Rosselli & Associates, the vintage pendant is from Dienst + Dotter, the cube table is a Maria Pergay classic, and the coffee table is a custom piece by Alex Papachristidis.

FOLLOWING SPREAD: A Cowtan & Tout fabric curtains the main bedroom. The bedside tables and bookcase are custom Alex Papachristidis designs. The bed is upholstered in a Studio Four fabric and outfitted with D. Porthault and Matouk linens. The carpet is by Beauvais, and the artwork is by Deborah Kass.

YOU MADE ME LOVE YOU

OPPOSITE: In the main bedroom, vintage chairs join an eighteenth-century bureau à gradin from Dienst + Dotter. ABOVE: Mosaic House tiles pattern the main bath, which features a Kelly Wearstler light fixture, a Waterworks tub, and D. Porthault towels.

GRAND CLASSICISM

One day a charming American woman with a Greek husband called me out of the blue and asked, "Would you come to Athens and decorate our apartment?" Of course, I said yes. She is a scholar of Greek antiquities, and what could be more relevant in an Athens residence than ancient statues and fragments—which I always like to use in my projects? Better yet, the couple's triplex turned out to have unobstructed views of the Acropolis. The commission had a built-in degree of familiarity, too, which always helps make a project fun: though we had never met, the clients knew other clients of mine and were friendly with my brother. They also turned out to be very trusting and committed to this project. For them, as for me, decorating is a joy rather than a burden.

We turned to the Greek architects MELKA, renowned for their impeccable craftsmanship. Very much on my mind was Villa Kerylos, a great early-1900s house in the South of France that a French archaeologist named Théodore Reinach had built for his family in the manner of an ancient Greek villa. It is a magical evocation of a long-lost time, but the Athens apartment would require an urban attitude rather than a seaside one, and with contemporary touches that would brighten its deeply rooted neoclassicism. The elevator, for example, opens to a vestibule paneled with mirror and trimmed with brass, and that leads to a charcoal-dark entrance hall where black-marble fluted pilasters frame walls painted with terracotta-and-gold motifs taken from historical Greek design; the Italian Empire tables are supported by winged female forms, mythological embodiments that underscore both the regional culture and the client's scholarly interests.

OPPOSITE: The mirrored elevator foyer is graced with an Hervé Van der Straeten ceiling fixture and an umbrella stand from Niall Smith Antiques.

28

RIGHT: Decorative artist Delphine Nény painted the marble-floored entrance hall with classical motifs that complement nineteenth-century console tables from the Chinese Porcelain Company. The Empire pendant is from Galerie Philippe Delpierre in Paris, and the statuary fragment was found at Galerie Chenel in Paris. An Italian marble profile relief from Christie's London was mounted in a custom giltwood frame by Atelier du Bois Doré.

More fluted pilasters—this time white—ring the grandly scaled living room, where the entrance hall's moody palette gives way to a sunnier situation, literally and figuratively. Instead of curtains, I screened the windows with see-through bronze panels forged in the manner of the ones that architect Emmanuel Pontremoli designed for Villa Kerylos; in the client's living room and dining room, the lacy panels regulate sunlight while also providing access to the wraparound terrace. We decided not to use carpets in the living room either; instead, the floor, paved with black marble veined in white in a parquet de Versailles pattern, feels as cool as a temple.

Though the eighteenth- and nineteenth-century paintings in the living room depict classical scenes, from mythology to hunting, the furnishings range widely in terms of style and materials—mixing periods always makes for a livelier space and a more satisfying experience. A 1970s Coque chair by Philippe Hiquily stands alongside a Knole-style damask-clad sofa that is a variation of a huge one that I once saw in Venice, while one of the room's embroidered blue-velvet sofas is flanked by a ceramic table in the shape of an elephant. Sculptor Ingrid Donat, a modern-day Diego Giacometti,

LEFT: Artist Eve Kaplan made sconces for the powder room; the chandelier is from Galerie Philippe Delpierre in Paris, and the wastepaper basket is a Piero Fornasetti model. The custom sink vanity and stone floors are by MELKA. OPPOSITE: Delphine Nény hand-painted a corridor with classical panels and pilasters.

made both of the cocktail tables in different styles, contemporary bronze works that fit in perfectly because they look as if they might have been discovered on an archaeological dig.

More of the distant past has been reinterpreted for the dining room. I didn't want to install a garden wallpaper that was out of keeping with the setting, so artist Delphine Nény conjured an imaginary landscape based on a Pompeian fresco to which she added grace notes that mean a lot to the clients. Four sculptures that illustrate a book that the lady of the house wrote are nestled amid the fruiting trees and flowering plants. Porphyry is a stone beloved across the ancient world, so I commissioned a gilded-bronze dining table with a verre églomisé faux-porphyry top and banked it with Regency mahogany chairs that I had gilded in a soft matte finish.

The roof terrace is by far the most modern space in the apartment, but it, too, has an updated classical air. We wrapped the space in an elegant cornice that also camouflages a structural beam; instead of interrupting one's enjoyment of the Parthenon in the distance, the beam now frames it like a painting, as if it was always meant to do that. The furnishings are as ageless as the scene beyond, whether it is the simple white-painted iron seating or the lion's-paw console table by John Dickinson, an American genius who could always make classical design feel new and adventurous.

PREVIOUS SPREAD: Accented with cushions made from an eighteenth-century fabric, the living room sofas are covered with a Brunschwig & Fils silk velvet. A vintage Japanese silk covers an eighteenth-century gilded armchair, while Ingrid Donat made the coffee table. The marble floor is inlaid in a parquet de Versailles pattern. OPPOSITE: A Louis Cane tree sculpture from Galerie Yves Gastou and a Nancy Lorenz box stand on the Ingrid Donat polished bronze coffee table from Carpenters Workshop Gallery. The giltwood console table from Carlton Hobbs hosts a François-Xavier Lalanne rhinoceros from Galerie Yves Gastou; the mirror is from Clinton Howell Antiques, and the painting is by Raffaello Sorbi.

37

ABOVE: A Brunschwig & Fils satin was used on an eighteenth-century armchair. The Turkish-style pouf is a custom Alex Papachristidis design. The painting *The Battle of the Lapiths and Centaurs*, by Sebastiano Ricci, came from Trinity Fine Art in London. OPPOSITE: A mirror from Clinton Howell Antiques hangs above an eighteenth-century commode from Laurent Chalvignac in Paris. Porcelain flowers from Dior Maison are planted in a Christopher Spitzmiller cachepot, and the Swedish porphyry urns were discovered at Christie's.

PREVIOUS SPREAD: A custom Alex Papachristidis sofa dressed in a Claremont Furnishing fabric faces, from left, a Philippe Hiquily chair, a pair of armchairs from Carlton Hobbs, and a custom Louis XVI–style chair by Alex Papachristidis. Over the sofa hangs a nineteenth-century Italian painting titled *Ulysses at the Court of Alcínous* by Pelagio Palagi, from Trinity Fine Art in London. Eve Kaplan made the lamps, and Frederick P. Victoria & Son created the games table at right. RIGHT: A custom Beauvais handwoven high-low wool carpet anchors the library. The foreground sofa is covered in a Claremont woven, while the other is clad in an Edelman suede. The coffee tables are a white-and-gold work by Hervé Van der Straeten and a vintage round Laverne design. Christopher Spitzmiller made the golden lamps; the Lynn Chadwick candlesticks were purchased in London.

OPPOSITE: Delphine Nény painted the dining room with a garden mural; the marble floor pattern was inspired by the floors of the Pantheon. Antique chairs from Avery & Dash Collections were custom-gilded and placed around a custom-made dining table by Eve Kaplan and Gerald Bland. Carlton Hobbs supplied the eighteenth-century neoclassical Italian inlaid commode. ABOVE: In the dining room, an Hervé Van der Straeten cabinet hosts lamps fashioned from nineteenth-century Greek vases.

RIGHT: The dining room chandelier was commissioned from Eve Kaplan. A Cowtan & Tout fabric upholsters the chairs, and the table is set with glassware by Dior Maison and antique silver, porcelain, and napkins from Everyday Elegance.

OPPOSITE: A Louis Cane pendant illuminates the breakfast area. Frederick P. Victoria & Son chairs are upholstered with a laminated Cowtan & Tout fabric and a John Rosselli &Associates textile. The table is a Saarinen design by Knoll. ABOVE: A Circa pendant hangs in the kitchen, which features Gaggenau ovens and Waterworks faucets.

ABOVE: The main terrace's seating is by Heveningham Collection, while the coffee tables
and dining table are from McKinnon and Harris. The square side tables are John Dickinson,
the outdoor fabrics are Jasper by John Rosselli & Associates and Giati, and the trims
are Samuel & Sons. OPPOSITE: Jamb sconces are mounted above a John Dickinson console.

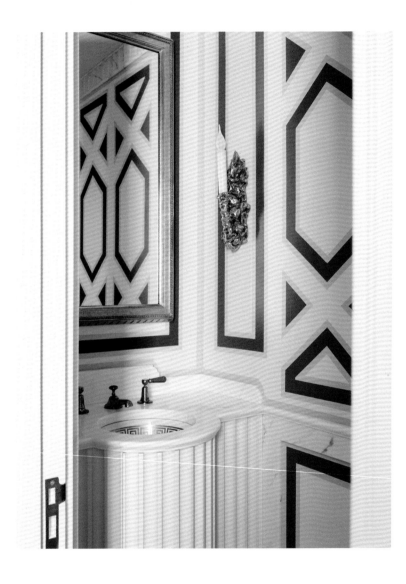

ABOVE, LEFT: In a powder room, an Eve Kaplan sconce joins a mirror in a J. Pocker frame. ABOVE, RIGHT: Christopher Spitzmiller cachepots top antique stands from Galerie Steinitz. OPPOSITE: Nineteenth-century gouaches by Luigi Ademollo depicting episodes of Homer's *Iliad* hang in a felt-walled sitting room; Delphine Nény painted the ceiling. An antique chair from Jonathan Burden is cushioned with Pierre Frey Le Manach silk velvet, while the custom sofa is an Alex Papachristidis design finished with a Cowtan & Tout fabric. The custom handwoven wool carpet is by Beauvais.

ABOVE: A Fortuny-clad armchair and a table lamp, both by Liz O'Brien Editions, meet in the dressing room; the light fixture is by Tisserant Art & Style. OPPOSITE: A John Rosselli & Associates bed is curtained with Carolina Irving fabric and dressed with custom Matouk linens and a John Robshaw throw. The Maison Charles lamp stands on a side table from Objets Plus. Beauvais made the custom handwoven carpet in hemp and wool.

ABOVE: A plein air table is set for lunch with Everyday Elegance. RIGHT: Custom trelliswork ornaments a featureless wall on another terrace. The furnishings are by Walters Wicker and McKinnon and Harris, with outdoor fabrics by Peter Dunham Textiles and Perennials.

56

REFINED
RADIANCE

A few years ago, my sister and brother-in-law decided that it was time to rebuild their beachside dwelling near the village of Bridgehampton, New York, and they wanted something simple but luxurious. Since my family is Greek—and we all love oceans and seaside living—I began thinking about some of the Aegean villas that affected me back in the 1970s, when I was coming of age, houses that were commissioned by shipping magnates like Aristotle Onassis and Stavros Niarchos. Imagine the Parthenon brought into the present day: sandy color schemes, pale limestone, beautiful bleached wood, and splashes of brass, bronze, and steel that made a shiny juxtaposition with the matte surfaces. Though that look certainly has roots in the 1970s, it has a timeless quality too, like ancient Greek temples.

My sister made three requests for her new home: it needed to be distinctively different from the family's other homes; have a gold, silver, and white color scheme; and limestone should not only be a primary material, but it should also flow from the inside out. Hamptons architect Kathrine "Kitty" McCoy and I developed a beach house that seems to disappear into the sand because the exterior is finished with stucco. The structure also blends with the landscape in other ways, largely because it has been built into a slope; it fools the eye when you arrive. What looks like a one-story

OPPOSITE: An oak balustrade rises to the main floor from the limestone-and-stucco entrance hall. Nancy Lorenz mirrors and a Rob Wynne exclamation point sparkle above a vintage Dorothy Draper console. The John Dickinson chair, in the Egyptian Revival style, came from Liz O'Brien, and the French barometer is from R. Louis Bofferding.

RIGHT: In the entrance hall, Maison Charles sconces flank a Marc Bankowsky mirror from Maison Gerard. The John Dickinson console from R. Louis Bofferding features a pair of Diego Giacometti lamps. The stool is from Jeffrey-Marie Antiques in West Palm Beach; the Saint Clair Cemin sculpture is from Kasmin Gallery.

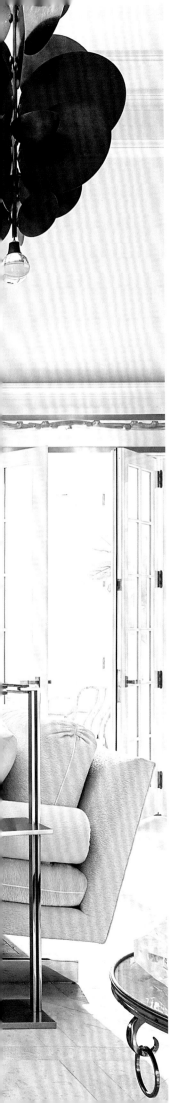

LEFT: In the living room, an Anish Kapoor sculpture hovers above a custom chimneypiece. The pendants are by Hervé Van der Straeten, and the curtains are of a Fabricut voile. The walnut and mirror coffee table is from Lamberty. The custom sofas were designed by Alex Papachristidis and the Ginkgo chair is by Claude Lalanne. ABOVE: A Nancy Lorenz painting shimmers behind eighteenth-century French armchairs and a games table from Gerald Bland. The candelabra is from R. Louis Bofferding; the Claude Lalanne *Pomme Bouche* is from Galerie Chastel Maréchal. FOLLOWING SPREAD: Brass-strapped lacquer walls define the living room. An Eve Kaplan mirror and a Rudolf Stingel painting hang above the sofas, which are upholstered in a Larsen Fabrics lamé. Ingrid Donat made the coffee tables.

63

ABOVE: A Gracie wallpaper transforms the central corridor into a work of art.
OPPOSITE: A composition of gilded honeycombs by Sophie Coryndon is mounted above
a stone architectural console from HB Home; the pendants are by Eve Kaplan.

66

RIGHT: An Anya Larkin hammered silk sheathes the sitting room. Cushions made of custom gold John Robshaw fabrics accent the custom sofa. The framed *Venetian Baroque Series I* photograph by Jean-François Jaussaud is from Maison Gerard, the framed collages are by Jean-Charles de Ravenel, the nineteenth-century rope twist chair is upholstered in an Edelman leather, and the Beauvais carpet is made of woven metallic leather.

house that you can barely see, in any case, is actually two levels; the cedar-shingled roofline, bleached by the sun and salt air, is really all that is visible. When you step up to the front door, walk into an entrance hall paved with Jerusalem limestone (Kitty chose every piece of stone for the house on a trip to Israel), and then ascend a cerused oak staircase, you end up with a surprise: the most important side of the house is the one you can't see. The main rooms open to a long, low limestone terrace that wraps around a swimming pool and offers a view of the marshes and the ocean beyond.

The decoration is all about the juxtaposition of glossy and sunbaked surfaces, glamorous but also soothing, with an organic quality that is especially appropriate at the beach. Some of the interior walls are covered in stucco, too, which is difficult to get right; it can often be too smooth, which sort of defeats a wonderful material, or too textured, which proves distracting. Instead, we created stucco walls with a slightly gritty surface that reminds you of the limestone. The big living room is the heart of the house. It is thirty feet long by twenty-two feet wide, and quite high, but it wanted a degree of visual organization, so it did not feel overwhelmingly large. I have always loved Albert Hadley's red-lacquer-and-brass library for Brooke Astor—it is a high-water mark of

LEFT: Laminated Fortuny fabric wraps a writing area in the dressing room. Miriam Ellner created the reverse-painted glass panel, and the lamp base is a Louis Comfort Tiffany original.
OPPOSITE: Eve Kaplan devised the golden details in an extravagant marble powder room inspired by the Grotto Hall in Potsdam's New Palace in Germany. P.E. Guerin made the custom shell faucet.

ABOVE: Artist Nancy Lorenz created the dining room's wavelike paintings.
RIGHT: An antique chandelier from Therien hangs above a custom table that
was designed by Eve Kaplan and Gerald Bland. Vladimir Kanevsky made
the porcelain peonies, and the Frederick P. Victoria & Son photophores stand
on pedestals once owned by collector Robert de Balkany. Alex Papachristidis
adapted the giltwood chairs from a Jean-Michel Frank design.

ABOVE: The Boffi kitchen is lit by chandeliers from H.M. Luther. RIGHT: A Soane table stands in the breakfast area, with chairs covered in a Jim Thompson gold lamé and a banquette upholstered in a Cowtan & Tout fabric. A Tommaso Barbi leaf pendant from John Salibello echoes a Scott Rudin photograph. FOLLOWING SPREAD: Rob Wynne bubbles dapple the walls of the main bedroom. The Venetian-glass chandelier came from R. Louis Bofferding, the desk is by Chris Schanck Studio, and the bedside commodes are a Frederick P. Victoria & Son design.

twentieth-century decoration—so I decided to create an homage with brushed brass strips framing panels of ivory-white lacquer, the same color as the inside of a seashell. All of the fabrics in the room are in varying degrees of white, including white velvet. But one of them is a linen lamé, a "wet" finish suggestive of pearls that dresses a pair of sofas. From Hervé Van der Straeten chandeliers that resemble glorious earrings to a striking gold concave mirror by artist Anish Kapoor that shines over the mantel, this comfortable space is radiant.

Ceramist Eve Kaplan fashioned a wonderful William Kent–style mirror to hang above one of the living room sofas; she also created a spectacular grotto-style powder room, all gold and limestone, inspired by a shell grotto in Potsdam that my family visited a few years ago. For the powder room, I took actual shells to P.E. Guerin, the legendary Manhattan foundry, which they cast into a faucet and levers. Decorating is all about invention and reinterpretation. Once again, when the shape of a piece of furniture is perfect but the finish is not, I am happy to alter it. On a shopping trip to London, I found the 1940s cocktail table that stands in front of the living room's brushed-steel-and-brass mantel. The shape was wonderful, but the wood was dark mahogany, so I had it bleached to a sandy pallor and gave it an inset mirror top; for the nursery, I came across a wonderful tree-branch chair at John Rosselli Antiques and gilded it. Gold touches are everywhere—a Claude Lalanne Ginkgo chair, curtain rods in the shape of branches, a hauntingly beautiful work of art by Sophie Coryndon in the form of gilded honeycombs—but in a way that feels sophisticated and confident rather than flashy.

The dining room is paneled with oak, which abstract painter Nancy Lorenz inset with beautiful evocations of swirling water and ocean currents. A spectacular steel-topped table with a custom gilded ceramic rock-form base, designed by Eve Kaplan, is paired with lean chairs inspired by the work of 1930s French designer Jean-Michel Frank. On the table stands a garden of overscale porcelain peonies (the client's favorite flower) by Vladimir Kanevsky, commissioned especially for

OPPOSITE: In the main bath, Baguès sconces in the form of elaborate bouquets are mounted on Miriam Ellner verre églomisé panels that are also set into the custom-made vanity's doors and drawer fronts. The ceiling fixture is by Sherle Wagner.

ABOVE: In a guest room, a Syrie Maugham armchair stands in front of windows curtained with an Osborne & Little fabric. RIGHT: Carole Gratale made the bed, adapting it from one designed for tastemaker Pauline de Rothschild. An Osborne & Little fabric, "Walk in the Park," was used for the walls and the bed, and Christopher Spitzmiller lamps are placed on the eighteenth-century French (left) and Syrie Maugham (right) bedside tables. The custom wool and silver Lurex carpet is from Marc Phillips.

the space. The main bedroom is also paneled, in the style of Jean-Michel Frank, but to add a sense of whimsy—and another echo of the ocean—I decorated the walls with an installation of silvered glass bubbles by artist Rob Wynne.

An important aspect of decorating for me is the relationship of floors from room to room. A floor should define a particular space but without being jarring when it meets the neighboring spaces. In my sister and brother-in-law's Hamptons beach house, most of the floors are limestone, but each one is laid with a different pattern, from herringbone to parquet de Versailles to the classic circle-in-square you see in Roman palazzos. That latter motif spans the bedroom corridors that bisect the house, and it is literally reflected in the corridors' ceilings, where the circles are made of mirror and set into plaster squares. It is a very structured and formal pattern, in total contrast with the walls, which are covered with a Gracie wallpaper mural of crashing waves in sepia neutrals and gold. That roiling motif reminds me of *The Great Wave*, the famous nineteenth-century print by Japanese artist Hokusai—it also gives the long passages a lot of visual drama that references the house's setting in a way that is elegant, transporting, and, like watching the sea itself, a bit hypnotic.

LEFT: Custom tiles ornamented with a Fortuny pattern line a bath, which features a Waterworks vanity and mirror. Remains Lighting provided the pendant and sconces. OPPOSITE: A Gracie Japanese cherry blossom paper was used in a guest bedroom, where a Larsen Fabrics gold lamé fabric upholsters the custom bed. The curtains are made of a Larsen Fabrics material, the chair is a Frederick P. Victoria & Son design, and the custom woven wool carpet is from ALT for Living.

OPPOSITE: The playroom is tented with a Lulu DK fabric, while Boxton Design Group painted the floor. The giltwood sofa is Maison Carlhian from Christie's Paris, and the bookcases are Alex Papachristidis designs. The rock-crystal chandelier is from Liz O'Brien. ABOVE: A mirrored sculpture by Andy Diaz Hope from Maison Gerard is mounted onto de Gournay–papered walls. The Bielecky Brothers bed was silver-leafed, Eve Kaplan and Alex Papachristidis created the bedside table, and the lamp is vintage John Dickinson.

ABOVE: A Chris Schanck Studio chair stands in a bathroom layered with custom giraffe wallpaper by Studio Four, a Remains Lighting pendant, and a Kelly Wearstler sconce. OPPOSITE: A Stephen Antonson mirror from Liz O'Brien oversees an Empire bed found at Patrick Perrin Antiques in Paris. The pendant is by Remains Lighting, and Christopher Spitzmiller lamps stand on John Dickinson side tables from R. Louis Bofferding.

LEFT: A golden sculpture by Serge Lutens from Liz O'Brien floats above custom headboards in a bedroom lined with a Kelly Wearstler wallpaper from Brunschwig & Fils; brass table lamps from Vaughan rest on a cast-iron and marble-top bedside table from Christie's, and the custom bed linens are by Matouk.
ABOVE: A coquina vanity and mirror make a bold statement in a bathroom. Vaughan Twig sconces are mounted above a Waterworks matte gold finish faucet.

ABOVE: An Ugo Rondinone sculpture frames an ocean view. The vintage table and chairs are from the Antique and Artisan Gallery. RIGHT: Bielecky Brothers seating is arranged around a vintage coffee table from Roark. The *faux bois* garden seat was purchased at Doyle.

ABOVE: A luncheon tabletop blends vintage Venetian glassware and tableware from Aerin and Everyday Elegance. OPPOSITE: The pool terrace's mirrored dining tables were custom-made by Gerald Bland, while the gold-tone aluminum klismos chairs were discovered at CB2.

CONTEMPORARY FLAIR

Keeping a sense of history in a new house is important to me, so I love incorporating furnishings that mean something to the people I work for. Objects that you have lived with and loved forever add a layer of familiarity, even if the house or apartment has been designed in a totally different style or feeling from your previous residence. I am always telling clients not to buy anything they aren't prepared to live with forever—we can always refresh and reinvent furniture as time goes by and as addresses change.

For clients in the Hamptons, architect Mark Zeff and I created a barnlike house with a spirit that is sleek and modern—I would even say breezy. But it is also a warm and happy home that really celebrates life and hospitality. The couple have three children, plus extended families who are always visiting, so their old place, a country cottage, felt too small. They decided to tear it down and build a place that could accommodate more guests, more dinners, more parties. It is always full of people, and I think that the rooms really welcome that kind of energy. Where possible, we used furnishings they already owned so the brand-new rooms had fond memories.

OPPOSITE: A colorful abstract painting by an unknown artist that has been in the clients' family for generations surveys the entrance hall. Extra brass dining chairs from Jonathan Adler stand beside the Minotti console; the same company made the pendant. Eve Kaplan created the sunburst mirror.

RIGHT: A brass-paneled fireplace separates the entrance hall from the dining room. Above the vintage Chinese-style metal chair, found at the Antique and Artisan Gallery, hangs a leaf sconce by Tommaso Barbi. The floor is polished concrete. FOLLOWING SPREAD: The living room features a geometric pendant from Design Within Reach, brass floor lamps from CB2, and a custom high-low carpet by Beauvais. A Brunschwig & Fils print upholsters the Victorian chairs flanking a custom sofa, while a potted fern occupies a classic John Dickinson draped-metal table. The coffee table is a Vaughan design, and the Syrian armoire is from John Rosselli & Associates. The leather chair came from Minotti.

From classic Chinese ceramic garden seats (one is shaped like an elephant) to batik-covered chairs with a Louis Philippe silhouette, familiar objects have been juxtaposed in the living room with clean-lined contemporary seating and eye-catching brass accent pieces, such as a pair of towering floor lamps. A custom-made carpet, sculpted like overscale plush trelliswork, grounds the space. It is a fun mix that feels casual, but it is very well balanced—soft here, hard there, a bit of shine, a bit of texture: a decor that won't look dated in a few years.

Brass is a leitmotif throughout the rooms, which are decorated in shades of blue, from smoke to periwinkle, which is the clients' favorite color. Lighting, tables, large and small, the frames of chairs, even the spherical feet of an upholstered bed—brass is everywhere. The biggest dose is a see-through, floor-to-ceiling chimneypiece composed of patinated panels that separates the entrance hall from the dining room. We framed the metal with a natural wood ceiling and a polished concrete floor that flows into the graphic blue-and-white kitchen as well. Concrete is not necessarily something people associate with my work, but I love how cool an industrial-strength material can look when used as a background for sophisticated gestures. Custom-made carpeting for the private spaces echoes the concrete's milky tones, so passing from room to room is a seamless experience.

The barn-wood accent wall in the main bedroom serves much the same contrasting purpose. Its washed gray-blue finish and rugged grain set off blue lacquered side tables and fabrics that are different in pattern—stripes, diamonds, and more, incorporating doses of blue—but complementary in scale and palette. A shapely Louis XV–style bergère brings another kind of history into the equation.

OPPOSITE: Remains Lighting Tony Duquette brass pendants are suspended from the dining room's wood ceiling. Warren Platner tables and chairs share the space with Jonathan Adler brass chairs cushioned with a blue velvet that echoes the Matthew Chambers painting.

RIGHT: Dressed with a Phillip Jeffries cork wallcovering, which creates a cozy atmosphere, the library is crowned by a dramatic Serge Mouille ceiling lamp. A painting by Kaves is displayed above the Minotti sofa. The modern dhurrie carpet is by Beauvais.

RIGHT: In the kitchen, the custom cabinets are painted in Benjamin Moore Hale Navy. The lighting includes a Kelly Wearstler pendant and spherical ceiling fixtures by Flos. The table and chairs are Saarinen designs by Knoll, the bar stools are by CB2, and a Christopher Spitzmiller golden gourd stands on the marble-topped island.

FOLLOWING SPREAD: Another living room, accented with a 1970s painting purchased in Stamford, Connecticut, opens to a glazed porch. A Minotti sofa faces a coffee table by the Lacquer Company for KRB, the latter flanked by vintage Lucite armchairs. Steel lamps found at a flea market in Paris are positioned on custom wood-and-Lucite side tables, and the ceiling pendants are from Schoolhouse Electric.

RIGHT: A blue-washed barn-wood wall rises in the main bedroom, which features a Kelly Wearstler chandelier. The fabrics that are used for the curtains and the custom bed are Jane Churchill designs from Cowtan & Tout. Design Within Reach sconces are positioned above side tables by the Lacquer Company, and the Louis XV–style armchair is a vintage piece upholstered in a Cowtan & Tout Larsen fabric. The photographs are by Alex Prager (above the bed) and Ricky Powell (above the sofa).

ABOVE: A custom-painted Room & Board bed frames vintage prints of marine life. The lamps are by Christopher Spitzmiller, and the coffee table is vintage. OPPOSITE: Another bedroom sets a modern tone with a Lucite-and-brass bed from Anthropologie. The pendant is a Kelly Wearstler design, the bedside lamp is by Christopher Spitzmiller, and the Roman shades are fashioned in a Jane Churchill print from Cowtan & Tout. The custom area rug is by Starr Carpet.

ICONIC ELEMENTS

The couple that lives in this New York City town house happily have sympathetic tastes: he likes the White House, she likes Versailles, his favorite color is blue, while she leans to purple and plum. They are young but also old-world romantics: they like beautiful furniture and objects, they love to entertain, and they really appreciate glamorous traditional rooms that feel layered and personal. Most collections like the ones assembled here—Régence giltwood furniture, eighteenth-century paintings of Venice, opaline glass and porcelains, a Jansen dining table that is almost a perfect twin of one that was made for the Duke and Duchess of Windsor, obelisks studded with cameos—take generations to gather, but this one was done relatively quickly. Still, it doesn't feel rushed.

Pretty was the operative word when we began working with Fairfax & Sammons Architects on the project, which was a complete renovation of a very contemporary West Village redbrick building that was constructed just a few years ago. French artisan Delphine Nény elevated the living room's simple strapped paneling with hand-painted flowers that bring to mind Indian *palampores*, though in a quiet palette of pistachio-green and ivory white rather than in the typical multitude of colors. One room, a vestibule off the faux-stone entrance hall, is encased in fanciful trelliswork—you can never be unhappy when you are surrounded by treillage—of the kind that was popular in the eighteenth century and brought into the twentieth century by the decorator Elsie de Wolfe. The decor contains a multitude of grace notes from the history of high style. On a landing, two 1930s chairs that were a hallmark of British tastemaker Syrie Maugham flank a grand mirrored Serge Roche obelisk of the same period. In

OPPOSITE: Recalling an eighteenth-century French tradition, custom treillage panels the foyer. The table is from Objets Plus, and the floor was stenciled by Boxton Design Group. The ceiling is the work of Atelier Premiere, and the mirror is from Yew Tree House Antiques.

RIGHT: The rusticated entrance hall is furnished with an Eve Kaplan mirror, through Gerald Bland, a Serge Roche console that hosts a Vladimir Kanevsky porcelain plum tree, and an eighteenth-century armchair upholstered in a Cowtan & Tout fabric. A Walter Gay painting hangs above a Syrie Maugham bench. The pedestal from the estate of Mario Buatta supports a terracotta bust that belonged to the client's grandmother.

the dining room, where Nény painted the mirrored pilasters with garlands of flowers, the table is banked with high-backed chairs that Jansen designed for the legendary Franco-Mexican aesthete Charles de Beistegui. I had them upholstered in a two-tone celadon velvet with a chevron pattern; the angularity of the motif makes a pleasing counterpoint to the chairs' sinuous Louis XV–style frames.

The interiors certainly embody the graciousness of another time—meaning that elegant reanimation of classic French decor in the 1950s and 1960s—but they do not feel stuffy or old. In the living room, for example, the gravitas comes from the antiques—among them a pair of eighteenth-century Cresson giltwood chairs—but the elegant and simple custom-made sofas acknowledge the time in which we live and the level of comfort that people want. You can be as formal as you like and still incorporate modern-day practicality. The kitchen chairs, a 1940s design by Samuel Marx, are upholstered in chintz but the fabric has been laminated for easy maintenance. The Chinese Chippendale staircase adds lightness and whimsy, as does the silvery chinoiserie wallpaper that joins it, even nearly three hundred years after both of them came into fashion: some of the most enchanting elements of interior decoration have everlasting shelf life.

LEFT: On the landing, Syrie Maugham chairs from Liz O'Brien flank a Serge Roche obelisk from Galerie Chastel Maréchal. The lanterns are by P.E. Guerin, and the sconces are by Frederick P. Victoria & Son. OPPOSITE: Against a Gracie wallpaper, Georges Geffroy tables flank an eighteenth-century settee; the clock on the staircase is from R. Louis Bofferding, the sconces are from Vaughan. FOLLOWING SPREAD: Delphine Nény painted the walls of the living room, where the windows are framed with a Cowtan & Tout satin.

ABOVE: A stool that belonged to decorator Mario Buatta is set beneath an eighteenth-century giltwood console. OPPOSITE: The custom sofa is upholstered in a Clarence House fabric that was embroidered by Penn & Fletcher. The painting, *A Ride in the Park* by Sir Robert Ponsonby Staples, is from Christie's; the carpet is an eighteenth-century wool and silk floral by Beauvais.

OPPOSITE: Master of the Langmatt Foundation Views' Venetian paintings from Sotheby's London are displayed above an eighteenth-century French chinoiserie painted commode from Christie's Paris by Jean Jerome Christophe Lemelle. The Louis XV giltwood fauteuil by Michel Cresson was found at Sotheby's. ABOVE: An antique clock, formerly in the collection of Howard Slatkin, stands on a marble chimneypiece from A&R Asta.

PREVIOUS SPREAD: Mirrored pilasters painted by Delphine Nény add dimension to the dining room. Cowtan & Tout fabrics were used for the walls and curtains, and the table is vintage Jansen from Christie's Paris. The Italian ormolu and cut-crystal chandelier are from Christie's. OPPOSITE: A Brunschwig & Fils fabric covers chairs once owned by Charles de Beistegui. The camel was found at Jonathan Burden, and the table features place settings by Everyday Elegance. The eighteenth-century Venetian School painting, *A Wooded River Landscape,* is from Christie's. ABOVE: A Christopher Spitzmiller cachepot atop an eighteenth-century giltwood console from Christie's holds a Vladimir Kanevsky porcelain rosebush; Eve Kaplan made the mirror.

ABOVE: Urban Electric Company pendants hang in the kitchen. The bar stools are a custom Alex Papachristidis design. OPPOSITE: Beneath a chandelier from KRB are Liz O'Brien Editions chairs, upholstered in a Brunschwig & Fils floral, surrounding a custom breakfast table. FOLLOWING SPREAD: The kitchen opens to a trellised terrace furnished, at right, with vintage Emilio Terry chairs and pieces from McKinnon and Harris.

OPPOSITE: An Eve Kaplan sunburst mirror hangs above a bed. ABOVE: The main bedroom
walls feature fabric custom-embroidered by Chelsea Textiles. The chandelier is from
Liz O'Brien, the eighteenth-century settee was found at the Chinese Porcelain Company
in fabric quilted by American Decorative Quilting, Frederick P. Victoria & Son made
the armoire, and the carpet is by Beauvais. The vintage coffee table is from David Duncan.

OPPOSITE: A Quadrille wallpaper lines a bathroom, and the chandelier was found at a Paris flea market. The client's clutch is by Scotstyle. ABOVE: Tisserant Art & Style ceiling fixtures and custom *faux bois* Beauvais carpeting were installed in the dressing room.

ABOVE: Ferran Textiles fabric from John Rosselli & Associates blooms in a bedroom furnished with a Frederick P. Victoria & Son *lit à la polonaise* that is dressed with Leontine Linens sheets; the pendant light is from the Urban Electric Company. OPPOSITE: A Napoleon III rope-motif chair stands next to a vintage Syrie Maugham table; a Rob Wynne unicorn horn is mounted on the wall.

OPPOSITE: Manuel Canovas patterns are used on the walls, window, cushions, and ottoman.
A Cowtan & Tout stripe appears on the chair, and a Le Manach woven upholsters the custom
sofa. ABOVE: A bedroom features wall upholstery in a Pierre Frey fabric. The curtains and
bed are composed of custom Le Manach fabrics, the side tables are vintage Jansen, and the
floral painting is by Gluck. The custom quilt is in a Pierre Frey ikat fabric.

A PASSION
FOR ART

Personal tastes change, sometimes radically, surprisingly, and, in this case, inspiringly. One of my oldest friends—she's the one who encouraged me, back when we were in our twenties, to become a decorator—along with her husband happen to be among my best clients and friends. The prewar Park Avenue apartment I did for them was elegant, with lots of antiques. A decade later, their contemporary art collection had grown, and they felt that the traditional decor, even though it had been refreshed not so many years ago, looked dowdy. That was tough for me, because I am such a lover of antiques. We came to an agreement: if the antiques had to go, then the apartment still needed gravitas. We would have to find furnishings and objects that were rare, striking, and special. I wanted iconic twentieth-century designs and custom-made complements that would harmonize with their collection of works by Elizabeth Peyton, George Condo, John Currin, Rebecca Warren, Rashid Johnson, Christopher Wool, and more; the art couldn't be everything and the furniture nothing. I told them, "This is going to be a hard-shop task," and they said, "We're up for it."

I love the idea of the same apartment being reinvented for the same or other owners, especially when we learn from each other. My friend's husband was not terribly interested in decorating; now he is obsessed with it, and he introduced me to contemporary art, which I never really cared much for and now adore. Here, in this redesign by architect Robert Morris, moldings were ripped out and replaced, architectural details were simplified or beefed up, and monolithic new marble and plaster chimneypieces were custom made; original parquet floors were stained gray, and doors ebonized. As for the decoration, when I am forced to go outside my comfort zone, I do research. That meant studying how art of all kinds was used most successfully in mid-twentieth-century interiors.

OPPOSITE: In the foyer, a vintage Grosfeld House table from Donzella stands amid walls layered with a Phillip Jeffries tea paper. The Jacques Duval Brasseur pendant light and Georges Jouve sconces are vintage from Galerie Yves Gastou in Paris, and the marble floor mirrors an Emilio Terry carpet design. The sculpture is by Rebecca Warren.

RIGHT: We commissioned custom lanterns by Démiurge in the manner of Diego Giacometti for the art-filled gallery. A Christopher Wool artwork is placed between the bookcases, while Maurizio Cattelan pigeons whimsically perch here and there. The Roberto Giulio Rida cabinets are from H.M. Luther. The sculpture on the pedestal is by Mark Grotjahn. FOLLOWING SPREAD: Works by Richard Prince (above the mantel) and Rudolf Stingel (to the right of the mantel) and George Condo (above the sofa) are displayed in the living room. The mantel hosts a François-Xavier Lalanne fish. The metal chairs are by Maria Pergay, and the carpet was custom-made by Holland & Sherry. The coffee tables are by Karl Springer and Ado Chale; the lamps are by Andrea Koeppel. Artworks by Rebecca Warren, Elizabeth Peyton, and John Currin accentuate the room.

RIGHT: Paintings by
Richard Prince (left) and
John Currin (right) flank
the door to the library,
revealing a Joe Bradley
painting over the library
sofa and an eccentric
little Philippe Hiquily
table, which stands
like a sculpture. Eve
Kaplan made the gilded
ceramic base console,
and the chairs and games
table are vintage Jacques
Quinet designs from
Bernd Goeckler.

OPPOSITE: A Warren Platner chair offers access to a Gabriella Crespi desk surmounted by a John Currin painting. Jean-Michel Frank designed the vintage desk lamp. Another Elizabeth Peyton painting adorns the windowsill. ABOVE: One of Maurizio Cattelan's trophy-wife sculptures emerges from the library paneling, above the Elizabeth Peyton drawings lining the mantel. A Claude Lalanne Crocoseat chair stands in front of the fireplace, and the satin-covered Ward Bennett swivel chair is vintage. The custom coffee table is by Brian Thoreen and the lamp is by Roberto Giulio Rida.

RIGHT: Flanked by large Rudolf Stingel canvases, a reflective Anish Kapoor sculpture makes a dramatic impression in the dining room. Jeff Koons's puppy vases perch on the mantel. The chandelier came from Liz O'Brien, and the vintage Swedish chairs, discovered at H.M. Luther, are upholstered in glazed linen. The custom granite top dining tables are by Paul M. Jones from John Boone.

ABOVE: A George Condo sculpture sits on a pedestal in the dining room.
RIGHT: A Rudolf Stingel work is seen above a console from Galerie Yves Gastou, while a Christopher Wool creation hangs on the adjoining wall.

The living room's graphic gray-and-white carpet, for example, was sparked by the fact that some of the greatest art deco interiors included important African masks and sculptures, so I came up with a geometric tribal motif that pays homage to those works. The curtains are fashioned of gray satin (it looks like mercury). There are two polished steel chairs by modern master Maria Pergay, an aluminum cocktail table by Karl Springer, and a side table in the living room as well as a Z-desk in the library, both designed by 1970s iconic designer Gabriella Crespi. It's all about "dry" and "wet" textures: velvet with satin, matte lacquer with polished metal. The combination, one of my favorites, reminds me of the glamour of Fred Astaire and Ginger Rogers' movies. We also found a vintage Jacques Quinet card table and matching chairs, then refinished them in gray lacquer and reclad them with silver leather. The leather brings back the days when my friend and I went to Studio 54; it is a subtle *aide-mémoire* that reminds us of who we are and how we got here.

The apartment's gray-and-white palette, specified by the clients, delights the eye from room to room. That is because of the juggling of tones and subtle differences in textures, from the entrance hall's tarnished-silver tea-paper walls and inlaid marble floor—the interlocking design is based on a 1930s Emilio Terry carpet, a transposition of materials that's something of a signature of mine—to the mushroom-gray velvet walls in the main bedroom.

Periodic shots of gold or brass (here I mix metals) add relief as well as warmth, such as a gilt-resin François-Xavier Lalanne fish that sits on a mantel, the golden Warren Platner chair in the library, and small tables by French designer Philippe Hiquily, one of my obsessions. The antique chandelier in the dining room, which used to be in the entrance hall and was too beautiful to jettison, is encrusted with drops of rock crystal, which has a gray cast, as does the chairs' glazed-linen upholstery, with its pearly shimmer. The same silver leather used on the Quinet table and chairs shows up in the main bedroom, where I had it tooled and applied to the bedside tables. I rarely repeat a fabric from one space to another but when you do so and tinker with it, as I did with the leather, it doesn't read the same way.

OPPOSITE: Pendants from Remains Lighting add a whimsical note to the kitchen, which features a Wolf range. The breakfast area is furnished with a Saarinen table and chairs and curtained with a Quadrille fabric. Paris Ceramics supplied the floor tile.

LEFT: The main bedroom is walled with a Holland & Sherry velvet. A Philippe Hiquily chair upholstered in Fortuny fabric stands alongside a Rebecca Warren totem sculpture, and a Maria Pergay chair graces the foot of the bed. The button-tufted bed and side tables, wrapped in a tooled Edelman leather, are custom; the custom Tencel area rug is by Beauvais.

ABOVE: Calcutta marble panels the main bathroom. The sconces and faucet are by Waterworks, a Jeff Koons sculpture stands on the counter, and the stool is vintage. OPPOSITE: A George Condo painting is paired with a Philippe Hiquily floor lamp and armchair.

FEARLESS PATTERN

One of my clients is a woman who is absolutely fearless: she knows what she likes and doesn't like, and she's not afraid of color. Bold colors—and lots of them—make her happy. She also understands and accepts challenges. The rooms at her family's house in the Hamptons are big, as they are in a lot of contemporary houses. They had to be handled with care, so that the square footage felt friendly, even cozy. My client's family is happy, easygoing, cheerful, and positive, and the décors needed to embody that vitality—a mix of solid and open shapes, a variety of textures, and some substantial, even beefy, furniture that would provide visual weight.

Confident pops of clear color—imagine a handful of beach glass—and patterned fabrics and textiles domesticate the white entrance hall. It's a grand space, baronial in its proportions, with a flying staircase and a dramatic grid of wainscoting. The fabrics—bold, graphic, multicolored but complementary—warm it up. A big, blue octagonal skirted center table set on a zigzag-patterned green-and-white carpet anchors the room like a fountain in a garden. Wing chairs aren't the sort of seats you usually find in an entrance hall, but their shape symbolizes security and refuge. You can imagine actually living in the space now rather than just passing through it, settling down to read a book or having a cocktail party.

The same sort of juggling act happens in a quieter way in the dining room. I love the vivaciousness of pattern-on-pattern spaces and the manner in which they envelope you. Have you ever seen one of Édouard Vuillard's room paintings? They're a master class in how to layer motifs and colors. In my client's dining room, blue-striped wallpaper meets curtains that are made from an exuberant fabric combining zigzags and a leopard print as well as polka dots and crowned by a

OPPOSITE: Pattern and color warm a soaring entrance hall, with Manuel Canovas fabrics for the curtains and the wing chair and a carpet by Madeline Weinrib. The plaster-and-steel chandelier is a Démiurge design, and the inlaid chest of drawers is Syrian. The painting is from the New York Botanical Garden's Antique Show. The stair runner is an Alex Papachristidis design for Langhorne Carpet in a custom colorway.

pagoda-shaped pelmet. I love chinoiserie, always have, and the pelmet's shape is echoed, culturally speaking, by framed chinoiserie panels depicting Chinese gardens. A caned fabric on a much smaller scale covers Georgian Revival chairs that were designed by the mid-century American architect Samuel Marx.

The boldness of color and form introduced in the entrance hall hits a crescendo in the living room. It's an incredibly fun retreat, a little bit retro but without being dated. The combination of green and turquoise, which I associate with chic houses on the Riviera in the 1950s, was stylish then and it is stylish now. It is a room where a lot is going on in terms of styles and origins and colors, what with an African stool I painted lime green to a big rattan chair by Gio Ponti and Lio Carminati, an overdyed Indian carpet, and ruffled chintz window shades. But at the end of the day, when the sun has set and the lights are low, it is incredibly relaxing and convivial—a caftan-ready, kick-back-and-relax retreat.

RIGHT: Gracie wallpaper panels bring the garden into the dining room. Above the custom lacquered Démiurge table, surrounded by Liz O'Brien Editions chairs, hangs a Tony Duquette chandelier from Remains Lighting. A bold Clarence House fabric was used for the curtains.

RIGHT: Manuel Canovas fabric curtains frame a view in the family room, where pagodas from JF Chen are mounted on ceramic elephants from John Rosselli & Associates. A custom pair of *faux bois* mahogany and lacquered mirrors from Lerebours Antiques hang above vintage Danish cabinets, by Børge Mogensen, from Paris. The spotted fabric is a Brunschwig & Fils classic, and the carpet is from ABC Carpet & Home.

RIGHT: Serena & Lily bar stools cozy up to the kitchen island, illuminated by Circa Lighting pendants. Knoll makes the Saarinen breakfast table, and the Jonathan Adler faux-bamboo chairs are upholstered in a laminated Manuel Canovas print.

FOLLOWING SPREAD: Custom upholstered pieces furnish the living room, from a baroque-inspired settee covered in a Brunschwig & Fils floral to a Turkish-style ottoman wrapped in a Schumacher ikat. The high-back Gio Ponti wicker armchair was found at a Paris flea market, the coffee table is by the Lacquer Company for KRB, and the carpet is from ABC Carpet & Home. The artwork includes prints by Josef Albers and an abstract painting purchased in Stamford, Connecticut. The mirrors are from Fortuny.

PREVIOUS SPREAD: A Syrian armoire adds an earthy tone to the main bedroom. The Louis XV–inspired armchair is a Syrie Maugham design, the console is an Alessandro Albrizzi creation from Liz O'Brien, and the custom bed features sheets and pillowcases by Leontine Linens. The floor covering is an Alex Papachristidis design for Langhorne Carpet Company. The Todd Alexander Romano coffee table came from Schumacher. ABOVE: A Christopher Spitzmiller lamp stands on an Alessandro Albrizzi desk found at Liz O'Brien. The watercolor painting by Sarah Graham is from Bunny Williams Home. OPPOSITE: A vintage bamboo settee from the Antique and Artisan Gallery adds a tropical note to a bedroom. The walls are covered in a Quadrille wallpaper, the custom bed is upholstered in a Cowtan & Tout fabric, and the needlepoint carpet came from John Rosselli & Associates.

BOHEMIA
BY THE SEA

When it comes to modernism, I'm drawn to Danish and Swedish furniture. There is just something so authentic about the shapes, as well as a sense of casual elegance and simplicity that seems so right for a family house at the seaside. My nephew, Michael, and his wife, Sabrina, bought the house of their dreams on Long Island, a charming farmhouse with wonderful floors, white walls, and barn doors. They lived in it for a while, but once they became parents, they realized that they needed more space. Instead of tearing down and starting from scratch, though, we lifted up the home and built a new house underneath, with the help of architect Kitty McCoy, preserving the upper floor and creating a playroom and bedrooms for the kids and guests downstairs.

The front door opens to a double-height living room, a glowing sunlit space that's all white with touches of indigo blue, from the carpet I had made in India to the pillows fashioned from a variety of Japanese fabrics. Except for a wonderful Papa Bear armchair by Hans Wegner that is dressed in a cozy, nubby fabric, I upholstered the chairs and sofas in a white linen. Sabrina founded Spring Café, an Aspen restaurant (now with a Manhattan outpost) that is all about healthy eating

OPPOSITE: Scandinavian touches greet visitors in the entrance hall. The Swedish settee is from Lief Gallery, and the Danish chest of drawers came from Arenskjold Antiques. Jonathan Burden supplied the round mirror, and the vintage white console is a Karl Springer design.

175

ABOVE: The angular lines of a Doyle New York auction-find bleached oak chair by Kelly Wearstler echo the folds of a John Dante Bianchi painting; the console is from C. J. Peters and the lamp is from Liz O'Brien. RIGHT: A Stephen Antonson "Angele" pendant illuminates the living room. In the foreground is a Papa Bear armchair by Hans Wegner, and the low nesting tables are by Maria Pergay. An Elizabeth Peyton lithograph is propped on the Karl Springer console, and the custom hand-knotted carpet is by Beauvais. Artwork by Colin Penno hangs above the L-shaped sofa (right). FOLLOWING SPREAD: The majority of the living room seating, from armchairs to the L-shaped, button-tufted sofa, was custom made and upholstered in natural white linen from Studio Four. The free-form "amoeba" steel coffee table is vintage. The artwork over the fireplace is by Jim Hodges.

LEFT: Vintage chairs upholstered in a Studio Four batik stripe surround a custom-made table from Jonathan Burden. The ceiling fixture is by Studio Van den Akker. ABOVE: A Matthew King painting hangs in the dining room over a vintage *faux bois* console.

ABOVE: Waterworks classic subway tiles encase the kitchen, where the grout has been toned to complement the gray-painted cabinets. The bar stools are from John Rosselli & Associates, and the ceramics are by Carolina Irving & Daughters. OPPOSITE: The pendant is from Circa Lighting, and a Cowtan & Tout sheer is made into café curtains.

ABOVE: On the glazed porch, a set of Serena & Lily café chairs encircle a Saarinen table. Circa Lighting made the sconces and ceiling fixture. OPPOSITE: The table is set with Everyday Elegance linen, flatware, dishes, and glassware.

and organic ingredients—she has described herself as an "earth mama"—so we used as many nontoxic elements in the house as possible, including special paints and stains. Family-friendly decor was important, too, so a lot of the furniture is softly rounded, with very few sharp corners, a concession to the reality that their young children will be running around.

Given the family's earth-friendly approach to life, I knew that vintage elements would be welcomed—recycling and repurposing is a form of green living. Dark-wood dining chairs were lightened to the color of sand, as was a vintage Swedish cabinet destined for the same room; a tree-branch console, another vintage find that has been painted white and topped with a slab of marble, brings nature indoors. We kept the original kitchen and repainted the cabinets a soft shade of gray, tiled the walls in white, and café-curtained the windows with pretty Ikat cotton. The space feels like a corner of Scandinavia.

Transitional spaces are important at a house in the country, so we added a screened porch that functions as a multipurpose den. One corner is anchored with the type of L-shaped sofa Sabrina loves; the shape feels homey and protective, like a room within a room. Classic café chairs stand around an equally classic Saarinen table—my favorite breakfast table in the world—ready for casual meals, art projects for the kids, or working from home. Everything is fresh, chic, and simple: what more could you want from a beach house?

LEFT: Organic fabrics from Studio Four are made into cushions and pillows for the L-shaped sofa by Country Casual Teak, which also made the ottoman. The marble-veined ceramic garden seats came from Christopher Spitzmiller.

PAGES 188–189, CLOCKWISE, FROM TOP LEFT: Vintage Jay Spectre tables flank a custom bed graced with Les Indiennes fabrics. A vintage sofa, chairs, and side tables gather around a custom Alex Papachristidis bench. Studio Four fabric covers a sofa from John Rosselli & Associates. A custom L-shaped sofa and a coffee table by Vincent Dubourg from Carpenters Workshop Gallery stand on a Beauvais cut-wool carpet; a vintage Arredoluce Triennale floor lamp and custom Lego wall installation accent the space. ABOVE: A Pierre Bergian painting hangs against wallpaper by Studio Four. T. H. Robsjohn-Gibbings tables flank the bed, as do adjustable light fixtures from Design Within Reach. The coverlet and throw pillows are from John Robshaw. OPPOSITE: In the nursery, a Circa Lighting pendant joins an Oomph Home crib, upholstery fabrics, and custom carpet from Studio Four. The watercolor is by Alexander White.

190

MODERN LUXURY

For a couple who lived on Central Park West, I decorated an apartment entirely in beige and taupe. After they parted ways a decade later (I decorated for each of them individually), the client who kept the apartment told me no more neutrals; he wanted to live with color now, lots of color. We also decided to change the layout, moving some walls to alter the purpose of certain spaces; the study became the dining room, and the dining room became a sitting room. Not everything from the past was forgotten, though. The pendant lights in the living room were kept but I re-covered the shades with remnants of the Fortuny fabric that had been part of the previous decor and alternated them with the rust-red wool I was using for the room's new curtains, creating a bridge between two parts of his life.

I love the juxtaposition of formal and casual, silk velvet and woven straw, bamboo and satin. I think I learned that from the great French decorating diva Madeleine Castaing, who knew all about dressy-casual. The living room reflects that, with angular carbonite-and-ebony Mattia Bonetti end tables that seem like a moody reincarnation of T. H. Robsjohn-Gibbings, a wonderful art deco chair and footstool in the cubist style, a soigné bronze cocktail table topped with porphyry, and a 1920s Swedish Grace cabinet that stands tall at the far end of the space. That latter piece breaks up the landscape, so to speak. You have to arrange furniture like you are building a mountain range, with peaks and valleys and mesas, so the room doesn't feel flat. The colors are varied, too—blues, reds, and yellows taken from a multicolored fabric on a comfy armchair. But the sofa I upholstered in a mystery

OPPOSITE: Brunschwig & Fils wool and satin fabrics were fashioned into custom curtains by New York Drapery for the living room. The wallpaper is a Phillip Jeffries design, and the vintage chairs and desk were found at the Winter Antiques Show. An Andy Warhol work hangs on the wall at right, while Boxton Design Group stenciled the floor. FOLLOWING SPREAD: A Louise Nevelson hangs above the fireplace, next to a vintage Swedish Grace cabinet. The black chair and ottoman are by Knoll, beside a Philippe Hiquily side table from Christie's Paris. Larsen print fabric covers the Louis XVI–style chairs, and a pair of lamps by Eve Kaplan rest on Mattia Bonetti side tables from David Gill Gallery in London. The painting over the sofa is by Cynthia Knott.

color. Is it brown? Is it peach? Is it somewhere in between? It is not really neutral, it's just interesting; I love using colors like that as part of a scheme.

We covered the walls in a variety of materials, again to define the spaces and give them their own distinct personalities: cerused oak paneling in the dining room, a dreamy wallpaper of clouds in a bedroom, a shiny green wallpaper in the sitting room, and another wallpaper, this one of black-and-white squares, in the main bath. Some people swear that paint is the easiest way to change a room, but for me, it is wallpaper. It gives you a lot of decorative effect for the investment—color plus pattern plus scale—and creates a little universe of its own.

ABOVE: The library's double-sided sofa is upholstered in a Clarence House fabric. Galerie des Lampes supplied the floor lamps, and the coffee table is by Soane. OPPOSITE: The vintage Egyptian Revival chairs are cushioned with a Jane Churchill fabric. The games table is an Alex Papachristidis design, while the green lamp is vintage.

OPPOSITE: The dining room's vintage pendant was found at H.M. Luther, while the American table and Danish chairs—clad in a Cowtan & Tout fabric overembroidered by Penn & Fletcher—are from an auction. Eve Kaplan made the sconces. The collage is by Louise Nevelson. ABOVE: The dining table is styled with Everyday Elegance tableware.

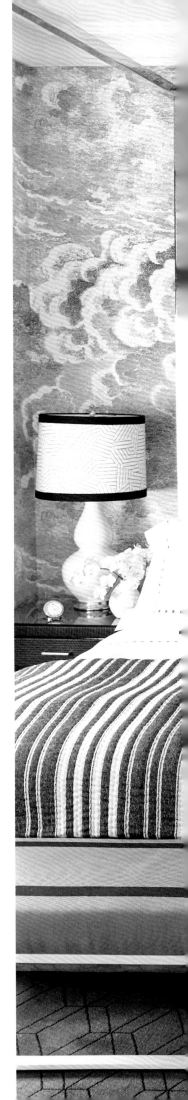

ABOVE: The main bath features a Kelly Wearstler wallpaper for Brunschwig & Fils, a Sputnik chandelier from John Salibello, and Vaughan sconces.
RIGHT: A wallpaper from Cole & Son provides a cloudy background for a custom brass bed by Alex Papachristidis, upholstered in a Schumacher geometric fabric. The photograph by Leonce Raphael Agbodjelou is from Jack Bell Gallery in London. The lamps are by Christopher Spitzmiller.

RHAPSODY
IN LAVENDER
AND BLUE

Making a statement at the entrance of any home is important; it sets the tone for the rest of the rooms. In a Manhattan apartment for my niece and her husband, the front door opens to a Venetian fantasy wallpaper of gondolas and strings of orange paper lanterns printed on sapphire blue. (Blue is his favorite color; hers are shades of purple.) It is rather dramatic—and a wonderful backdrop for a Renoir portrait of a boy—but my niece has never been afraid of bold decoration or of extreme makeovers. Working with architect Alan Orenbuch, we gutted the place and started over. I like defined rooms and defined relationships between those spaces, so we created a classic floor plan featuring a square central gallery off of which the main rooms open. Down went inlaid limestone floors, up went elegant plaster cornices, and we created tall doors to make the ceilings seem higher and the rooms grander. The furnishings hearken back to the 1950s, but the glamorous 1950s, when decorators like Henri Samuel and Stéphane Boudin were taking eighteenth-century style and giving it an à la mode spin. Louis XVI–style chairs are brought together with chic takes on neoclassicism— such as his dressing room's vintage bronze-and-stainless-steel John Vesey desk—and edgy contemporary art, like the gilt-framed Anish Kapoor color etchings in the dining area and the main bedroom. That effervescent combination of then and now, set within a saturated palette and touches of tiger-stripe velvet, makes a perfect background for an energetic young family.

OPPOSITE: The apartment's entrance hall evokes the romance of Venice's Grand Canal, thanks to a Cole & Son wallpaper. Beneath the Pierre-Auguste Renoir pastel portrait stands a nineteenth-century Régence-style settee from the Antique and Artisan Gallery; it is upholstered in an Edelman leather. Eve Kaplan made the sconce.

ABOVE: An arrangement of brilliant orange dahlias by Mieke ten Have is keyed to the color of the lanterns in the Cole & Son wallpaper. OPPOSITE: A Jasper fabric was used on Liz O'Brien Editions chairs in the dining room. Hanging on the wall is an Anish Kapoor digital print, framed in giltwood by J. Pocker. The table is from Objets Plus. Beyond is a glimpse of the purple library.

PREVIOUS SPREAD: Another Anish Kapoor digital print hangs in the living room, above a Schumacher *strié* velvet-clad sofa. A Tessitura Luigi Bevilacqua tiger-stripe velvet upholsters the Louis XVI–style chairs, which came from James Sansum. The table lamps are vintage Maison Charles. ABOVE: Extra dining chairs are kept in the study, which is centered on a vintage Louis XVI–style bureau plat designed by John Vesey. A gathered batik shade tops the vintage lamp. OPPOSITE: Clarence House and Brunschwig & Fils fabrics are combined on the library's custom sofa. A Pierre Frey print covers the Louis XVI–style chair by de Gournay. A print by Andy Warhol hangs over the sofa. The coffee table is vintage, and the custom dhurrie area rug is from Beauvais.

OPPOSITE: In the main bedroom, Anish Kapoor digital prints are placed on either side of the custom bed, which is covered in a Brunschwig & Fils pattern and dressed with Leontine Linens. The floor is clad in an Alex Papachristidis design for Langhorne Carpet Company. ABOVE: Brunschwig & Fils and Manuel Canovas fabrics are used in the nursery with a crib from Oomph Home and Beauvais Wilton carpeting.

FOR THE LOVE
OF COLOR

When you're handling patterns—because, honestly, who can say they love only one pattern?—the trick is to blend and balance, so that no one element dominates. For a Manhattan couple with three sons, I created a happy, fun apartment that is very easy to use and enjoy. Every room, from the entrance hall to the powder room, is layered with motifs, materials, and colors.

The floor of the gallery off the entrance hall is stenciled with blocky angles in three wood tones, a kinetic pattern that is inspired by the sculpted carpets of 1930s American textile designer Marion Dorn. A Mayan-style wallpaper that echoes the floor treatment, though with softer angles, covers the walls, complementing without clashing. The living room is even more pattern-rich and boldly colored, but it still feels serene. There I combined everything from a velvet with a cloudlike motif to another plush fabric bearing a design of tumbling blocks to a chinoiserie-style woven that cushions the Louis XVI side chairs—and all this is set atop a diamond-pattern carpet that recalls trelliswork. The lampshades are made of printed fabrics, and one of the coffee tables is painted to resemble python skin. Classic furnishings of suavely polished wood, largely 1940s designs by T. H. Robsjohn-Gibbings, provide a framework for the animated textiles, and the up-to-date attitude is grounded with traditional details like the ruffled curtain valances and a modern *gauffrage* pattern fabric.

OPPOSITE: The apartment's gallery is wallpapered in a Peter Fasano pattern from John Rosselli & Associates. A vintage octagonal mirror surmounts an inlaid cabinet, both by Paul Evans from Kelly Wearstler. The golden ceramic gourd and angular lamp are Christopher Spitzmiller designs, and the Jean Roger frog planter is from KRB. The vintage painted chairs are Syrie Maugham classics from Doyle New York, which have been upholstered in a Cowtan & Tout print. Boxton Design Group did a modern stenciled floor.

RIGHT: A large polychrome artwork by Alexis Marguerite Teplin, from Gavlak Gallery, is a vivid presence in the entrance hall. Beneath it stands a Claude Lalanne Crocoseat chair. A William Yeoward mirror from KRB is displayed above a 1970s Sirmos plaster console from Liz O'Brien that channels mid-twentieth-century rockwork designs by Emilio Terry and Serge Roche. FOLLOWING SPREAD: A Rob Wynne artwork is mounted above a custom sofa in the family room. Christopher Spitzmiller lamps stand on gilded demilune consoles by Banci for Gaspare Asaro, from Jeff Lincoln Art + Design. The upholstered club chairs are by Liz O'Brien Editions, and a Schumacher velvet cushions the vintage cockpen chairs. The television stands on a vintage T. H. Robsjohn-Gibbings cabinet from Liz O'Brien, and the pendant is by the Urban Electric Company.

That same balance of plain wood with color and pattern is felt in the dining room, family room, and bedrooms. Call it blissfully busy. The impression, though, is seamless, thanks to a consistent palette of pinks and blues, here vibrant, there pale. That way you can move furnishings from room to room if you like, such as taking the wonderful Syrie Maugham armchairs from the gallery and adding them to the dining table to accommodate a couple of extra guests; within the continuity, there is the possibility for change.

ABOVE: In the living room are several vintage furnishings by T. H. Robsjohn-Gibbings, including a coffee table and a lean armchair. Christopher Spitzmiller lamps top Scandinavian side tables by Fritz Henningsen. The painting is by Erica Baclawski, from Avery & Dash Collections.
OPPOSITE: A Schumacher velvet is used on a sofa, the Jean-Michel Frank–style coffee table has been custom painted, and the gilded lamp is an Andrea Koeppel design from Gerald Bland. A print by T. J. Wilcox, from Gladstone Gallery, echoes the vibrant, custom high-low area rug by Tibetano.

OPPOSITE: Custom chairs in a Schumacher chinoiserie fabric surround a vintage Italian lacquered faux-tortoiseshell games table from Avery & Dash Collections. A vintage Maison Charles lamp is on the mahogany pedestal, and the curtain fabric is by Manuel Canovas. ABOVE: Alex Papachristidis designed the vanity in the powder room, painted in a lapis lazuli motif. A Schumacher grass paper lines the walls, the sconces are by Kelly Wearstler, and the mirror is from J. Pocker.

ABOVE: The dining table place settings are from Everyday Elegance and feature custom-designed dishes by Alex Papachristidis and Lisa McCarthy. RIGHT: The dining room is curtained with a Jane Churchill fabric and wallpapered with a Schumacher abstract pattern, while a Fermoie fabric covers the "Alex" dining chairs from Liz O'Brien. Remains Lighting provided the chandelier. Centered on the Directoire mahogany dining table from Bonhams is an arrangement by Plaza Flowers.

223

ABOVE: Boxton Design Group stenciled the kitchen floor, and Lichten Architects made the custom cabinets; the pendants are by Circa Lighting. RIGHT: A swagged shade made of a Brunschwig & Fils print spans the breakfast room. The light fixture is by the Urban Electric Company, while the custom Saarinen table with wood top joins vintage American chairs wearing a laminated Schumacher fabric. Propped in the window is a work by Elizabeth Peyton.

ABOVE: The main bedroom stars a geometric pattern from Cowtan & Tout and a floor covering by Stark Carpet. Christopher Spitzmiller lamps are placed on vintage bedside tables. OPPOSITE: Another Stark carpet paves the dressing room, with Vaughan pendants and a Warren Platner chair by Knoll.

SALLE À MANGER GLAMOUR

Refreshing iconic designs for contemporary eyes is the soul of decorating. For the neoclassical space I created at the 2016 Kips Bay Decorator Show House that meant vastly magnifying Gracie's exacting reproduction of a Chinese Export wallpaper that Elsie de Wolfe used in a penthouse ballroom in the 1920s. Depicting a walled garden, it was also recolored *en grisaille* and the scale was enlarged at my request, the combination of smoky grays and hyperscale motifs putting an otherworldly spin on a typically traditional element. King-size chevron stripes painted across the floor balance the wallpaper's fruiting trees, a geometry-meets-organic collision that's a favorite way for me to add energy to a space, especially, in this case, a relatively neutral one. The bold juxtaposition is echoed in the gutsy yet elegant furnishings, from plump Turkish ottomans to a pair of eighteenth-century gilded consoles that once belonged to tastemaker Mona von Bismarck to the silvery rock-work dining-table base that was specially commissioned from artist Eve Kaplan. She even created strings of handmade, darkly metallic beads that Gerald Bland looped through the Georgian chandeliers to take them out of eighteenth-century England into twenty-first-century Manhattan. Quatrefoil bows in similar anthracite tones add jaunty grace notes to the creamy curtains, which tumble from the cornice like ball gowns. Lalanne, George Condo, Greek and Roman antiquities, and French eighteenth-century furniture were all in the mix to create a lush collected interior.

OPPOSITE: A Christopher Spitzmiller ceramic lamp is centered on an elaborate antique giltwood console table from Dalva Brothers. The latter is one of a pair that belonged to the celebrated American fashion icon Mona von Bismarck—among the furnishings of her apartment in Paris's Hôtel Lambert.

RIGHT: A hand-painted grisaille wall covering by Gracie representing a walled Chinese garden wraps the lofty multipurpose space. The eighteenth-century chandelier, one of a pair, came from dealer Gerald Bland, and artist Eve Kaplan laced it with metallic ceramic beads. Around the Eve Kaplan table stand eighteenth-century French giltwood chairs from Dalva Brothers, while the bronze Crocoseat chair at left and Crococurule stool at right are Claude Lalanne works of art from Jane Holzer.

ABOVE: An ancient statuary fragment from Galerie Chenel stands on a vintage table with a Claude Lalanne candelabra. OPPOSITE: Vintage Serge Roche obelisks from Liz O'Brien punctuate the marble mantel, flanking an eighteenth-century gilt-bronze clock from the Chinese Porcelain Company and a work by George Condo.

RIGHT: Frederick P. Victoria & Son made the coffee tables, which have custom tops fashioned by artist Nancy Lorenz; one bears a ceramic gourd by Christopher Spitzmiller. In addition to the eighteenth-century Italian giltwood chairs from Dalva Brothers with unusual heart-shaped backs and a fringed sofa wearing a Cowtan & Tout fabric and trims from Samuel & Sons, the space offers additional seating in the form of Turkish-style poufs. The carpet, from Beauvais, is made up of antique Turkish tent panels.

BECOMING THE
PERFECT HOST

Big dinners in the city, family luncheons in the country, summer buffets in the garden, birthday parties anywhere: I love entertaining and, believe it or not, all the effort that goes into it. To my mind, the greatest expression of friendship is to be invited into someone's home and to know that everything that makes the visit special—the flowers, the drinks, the food, the table setting—was created to please you. That is the cardinal rule of being a good host: thinking of others.

My mother taught me that anticipating is a big element of hospitality. I don't drink Scotch, but I have it on hand for people who do. I don't eat hors d'oeuvres, but they're my partner's favorite so we serve them anyway. There is always a vegetarian choice for dinner guests who don't eat meat, but I rarely serve fish (too controversial) or shellfish (too many allergies). Table settings should delight the

OPPOSITE: Alex
Papachristidis in his
Manhattan dining room,
which is lined with a
fabric studded with
Houlès nailheads and
curtained with an Oscar
de la Renta satin by
Brunschwig & Fils.
The cabinet on a stand
was found at Doyle New
York, and the chandelier
came from John
Rosselli & Associates.
RIGHT: Antique Chinese
Export ceramics with
Everyday Elegance napkins.

RIGHT: Readied for a buffet dinner, the dining table bears flower arrangements by Zezé, the Manhattan florist, who created fireworks of orchids, pomegranates, dahlias, hydrangeas, and more. The brilliant array of colors is a dramatic contrast with the Chinese Export plates and serving pieces. Boxton Design Group stenciled the floor.

eye, so I have a variety of tablecloths that go down to the floor, a multitude of napkins in all colors and patterns, and lots of china; by mixing and matching, you can create new looks and varied moods. Whether you are planning a dinner for six or a cocktail party for a hundred, the same level of attention applies. Mixing and matching helps when you plan the seating, too: I always place guests between somebody they know and somebody they don't know but will adore. Having wonderful conversations is the goal, so avoid hiring a band or musicians—the person next to you should be the entertainment.

Every host has his own style. Mine are gatherings that are casual and relaxed in tone yet beautiful and formal in the details. I still love seated dinners and black tie. The end of civilization as we know it was the invention of casual Friday. People really do love to get dressed up, to look their best—I think we behave differently when we are dressed well—and to see others doing the same: that is also part of the entertainment. My advice? Start your planning early, overlook nothing, and put yourself in the place of your guests—that way, your entertaining will be just as pleasurable for you as for them. It is important to be a relaxed and charming host as you set the tone for the occasion.

LEFT: Cocktails are served from a vintage Jansen commode set with Chinese porcelain cockerels and fanciful embroidered cocktail napkins, custom made for an Alex Papachristidis trunk show for Moda Operandi. OPPOSITE, CLOCKWISE, FROM TOP LEFT: Ormolu-mounted blue-and-white Chinese porcelain candlesticks from the collection of Alberto Pinto from Christie's Paris set the mood. A woodgrain Nobilis wallpaper complements a fireplace framed with Delft tiles from Country Floors; the custom tablecloth is made from a leopard-spot Cowtan & Tout fabric.

ABOVE, LEFT TO RIGHT: Vintage chairs bank a table draped with a Cowtan & Tout fabric. Everyday Elegance tableware is punctuated by a centerpiece from Sag Harbor Florist. OPPOSITE: The same table set for a dinner party, with a Cowtan & Tout fabric tablecloth and Bielecky Brothers chairs cushioned with laminated Quadrille fabric; the chinoiserie figures are from John Rosselli & Associates, the flowers are by Sag Harbor Florist. FOLLOWING SPREAD: A plein-air summer luncheon inspired by the wonders of Asia. A Cowtan & Tout fabric has been made into tablecloths. The centerpieces are towering porcelain pagodas from John Rosselli & Associates and obelisks from JF Chen. The result is a festive atmosphere that brings to mind a garden of follies à la tastemaker Charles de Beistegui's legendary Château de Groussay.

OPPOSITE, TOP: Aptware plates from La Tuile à Loup with Everyday Elegance tableware embellish the custom tablecloth, done in an ikat fabric from Bermingham & Co. ABOVE: An outdoor dinner in the adjacent garden, overlooked by an Igor Mitoraj sculpture. The tables (here and opposite below) feature antique silver from Christie's and Sotheby's auctions and a blend of Everyday Elegance and Dior Maison designs.

A COUTURE PLAYHOUSE

A century ago, parents often commissioned charming playhouses, miniaturized morsels of architecture that also served as follies. For clients on Long Island who wanted a classic playhouse for their young granddaughter, architect Kitty McCoy and I pored over captivating examples from the past, because even a frivolous building requires thoughtful detailing, especially one that will be a focal point in a garden. Built off-site and brought in on a flatbed truck, the cottagelike playhouse sits on a foundation and has electricity, air-conditioning, even a telephone. Board-and-batten siding dresses the exterior, and double-hung diamond-pane windows reference fenestration on the family's main residence. The Dutch door opens to a soaring space washed with a confectionary palette of pink, fuchsia and Marie Antoinette blue and outfitted with fanciful antique and vintage child-scale furniture I picked up at auctions and had repainted. It's so good I honestly wouldn't mind adapting it into an actual house.

LEFT: A window box brims with geraniums. OPPOSITE: A charming board-and-batten folly with diamond-paned windows and operable shutters, the playhouse was designed by architect Kitty McCoy with Alex Papachristidis.

ABOVE: The colorful decor evokes storybook illustrations, with curtains of dotted swiss and a rabbit lamp that was a gift from decorator Mario Buatta. OPPOSITE: A Manuel Canovas toile wallpaper lines the walls of the vaulted interior, where the floor was painted by Boxton Design Group in homage to one that decorative artist Graham Carr painted for Pauline de Rothschild in the 1970s.

This book is dedicated to Ophelia Rudin,
my incredible and inspiring sister.
Her love, support, and belief in me from the beginning of my career
have allowed me to become the decorator that I am today.

ACKNOWLEDGMENTS

This book would not have been possible without the insights and encouragement of so many people: friends, family, clients, and more.

My mother and my father. My sisters Ophelia Rudin, Aurora Christidis, and Thaleia Christidis. My brothers-in-law Bill Rudin and Rob Klepper. My partner, Scott Nelson, and his mother, Donna. My niece Samantha, her husband, David Earls, and their daughter, Elle; and my nephew Michael Rudin, his wife, Sabrina, and their sons, Dylan, Lukas, and Oliver. My nephew Rafe. My brother, Basil Papachristidis, and my sister-in-law, Patrizia. My niece Tatina, her husband, Thomas Braziel, and their children, Amalia and Alfredo. My nephew Phrixos Papachristidis and his children, Alessandra, Basil, Elisabetta, and Leonia. Our dog, Teddy, who gave us eighteen years of joy and love, and our new puppy, Cooper, who puts a smile on our faces every day.

There would be no book without my wonderful clients, including my dear friend Laura Broumand, who first told me I should be a decorator, and her family—husband Stafford and sons William, Henry, and Charles. And of course, our amazing and talented vendors: Jose Quintana, Aldo Manrique, Cecilia Garzon, Andy Holland, and Eric Englebert.

My thanks to the team that helped me put this book together: Rizzoli publisher Charles Miers, editor Sandy Gilbert Freidus, designers Doug Turshen and Steve Turner, writer Mitchell Owens, and all the incredible photographers whose work is featured in these pages.

I owe a debt of gratitude as well to my longtime friend Harry Slatkin, who wrote the foreword, his wife, Laura, their daughter, Ali (my goddaughter), and their son, David. And to the enthusiasm of Lisa McCarthy, my Everyday Elegance business partner.

Thanks also to Amy Astley, Alison Levasseur, Stellene Volandes, Steele Marcoux, Margaret Russell, and Michael Boodro, who have featured my interiors in *Architectural Digest*, *Elle Decor*, *Veranda*, and *Town & Country*, and to Anita Sarsidi, an extraordinary stylist who helps my rooms always look their best.

Last but not least, I could not do what I do without my team, both past and present: Antonina Papis, Liljana Ndoka, Michael Rayhill, Amber James, Kate Brown, Patricia Spado, Joyce Marlow, Alice Minnich, Kaitlin Gwock, Zoe Stolper, Lena Jacobs, Frannie Hall, and Gillian Warner.

DESIGN RESOURCES

MADE TO MEASURE

Atelier Premiere
atelier-premiere.com

Beauvais Carpets
beauvaiscarpets.com

Boxton Design Group
boxtondesigngroup@gmail.com
(917) 744-2598

David Monn LLC
davidmonn.com

Fairfax & Sammons Architects
fairfaxandsammons.com

Ferguson & Shamamian Architects
fergusonshamamian.com

Frederick P. Victoria & Son Inc.
victoriaandson.com

Gracie Studio
graciestudio.com

J. Quintana Upholstery
43-02 22nd Street, Suite 115
Long Island City, NY 11101
(718) 361-0946

Kathrine McCoy Architect
kmccoyarchitect.com

Leontine Linens
leontinelinens.com

Lichten Architects
lichtenarchitects.com

MARKZEFF
markzeff.com

MELKA
melkaltd.gr

New York Drapery Inc.
nydinc.com

Sag Harbor Florist
sagharborflorist.net

Scotstyle
scotstylebracelets.com

FURNITURE, FURNISHINGS, AND TABLETOP

Carpenters Workshop Gallery
carpentersworkshopgallery.com

Christopher Spitzmiller Inc.
christopherspitzmiller.com

Circa Lighting
circalighting.com

Claremont Furnishing
claremontfurnishing.com

Cowtan & Tout
cowtan.com

D. Porthault
dporthaultparis.com

de Gournay
degournay.com

Demisch Danant
demischdanant.com

Démiurge New York
demiurgenewyork.com

Dienst + Dotter
dienstanddotter.com

Everyday Elegance
everyday-elegance.com

F. Schumacher & Co.
fschumacher.com

Fortuny Inc.
fortuny.com

Galerie Yves Gastou
galerieyvesgastou.com

Hervé Van der Straeten
vanderstraeten.fr

I. J. Peiser's Sons
ijpeiser.com

Jeff Lincoln Art + Design
collectiveartdesign.com

John Robshaw
johnrobshaw.com

John Rosselli & Associates
johnrosselli.com

Kelly Wearstler
kellywearstler.com

KRB
krbnyc.com

La Tuile à Loup
instagram.com/latuilealoup

Lee Jofa
kravet.com/lee-jofa

McKinnon and Harris
mckinnonharris.com

Nancy Corzine
nancycorzine.com

Osborne & Little
osborneandlittle.com

P.E. Guerin
peguerin.com

Pierre Frey
pierrefrey.com/en/

Quadrille Wallpaper & Fabrics
quadrillefabrics.com

Remains Lighting
remains.com

Samuel & Sons Inc.
samuelandsons.com

Schweitzer Linen
schweitzerlinen.com

The Urban Electric Company
urbanelectric.com

ANTIQUES AND VINTAGE

ARF Thrift & Treasure Shop
shop.arfhamptons.org

Avery & Dash Collections
averydash.com

Bernd Goeckler
bgoecklerantiques.com

Carlton Hobbs
carltonhobbs.com

Casa Gusto
getthegusto.com

Christie's
christies.com

Clinton Howell Antiques
clintonhowellantiques.com

Doyle New York
doyle.com

Galerie Chastel Maréchal
chastel-marechal.com/en/

Galerie Chenel
galeriechenel.com

Galerie Kugel
galeriekugel.com/en/

Galerie Perrin
galerieperrin.com

Galerie Steinitz
steinitz.fr

Gerald Bland
geraldblandinc.com

Hyde Park Antiques
hydeparkantiques.com

JF Chen
jfchen.com

James Sansum
jamessansum.com

Jonathan Burden
jonathanburden.com

Lerebours Antiques
lereboursantiques.com

Liz O'Brien
lizobrien.com

Maison Gerard
maisongerard.com

Objets Plus Inc./Daniel Barney
danielbarney.com

R. Louis Bofferding
bofferdingnewyork.com

Soane Britain
soane.co.uk

Sotheby's
sothebys.com

Stair Galleries
stairgalleries.com

ART

Atelier Delphine Nény
7 Rue du Château
72330 La Fontaine-Saint-Martin, France
+33 6 09 24 61 10

Gagosian Gallery
gagosian.com

Galerie Mitterrand
galeriemitterrand.com

Gavlak Gallery
gavlakgallery.com

Gladstone Gallery
gladstonegallery.com

Jean-Charles de Ravenel
jcderavenelcollages.com

Kasmin Gallery
kasmingallery.com

Nancy Lorenz
nancy-lorenz.com

Pierre Bergian
pierrebergian.com

Rob Wynne
robwynne.net

Vladimir Kanevsky
thevladimircollection.com

PHOTOGRAPHY CREDITS

William Abranowicz: jacket (front cover), pages 58, 60–77, 79–93

Pieter Estersohn: pages 1, 10–27, 95–99, 101–111, 161–174, 176–191, 193–201, 212, 214–227, 243–247

Tria Giovan: jacket (back cover), pages 2–3, 229–235

Mark Glenn: page 240 (courtesy of Moda Operandi)

Thomas Loof: pages 6, 236–239, 248–251, 255

Ngoc Minh Ngo: jacket (back flap), pages 4, 112, 114–139, 253

Richard Powers: pages 141–153, 155–159

Mikkel Vang: pages 203–211

Simon Watson: pages 9, 29–36, 38–57

Weston Wells: pages 241, 242

PAGE 1: In a Long Island house, Josef Albers prints are gathered above a custom sofa upholstered in a Brunschwig & Fils floral. The carpet is from ABC Carpet & Home.

PAGES 2–3: A Kips Bay Decorator Show House space by Alex Papachristidis is wrapped in a Gracie wallpaper. A sofa in a Cowtan & Tout fabric faces custom Frederick P. Victoria & Son coffee tables with Nancy Lorenz tops.

PAGE 4: A Gracie wallpaper transforms a Manhattan entrance hall into a fantasy garden.

PAGE 6: Everyday Elegance dishes and a François-Xavier Lalanne bird enliven a table in Alex Papachristidis's apartment in New York City.

PAGE 9: Murals by Delphine Nény establish a classical tone in an Athens entrance hall. A Kangxi vase from Laurent Chalvignac stands on the Northern Italian console from the Chinese Porcelain Company.

PAGE 253: A New York City breakfast area features a Cowtan & Tout fabric and a stenciled floor by Boxton Design Group.

PAGE 255: In Alex Papachristidis's apartment, a Chinese mirror painting from Ariane Dandois hangs against a wall clad in a JAB wool and trimmed with Houlès nailheads. Elephant vases hold Vladimir Kanevsky porcelain kumquats.

ENDPAPERS: Stenciled floor renderings by Boxton Design Group. FRONT SPREAD: A pattern inspired by the Salon Hollandais at Château de Groussay; BACK SPREAD: Parquet de Versailles.

First published in the United States of America in 2022 by Rizzoli International Publications, Inc.
300 Park Avenue South
New York, NY 10010
www.rizzoliusa.com

Text and photography © 2022 Alex Papachristidis

Publisher: Charles Miers
Editor: Sandra Gilbert Freidus
Editorial Assistance: Hilary Ney, Kelli Rae Patton, Rachel Selekman
Design: Doug Turshen with Steve Turner
Design Assistance: Olivia Russin
Production Manager: Alyn Evans
Managing Editor: Lynn Scrabis

Printed in China

2022 2023 2024 2025 / 10 9 8 7 6 5 4 3 2 1

ISBN: 978-0-8478-7253-4
Library of Congress Control Number: 2022935636

Visit us online:
Facebook.com/RizzoliNewYork
instagram.com/rizzolibooks
twitter.com/Rizzoli_Books
pinterest.com/rizzolibooks
youtube.com/user/RizzoliNY
issuu.com/Rizzoli